DANCE AND THE
CHRISTIAN FAITH

DANCE AND THE CHRISTIAN FAITH – DANCE: A FORM OF KNOWING

by Martin Blogg

A critical discussion, both theoretical and practical, into the nature and conditions of religious dance seen within the disciplines of SCRIPTURE, EDUCATION and ART.

Although centred on dance much of the discussion is directly relevant to the performing arts in general.

HODDER AND STOUGHTON
LONDON SYDNEY AUCKLAND TORONTO

British Library Cataloguing in Publication Data

Blogg, Martin H.
   Dance and the Christian faith: a form of
   knowing.
   1. Public worship   2. Dancing – Religious
   aspects – Christianity
   I. Title
   264   BV15

   ISBN 0 340 35173 X

CONTENTS

SECTION II   DANCE AND EDUCATION 157

SECTION III   RELIGIOUS DANCE – PRACTICAL 207

'To you, O Lord, I offer my prayer. In you, my God, I trust'
(Ps. 25:1). 'Our Father who art in heaven' (Matt. 6:9).

FOREWORD

A pioneer has to have special qualities, and a Christian pioneer even more so. Miss Cable and Miss French across the Gobi desert, C. T. Studd to Africa, Dr. Albert Schweitzer to Lambarene or today, Dr. Cecily Saunders, pioneering the Christian and medical work of St. Christopher's Hospice.

Martin Blogg in his modest way might disavow that he was cast in such a heroic mould, but a pioneer must be supremely confident in his cause courageous, to overcome discouragement, and of special competence in his chosen field. A Christian pioneer needs to discover the twin track of the Christian way, which experience the resolution Christ offers us, and the sacrifice Christ demands of us.

Without peradventure, ever since Martin Blogg came to faith in Christ, and then began relating his faith to his profession of teaching Dance Drama he has steadily and persistently pioneered the task of relating the disciplines of a highly professional dancer to the study of the doctrines of the Christian faith (he has spent much time, studying at Oak Hill Theological College, with the encouragement of the former Principal, Canon David Wheaton).

As a side issue, the two well known colleges of Trent Park and Oak Hill, on opposite sides of Chase Side near Cockfosters have benefitted by this living express of synthesis, as Martin Blogg has travelled backwards and forwards across this roadway.

'Dance and the Christian Faith' with its clear sections on
1. Dance and Scripture
2. Dance and Education
3. Religious Dance and its practical training.
is a tribute to the work which Martin Blogg has pioneered in

his own person. His non-verbal approach to Christian dance will open new avenues for the expression of the Faith, in parallel with the traditional ones of speech and liturgy and sacramental express.

Maurice Wood, Bishop of Norwich

INTRODUCTION

The second half of this century has witnessed something of a quiet revolution within the Church in the way that liturgy and religious communication have accommodated the growth and development of the performing arts as a means to prayer and worship, outreach and renewal. This represents a liturgical innovation unknown in the history of the Church, at least since the Reformation.* The sixties saw a careful and modest but nevertheless very real innovation within one of the most established and traditional of church arts – music. This was followed in the seventies by a slightly more radical innovation in the form of drama as a means of coming to know and express the Christian faith. And more recently in the late seventies and early eighties, we see the most radical of innovations, that of dance as a means to worship and communication. Although, perhaps, not quite so spectacular an innovation as music and drama and by no means as acceptable and uncontroversial, dance has nevertheless begun to make itself known and felt within the Church.

Yet there were many explorations of dance as a means of religious expression long before this time. This is shown in the writings and work of the early modern dance pioneers in the United States and on the Continent, as well as in this country. A most extraordinary, if not unique, spiritual focus within dance as art and dance as education occurred during the first half of the twentieth century. In more recent

---

* In some aspects a return to ancient roots; liturgical dance, drama and music have always had a prominent role in Ethiopian, Egyptian and Armenian Christianity.

times there are such names as Dr. V. Bruce, the first Ph.D. in Dance in this country; Janet Randell, who established one of the early professional dance companies in religious dance, at that time called the Cedar Dance Theatre; Anne Long, who made a very significant contribution in laying the foundations for the present developments in dance; and many more to whom we owe much.

But it is, I believe, only within the last five years or so that the Christian faith has witnessed something of a sacred dance explosion corresponding to the dance explosion in society generally. While it is by no means on a scale with secular dance, there has never been as much interest in the practice and theory of religious dance as there is today. I do not know how many religious dance groups exist in this country, but there are at least three full-time professional dance companies and many amateur companies. I know also from the major religious festivals and dance workshops around the country that dance is being received most enthusiastically. More and more churches are considering using dance as a means of expression and the growing number of publications on the subject reflect this interest. But it has to be admitted that dance does not yet have the established place or widespread credibility enjoyed by music and drama. Indeed, sometimes quite the opposite, for it appears that alongside the growing interest is a corresponding fear and scepticism (see the church press!). For many Christians, dance seems to be the most difficult of the performing arts to accommodate within the liturgy. Whereas music and drama have become more or less established as legitimate and credible forms of religious expression, dance has still to prove itself and be accepted by the Church generally.

This book is written in response to this paradoxical attitude of Christians who on the one hand express a growing interest and enthusiasm for the arts in worship, and yet on the other, an equally growing fear and scepticism of dance.

It aims primarily, however, to give wholehearted encouragement, love and support to those already committed to dance and the Christian faith within the Church, education and community, and to those who are seeking to become committed. It seeks to share, in both theoretical and practical terms, a modest, disciplined and critical exploration into the nature and conditions of religious dance. It does so through three major disciplines: scripture, education and dance as art. It does not purport to represent an all-embracing, definitive account of dance and the Christian faith, either in scriptural, educational or dance terms. Nor does it in any way seek to 'put down' or undermine the many and varied positive explorations that already exist or are still being worked out. Rather, it seeks to contribute, in as positive a way as possible, to an already existing and ongoing debate within the Church both in this country and abroad.

GENERAL STRUCTURE

The book is divided into three major sections each with its own particular focus but all, in different ways, concerned with dance in the Christian faith.

Section I   Scripture

Section I is concerned with dance as seen within the Bible and is divided into two parts.

The first part focuses on explicit references to dance and discusses critically conditions of such expressions within the context of twentieth-century worship.

The second part focuses on biblical principles from which dance may be justified. I intend to offer here a scriptural justification for dance within the Christian faith.

Section II   Education

Section II is concerned with dance seen within education. It is also divided into two parts.

The first part focuses on what is sometimes termed the 'knowledge centred curriculum theory'. I will be arguing that dance represents a form of knowing and as such constitutes, necessarily one of many forms of knowing that together make up an educational curriculum.

The second part focuses on what constitutes an initiation into dance as a form of knowing; what is the form and content of such an initiation and how this can be related to dance within the Christian faith.

Section III   Dance

Section III is concerned exclusively with practical dance and is designed specifically to be used within the Church, education and community. The practical material arises out of the previous critical discussion and is intimately related to the real worlds of dance and the faith.

This section is again divided into two parts.

The first part focuses on set dances. These dances are firmly rooted in scripture and have already been choreographed and proved within the fields of the Church, school and community. They range from very simple movement expressions in which all can easily join, to more demanding and skilful dances designed to stretch the more experienced.

The second part focuses more on dance/scripture ideas. Here the emphasis is on 'creative dance' and the reader is encouraged to work out his or her own ideas. The structures are clear and supportive and there are many ideas and possibilities for individual development.

The bibliography provides a very useful list of dance books for further reference.

The distinctions between the three sections are more conceptual than real, for while each concentrates specifically upon certain questions and moves within distinct focus and logical thought patterns, all are intimately inter-related. The focus of all three sections remains the same – dance and the Christian faith.

THREE CO-ORDINATE SPECIES
OF KNOWING

I have tried to keep a careful balance between theory and practice within scripture, education and dance. A conceptual structure which is sometimes referred to within philosophy as 'three co-ordinate species of knowing' underlies much of the thinking in all the sections and refers to this concern for balance.

   (i) Knowing 'that' – is propositional knowledge; knowledge *about* the faith and *about* dance.
  (ii) Knowing 'how' – is practical or procedural knowledge in relation to the faith and dance.
 (iii) Knowledge 'of' – is knowledge by acquaintance which refers to the existential, the inner, heartfelt and ineffable nature of knowledge.

Throughout the book, theoretical knowledge is seen very much as a means to the end of a practical working knowledge and understanding of dance within the Christian faith.*

ACKNOWLEDGMENTS

This book arises out of my experiences as a Christian, as a performing artist and educationalist.

   Above all it arises out of my first-hand practical experiences of working with Springs Dance Company, a unique group of professional dancers, choreographers and teachers, all of whom are committed Christians, devoted to the propagation of the Christian faith and dance within the Church, education and community. The company has travelled widely both in this country and abroad expounding, performing, teaching and leading dance workshops – all the time trying to bring about a disciplined knowledge in practical and theoretical terms of dance and religion. To

---

* For a depth discussion into this notion of three co-ordinate species of knowing the reader is directed to at least two books: (i) *Knowledge*, K. Lehrer, Clarendon Press, Oxford, 1974   (ii) *The Theory of Knowledge*, D. W. Hamlyn, Macmillan, 1970.

this dedicated, special band of Christian friends, I owe more than words can tell. This book is very much a product of their extraordinary professional commitment, love and sacrifice, and I am greatly indebted to them in every possible way. I wish to acknowledge also the special inspiration of St. Helen's Church, Bishopsgate, and the inspired teaching of the rector, R. Lucas; Bishop Maurice Wood, patron of Springs Dance Company, who from the beginning has been a constant source of encouragement, strength and support both for the company and myself; St. Gabriel's Educational Trust and Hockerhill Educational Trust for sponsoring my sabbatical in order to write this book; to Rev. Dr. J. Watson, a dear friend and professional colleague who patiently worked through the original manuscript and helped clarify much of the material; to Scargill Community and Oakhill Theological College, and finally, to Canon David Watson, who, unbeknown to him, firstly turned my world upside down and brought me painfully to the foot of the cross and then, by his extraordinary example both as a Christian and as one so wholeheartedly committed to the use of the performing arts in the faith, inspired me to pick myself up, take up the cross again and, among other things, write this book.

It is my prayer that this book, and all the love, encouragement and support that surrounds it, will in some modest way contribute towards a better knowledge and understanding of dance within the Church, education and community.

> Martin H. Blogg
> Trent Park, 1984.
> Middlesex Polytechnic
> Cockfosters
> Barnet Herts

(i) Scriptural quotations throughout are taken, in the main, from the New International Version of the Bible, Hodder and Stoughton, 1978.
(ii) All the enclosed photographs are of the Springs Dance Company and were taken by the author.

'God did not give us a spirit of timidity, but a spirit of power, joy and self discipline' (2 Tim. 1:7). 'My heart leaps for joy' (Ps. 28:7). 'Come, let us sing unto the Lord, let us heartily rejoice in the strength of his salvation' (Ps. 95). 'It is fitting for the upright to praise him. Praise the Lord with the harp; make music to him on a ten-stringed lyre . . . play skilfully and shout for joy' (Ps. 33).

SECTION I
DANCE AND SCRIPTURE

Part I

Dance as explicitly recorded in scripture

1. BACK TO BASICS: 'It is written'

Whenever a question is raised within the Church concerning the rightness or wrongness of an action it is not the Church as such that constitutes the fundamental authority. My conviction, and the foundation of all that follows, is that the Bible alone constitutes the divine rule for Christian faith and practice. This is to affirm no more than the Lutheran cry at the Reformation, '*Sola Scriptura*'. While we must always recognise the importance of the local church, which represents its members' unique and peculiar cultural realisation and expression, the first authority is the Bible – that most precious heritage and unique collection of sixty-six books, written over a period of some 1500 years by some forty different personalities from different cultures, languages and traditions.

This book which is above all books and which contains the 'written word' of God, reminds us again and again that our faith must be rooted in scripture. It is quite consistent on this point. 'It is written . . .' in its various guises is a phrase that occurs many times.

Since all scripture is God-breathed we can rely on it. We are exhorted to commit our whole being – minds, hearts and bodies – to the written word. The scriptures are the one sure sufficient foundation for all men, at all times and in all places. Accordingly this first section of our discussion on dance is devoted primarily to scripture.

2. DIFFERENT USES OF THE TERM 'WORD' IN SCRIPTURE

I should make it clear that at the moment I am using the term 'word' in its everyday, literal sense. It is important for this critical discussion to recognise that 'word' in scripture is used in several different ways:

> John 1:11: 'In the beginning was the Word and the Word was with God, and *the Word was God*'.
> John 1:14: '*The Word became flesh* and dwelt among us'.
> John 6:63: '. . . the words that *I speak* unto you'.

These distinctions are more conceptual than real. In reality they are intimately interrelated. For the moment, however, I want to focus upon 'the words that I say unto you', the *written word* as expressed in the scriptures to emphasise the fundamental source of authority for any Christian in the belief that all too often within the Church controversies are conducted within parameters which are not always scriptural and which sometimes lead to a distortion and serious undermining of the truth.

3. THE WORD IN THE OLD TESTAMENT AND THE NEW TESTAMENT

Another important point arises from many of the contemporary rejections and criticism of dance. It is not infrequently argued that today's Church is a New Testament Church and therefore Old Testament records of dance are unreliable or in any case invalid. In terms of dance this means that the many vivid references to religious, communal expression, as well as to worship and the faith generally, are dismissed. It can also sometimes mean a rejection of the essential and fundamental feeling element of the faith which was so characteristic of Hebrew worship.

Jesus was a Jew and as such the Old Testament was his prayer book and teaching. Since he was a Jew it is certain that he danced as it is that he wore a beard. Dance was a normal, everyday occurrence and an intimate part of Hebrew culture which did not make as much distinction between religious and secular as we do today. All life, including dance, was religious by nature. The three quotations I presented to illustrate three different uses of the term 'word' all come from the New Testament but that is not meant to imply that they are exclusive to the New Testament. It is quite clear in the Bible that the Word belongs to both the Old and the New. 'The Bible for Jesus *was* the Old Testament, and whatever doubts men may have concerning the value and trustworthiness of the Old Testament, those doubts were not shared by the Lord' (B. H. Edwards).[1] 'It is clearly inconsistent for one who calls Jesus, "Lord", to think lightly of those scriptures which were for him the supreme revelation of God' (R. Frances).[2]

Christ frequently made use of the Old Testament. He used it to introduce himself to Luke (Luke 4:16), to fight Satan (Luke 4:1–12), to silence his enemies (Matt. 26:31), to instruct his hearers (John 6:25–34), to warn his disciples (Matt. 26:31) and teach salvation (John 3:14). He consistently quoted scripture and without question he accepted its accuracy and authority. He also made it quite clear in Matthew 5:17 'that he did not come to abolish the Law and the Prophets, but rather to fulfil them', and that 'until heaven and earth disappear, not the smallest letter, not the least stroke of the pen, will by any means disappear from the Law until everything is accomplished'. Recorded in the gospels are at least thirty-six different passages of the Old Testament, taken from thirteen different books. Roger Nicole[3] claims to have counted in the New Testament 224 quotations from the Old Testament. Lorraine Boattner[4] states there are 370 allusions to Old Testament passages. Finally, Kenneth Hawkins[5] says, 'Some people reject the Old Testament, as being non-Christian or sub-Christian. This is no new idea. In the first place, the Christian's view of the Old Testament must be Christ's view of it. It is clear that he accepted its authority and validity. The question is whether Christ and Christianity have presented a new or truer view of God which invalidates the Old Testament?'

In certain respects, of course, the Old Testament *is* now invalidated. Animal sacrifices, for example, are no longer necessary since Christ made the final sacrifice, once and for all. The only sacrifice that we as a New Testament Church are exhorted to make, is that of praise. Similarly much of the Jewish ceremonial and legalities are superseded, but this does not mean that those Old Testament rituals such as music and dance should now be completely ignored. They reveal to us a great deal about ourselves and society and also something permanently true about the nature of God and man's relationship to him. Many of the Old Testament expressions of truth as recorded in the written word have changed but the Word, i.e. the truth, remains absolute, universal and unchanging. Above all in the Old Testament the inner, feeling nature of man remains fundamentally the same. When twentieth-century man reads the Psalms, he reacts with mind, heart and body, much as man did before him.

4. BIBLICAL COMMANDS AND BIBLICAL PRINCIPLES

My third and final point springs directly from our previous discussion and concerns an important conceptual distinction between what I call a 'biblical command' and a 'biblical principle'.

The failure to distinguish between the two can sometimes result in an extraordinary naivety when translating the scriptures into everyday twentieth-century terms – and dance particularly. When reading about justifications or rejections of dance based upon specific references from the Bible I have for some time now felt slightly uncomfortable about the reasoning. It always seemed to me, for example, that the traditional scriptural justification for dance, of David dancing before the ark (2 Sam. 6), while constituting a *necessary* reason for referring to the Bible and giving due attention and respect to this event, was not a *sufficient* reason for the dance today. Similarly, the traditional rejection of dance, based upon the scriptural references to 'worshipping the golden calf' (Exod. 32) or the 'dancing of Herodias's daughter' (Matt. 14:6) while constituting a *necessary* reason for looking at the biblical reference was not a *sufficient* reason for rejecting dance. This distinction between 'command' and 'principle' will, I hope, help us in identifying this uncertain and rather uncomfortable situation with regard to justifying contemporary sacred dance.

B. H. Edwards[6] provides a basic key with which to unlock a more reliable and valid justification for dance. Edwards asks the question:

'What is the purpose of the Bible?' If its purpose were to be a complete handbook for the space engineer, surgeon, the business man or the building contractor (or dancer) then we would expect it to say everything and could rightly criticise it for anything left out. But in fact, the Bible is first of all a book about God. It tells us all we need to know, and all we shall ever need to know about God: who he is, what he is like, what he does and so on. In this area it is sufficient: it is enough. It tells us accurately about man and salvation. It tells us accurately and in detail what man is like, not physically because that is only a part of man, but spiritually, in his soul and character. It tells us where and why man has gone wrong, and where and how he can put it right. On these subjects the Bible is sufficient. The sufficiency of scripture does not mean this scripture is everything we need to know on a subject. It does mean, however, that it says everything we need to know on the chief subjects of the Bible. Clearly there are many subjects on which the Bible is silent, and in all these areas such as living the Christian life in the modern world, or organising the local church, the scripture gives us *principles* that are sufficient to guide us in any way and every situation.

There are no subjects upon which scripture has nothing to say either by direct command or indirect principle. Both in our critical analysis of specific biblical references and a more general analysis within contemporary society, a recognition of this distinction is important to our justification of dance. It may be that while there are no clear *biblical commands* – and this is, perhaps, particularly true of the New Testament – there may nevertheless be any number of *principles* which constitute sufficient if not necessary reasons for dance. In the same way that there are few explicit and detailed *commands* with regard to worship, so, too, with dance. And just as there are any number of *principles* which can reliably and validly justify contemporary worship so, too, can there be for dance.

5.　GENERAL REFERENCES TO DANCE IN SCRIPTURE

In arguing for a return to the authority of the written word as expressed in scripture, let us first remind ourselves of two important points:

(i) The Word, although formulated and expressed in public propositional terms is always 'more than' and in a sense 'separate from' THE WORD. These written symbols of verbal utterances are always *about* God and are a means to that end. The Word is revered in a variety of ways and a variety of 'languages'. It is the purpose of this book to argue that dance represents one of these 'languages'.

(ii) The Word as expressed in writing and handed down to us, translated, interpreted and presented in its present cultural form is necessarily a product of a man-made, multicultured tradition, however inspired it may be. The Word as recorded in scripture is a combination of several linguistic socio-cultural traditions including Hebrew, Greek and Aramaic. These original languages had their own peculiar psycho-socio traditions. This is not to imply necessarily that they are wrong, but simply to remind ourselves that we have to try to put ourselves in the shoes of these writers if we are to understand truthfully the meaning and context of the Word. The written word by itself is not enough.

With this in mind we must be very much aware of the way we interpret dance today. Contemporary conceptions of dance are very different from yesterday's and if our critical discussion of biblical dance is to have any reliable meaning, we must try to rid ourselves of our ethnocentricity in order to understand the meaning in Old Testament terms. We are so bound to culture and traditions of today that it is sometimes very difficult to truly understand yesterday. Our contemporary social attitudes towards dance are almost totally alien to those of the Old Testament man. The distinction, for example, in our society between religious dance and secular dance simply did not exist in early times. Dance was bound up with life itself and life was intimately bound up with religion. Today, not only do we distinguish between secular dance and sacred dance, we also distinguish a wide variety of dance forms and functions.

Religious dance experts inform us that there are in either the restricted sense or the more extended sense no less than eleven Hebrew verb roots to describe dancing activities and to highlight the nuances of dance movements. 'This,' observes W. O. E. Oesterley,[7] 'in what is a relatively poor language is not without significance, and as well as indicating how large a role in its various forms dance must have played among the Israelites it surely points to quite an advanced stage of choreography among the Jews.' In the description of King David's dance alone there are four descriptive terms. Not only did he dance in the normal sense of the term *sahek*, he rotated with all his might, *karker*; he jumped, *pazez*; he skipped, *rakad* (2 Sam. 6:5, 14, 16; 1 Chron. 15:29). The other root words for describing the dance are: Leap or jump, *daleg*; jump with both feet, *kafoz*; go around, *savav*; skip, *pase'ah*; limp, *zala*; dance in a circle, *hagag*.

Encyclopaedia Biblica[8] informs us that the chief original Hebrew term for dance was doubtless *hag* – and that while the rendering 'feast' or 'festival' will suffice in most cases, it must be remembered that religious feasts necessarily included dance.

Encyclopaedia Judaica[9] makes the same point, arguing that *hagag* implies 'feast' and is used in designating the three great Jewish festivals distinguished by their dancing: *Hag ha Mazzoth* (Passover), *Hag ha Bikkurim* (Festival of the first fruits), *Hag ha Asif* (Harvest festival).

There are other such words which may seem unrelated to dance, but when we immerse ourselves in the etymology, history and tradition of the culture, we recognise that they mean much more than we first thought. The written word *represents*, it is a written record *about* something or someone and not *of* someone or something. One of these terms, which by tradition has been used as a synonym for dance, is *rakadu* which means 'to dance' and also 'rejoice'. It may be that the term 'rejoice' *is* a synonym for 'dance'. Professor D. Adams[10] argues strongly for this interpretation. For those who are interested in the etymology of the dance, I recommend Oesterley's work *The Sacred Dance*[11] which gives an excellent and thorough account of the Hebrew origins for the term 'dance'. This etymological study is in some ways a more convincing justification for dance than the more direct accounts. Also helpful is J. H. Eaton, *The Psalms Come Alive* (Mowbray, 1984), an introduction to the Psalms through the arts.

6. SPECIFIC REFERENCES TO DANCE IN SCRIPTURE

There are something like twenty-four explicit references to dance, depending upon which translation of the Bible you use; nineteen in the Old Testament, and five in the New. These twenty-four by no means represent all the examples of dance. As already indicated there are many references to dance by implication, association, custom and tradition. For many of the events described in the Bible, it was not necessary to mention dance specifically for it would be known that such events involved dance. We have already quoted several such terms – 'rejoice' and 'feast'. The timbrel was also frequently associated with dance. It seems that dance was such a normal, everyday event in Jewish life that it did not need mentioning! Hasidic Jews today maintain this tradition and dancing is common beside the Wailing Wall (the so-called Wailing Wall) in Jerusalem at ceremonies like a Bar-Mitzvah. The musical *Fiddler on the Roof*, portraying a *shtetl* in Poland, gives a more authentic picture of biblical dance than any modern conception. For the moment, let us identify the specific references to dance:

Exod. 15:20 Israel's deliverance from the Red Sea
Exod. 32:19 Worship of the golden calf
Judg. 11:34 Jephthah's return
Judg. 21:21 Women of Shiloh
1 Sam. 18:6 David's victorious return
1 Sam. 21:11 David's praise sung in music and dance
1 Sam. 29:5 David's victorious return
2 Sam. 6:14 David dances before the ark
1 Kgs. 18:26 Worship of Baal
1 Chr. 15:29 Same as 2 Samuel 6
Job 21:11   Children singing and dancing

Ps. 30:11	Weeping and wailing/dancing and rejoicing
Ps. 149:3	Praise him in the dance
Ps. 150:4	Praise him in the dance
Eccles. 3:4	Time to dance
S. of S. 6:13	Wedding dance
Jer. 31:4	Joyful dance
Jer. 31:13	Maidens will dance and be glad
Lam. 5:15	Dancing turned to mourning
Matt. 11:17	We played the flute for you
Matt. 14:6	Daughter of Herodias's dance
Mark 6:22	Daughter of Herodias's dance
Luke 7:32	We played the flute for you
Luke 15:25	We heard music – the Prodigal Son

It is not very helpful to try to classify these references to biblical dance within contemporary categories which distinguish between one dance form and another in terms of vocabulary, context, structure, function, etc., to produce classifications such as classical ballet, modern, contemporary, stage, ballroom, tap, folk, national, ethnic, educational, creative, spectacular, disco. Dance during biblical times was more a homogeneous phenomenon whereas today it is much more heterogeneous with a diverse and complex variety of movement expressions.

As far as it is possible to tell, no distinctions based on vocabulary, form and function existed within Israelite culture. There is the possible exception of Herodias's daughter, but this, by all accounts, was more to do with Roman and Greek than Hebrew culture. Although I feel sure that dance was in some limited sense codified, and by that I mean there were probably some established movements, forms, rhythms, etc., in the main it seems to have been much more interpretative, more improvised and intuitive than we know of today. With the exception of David's dance, possibly, and certainly with Salome's – dance was communal dance. It does not usually appear as an entertainment. It was a communal, religious expression and although everyone may not physically have taken part, all took part in spirit.

So to try to squeeze biblical dance into our present

systems of thought could hinder our understanding. There was no such thing as non-religious dance in the sense that we understand the term today, although no doubt there was dance and dancing that was unlawful (e.g. golden calf). Victory dances, nature dances, harvest dances, wedding dances, festivals, processions, worship and rejoicing were all occasions for religious celebration.

Let us now begin to examine in detail some of these specific references to dance and identify something of the scriptural principles that formed the basis of such expression.

7. **SOME BASIC QUESTIONS ABOUT THE DANCE**

Before we become involved in critical analysis of particular references, we should formulate some general basic questions to apply to all the examples to help us build a meaningful framework from within which to construct a contemporary justification for dance and the Christian faith, and a series of possibilities in terms of form and content for such a religious expression.

Examining each dance example we shall pose the following questions:

   (i) Who danced?
  (ii) Why did they dance? What was the occasion?
 (iii) What form did the dance take?
 (iv) What do we know about the dancer(s)?
  (v) What do we know about the occasion in general biblical terms?
(vi) What is the significance of this passage with regard to dance and the Christian faith today?

Example 1 Exodus 15:20–21 Miriam

'And Miriam the prophetess, the sister of Aaron, took a timbrel in her hand: and all the women went out after her with timbrels and with dances. And Miriam answered them:
  "Sing ye to the Lord, for he hath triumphed gloriously;
  The horse and rider hath he thrown into the sea."'

Who danced?

Miriam and the women danced.

Why did they dance? What was the occasion?

They danced to celebrate a great and glorious victory. The Israelites expressed their praise and thanksgiving for their triumph, and their relief to the Lord for their deliverance through the Red Sea and out of bondage in Egypt.

But it was more than a physical celebration. 'This was a celebration of a "new song" of a new redemption from the lips of a restored people. The nation rejoices in one who is their Maker, their King and their Saviour. The salvation here referred to includes more than simply rescue from national distress and victory. It points to a spiritual awakening and full recognition of the renewed relationship with God and the terms of the new covenant' (A. G. Clarke).[12]

What form did it take?

We do not know precisely the actual form of the dance. Clearly Miriam 'led' the other women who 'answered' her and this might very well imply a sort of Old Testament 'follow the leader' – not an uncommon dance form in Mediterranean countries today, and indeed in our own sixteenth-century farandole and branle as illustrated in the paintings of Bruegel. The leader initiates a movement and the others imitate and follow. At one level this can be in the form of a fairly constant repetition of a simple step or movement motif originally initiated by the dance leader and maintained throughout the whole of the dance. At another level it can be a series of steps and developing movement motifs which become more and more elaborate and demanding. This usually takes the form of a line dance involving a combination of geometric floor patterns and rhythmic steps. It may also be a situation where the solo or lead dancer does a series of steps separate from the chorus. The dance chorus could simply be a sort of refrain to the solo leader: this is not uncommon in folk dance.

The fact that all were carrying, and presumably playing, timbrels might imply that they were not in contact with each other. But maybe the timbrels were shaken with the movement of the body as they travelled and therefore one hand could have been resting on the person in front. No doubt the rhythm of the timbrels was related in some way to the dance.

This dance could also have taken several other forms, such as:

(i) A circle dance with the leader in the centre performing the same initiating role.

(ii) A combination of both a line dance and a circle dance (farandole and branle) moving from one form into the other. Again, this is not uncommon in folk dance.

(iii) The line dance could have taken the form of a procession of women rather than a single line – with the leader still out in front initiating the dance.

We know that the dance was accompanied by song, either solo and chorus or solo alone, and also by timbrels, but it could very well have been accompanied by many other musical instruments. This was a triumphal hymn of praise, so any number of celebratory elements could have been used.

All these possibilities constitute ideas for contemporary religious dance, both in terms of form and content.

What do we know about the dancer(s)?

We do not know much about the women who danced, except that they were rejoicing and giving thanks and praise. But we do know more about Miriam. She was not an ordinary tribal female: she 'led' and the rest of the women 'followed' or 'answered'. She was also a prophetess, although it is not always clear whether this was used in the sense of 'a female interpreter speaking for the deity' and one who gave oracular answers from God as, for example, Moses the prophet, or simply one endowed with the gift of song, as Deborah in Judges 4:4. However, it is clear that she was a person of high ranking social credibility. This and the fact that her dancing was not condemned but, indeed, was encouraged suggests that this dance experience was a lawful and significant one.

What do we know about the occasion in general biblical terms?

From all other references to dance in scripture and from our studies in Jewish history we know that dance was a normal and legitimate religious expression – any festival or celebration invariably involved dance. Almost all festivals included communal, physical expression, and occasions of victory, of which there are several accounts in the Bible, were especial occasions for the dance, e.g. Judg. 11:34, 1 Sam. 18:6, Judith 15:12.

Dance, it is clear, was one of the normal, traditional ways in which the Israelites expressed their victory. It was so respectable and accepted within religious expression that Miriam, sister of two very important members of the community, a prophetess and an accepted leader to whom all the women 'answered', was worthy enough to celebrate such an important and historically significant victory. Finally, it is noteworthy that there is nothing here to indicate the slightest hint of displeasure.

What is the significance of this passage with regard to dance and the Christian faith today?

In the first place, we can learn something about 'why' we should worship and give praise. Remembering that Miriam's dance has to be seen within the context of the event described in more detail by Moses in Exodus 15, we can recognise some of the following reasons for praise and thanksgiving:

What God had done for the Israelites.
What he was going to do.
He was their strength, their song, and their salvation.
He was their Lord.
His love was unfailing.
He was faithful in his promises.
He was greater than any other god.
He was ruler over all the universe.
He was a great deliverer and guide.
He was majestic, powerful – awesome and wondrous.

In the second place, we can learn something about 'how' we can express our praise and thanksgiving:

The Israelites sang.
The Israelites gave poetic utterance to their Saviour and
    Lord.
The Israelites made music with various instruments.
The Israelites came together and gave communal ex-
    pression to their God using their whole beings, bodies,
    hearts and intellect.
We read from other accounts of victory celebrations that
    they formed choirs of dancers.
The community formed a procession.
Men and women joined in the celebration of victory –
    'Everything that had breath, praised the Lord.'

All sang hymns of praise.
They sang loudly, joyfully, thankfully, praising him,
   exulting him.

There is very little here that is alien to us today, but these
expressions both in terms of form and content are foreign to
many churches. Yet the reasons for celebration are not
exclusive to a former culture and tradition: biblical principles of praise and thanksgiving are as fundamental to us
today as they were yesterday. 'Christians are redeemed
people of God [as the Israelites were at this time]. Their
hearts should be so brimful of praise to God, who has
stooped to seek and save them that it spills out of their
mouths in singing [and dancing]. Indeed one of the sure
signs of the fulness of God, of the Holy Spirit *is* singing and
making melody to the Lord with all our heart' (John
Stott).[13]

The deliverance from Egypt occupies the Old Testament
place of the resurrection in the New Testament. Our Easter
festival today is the equivalent of the Israelite festival.

The expression of Miriam, its form and its function, is as
much a legitimate part of worship today as it was yesterday.
So, 'Come, let us praise his name in dancing.'

Example 2   Exodus 32 Worship of the golden calf

'When Joshua heard the noise of the people shouting, he
said to Moses, "There is the sound of war in the camp."
Moses replied:
   "It is not the sound of victory,
   It is the sound of defeat;
   It is the sound of singing that I hear."
When Moses approached the camp and saw the calf and
the dancing, his anger burned and he threw the tablets
out of his hands, breaking them to pieces at the foot of the
mountain.'

Who danced?

Some of the people of Israel, a religious and redeemed people, led by Aaron.

Why did they dance? What was the occasion?

During Moses's long absence in the mountains, the people of Israel became sceptical and impatient and began to doubt the promises made to Israel as God's people. They persuaded Aaron the priest to allow them to build a more tangible and more traditional god, 'an idol cast in the shape of a calf' to whom they offered burnt offerings and danced.

What form did the dance take?

The Bible is not very clear as to the precise nature of the dancing itself. There is, however, a vivid picture of the general context within which it was performed. It would appear that the celebration took the form of an orgy, with excessive eating, singing, dancing and sexual intercourse.

> Eating and drinking (Exod. 32:6) could be innocent enough after a peace offering but the verb translated, 'play' or 'revelry' suggests sex play in Hebrew and we are therefore probably to understand drunken orgy. (A. Cole)[14]

> Sexual intercourse, by all accounts, was an important element in some primitive religious celebrations. The Canaanites believed that it would persuade the gods to grant fertility to the people, their flocks and their soil! The Israelites probably shared this sort of belief as they ate and drank and danced before the golden calf. (J. H. Dobson)[15]

What do we know about the dancers?

We know that they were an unfaithful people who:

(i) broke the promise   (Exod. 24:7)
(ii) disobeyed God   (Exod. 34:8)
(iii) exchanged the glory of God for the image of an ox that eats grass   (Ps. 106:20)
(iv) bowed down to the work of their hands   (Isa. 2:8)
(v) thought that they were worshipping God (Exod. 32:5, 6)
(vi) were taking part in dances and sexual practices like those of Canaanite fertility rites: such dances expressed the wrong idea of God, the wrong idea about the world and a wrong idea about sex.

What do we know about the occasion in general biblical terms?

The question of idolatory is a consistent and recurring one throughout the Bible. In 1 Samuel 13:13, we read that just as Moses rebuked Aaron with regard to the golden calf, so Samuel rebuked Saul and in the same way in 1 Kings 18:18 Elijah rebuked Ahab. (J. Blanchard[16] and J. White[17], two contemporary critics of the performing arts, take up a similar position.)

The Bible states clearly 'you shall have no other gods before me' (Exod. 20:3), 'that you shall not take for yourself an idol' (Exod. 20:4), 'that you should not turn to idols or make Gods of cast metal for yourselves . . . for he is the Lord your God' (Lev. 19:4), 'He is the first and the last; apart from him there is no God' (Is. 44:6), 'do not be idolators' (1 Cor. 10:7). The example of Herodias's daughter, to be discussed shortly, is yet another example of idolatory.

*What is the significance of this passage with regard
to dance and the Christian faith today?*

Firstly, we have a vivid picture of what the nature and
conditions of religious dance *are not*, or *should not* be. The
motivation for the dance, the context within which it is
used, and the general form and content of the associate
celebration are as alien to lawful worship today as yesterday. Perhaps even more tragic than the idolatory itself
was the fact that this was still motivated by worship.
The episode illustrates a position that I will be taking up
throughout this discussion, *that the misuse of a good thing is
not necessarily a reason for its non-use.*

However wrong this use of dance, it is nevertheless yet
another example of dance as a normal and legitimate part of
religious expression.

> This passage clearly and positively proclaims that danc-
> ing was considered as a part of the religious exercises,
> was observed in honour of the golden calf, and, hence, in
> so far as this was the case, a perversion from its legitimate
> use. The passage however does not convey the least
> intimation that Moses found fault with the dancing of the
> people on this festive day, but simply their worship of the
> golden calf. We have here another proof that the use
> of dance in the religious observance of the Jews, was
> not only *not* disapproved or censured by the chosen
> representative of the Old Testament theocracy, but evi-
> dently cordially sanctioned and seemed to be a promi-
> nent part of the elaborate ritualism of the Jewish faith.
> (D. H. Gross)[18]

Encyclopaedia Biblica[19] points out with regard to a similar
idolatrous situation of Ahab and 1 Kings 18:26, that, 'The
great religious crisis in the reign of Ahab is not the dancing
that Elijah disapproves, but its connection with the bad,
foreign religion. The prophets of Baal, we are told,
"leaped" i.e. danced, after a special rite – around the altar,
not eucharistically, but as suppliants.'

When today we accept or reject dance, let us consider carefully this point: nothing is unclean in itself; for the religious man, everything comes from God and is good. What makes dance unclean or clean is that which comes from our hearts. The New Testament particularly is very clear on this point.

But in defending dance, I am *not* condoning idolatory. I am trying to restore dance to its rightful place as a legitimate and proper manifestation of God's creation. Clearly within the performing arts and the contemporary Christian faith, there is evidence of some considerable abuse of the arts which come under the heading of idolatry in the same way as the golden calf did. The *Interpreters' Dictionary of the Bible* states, 'What gives this story such a cutting edge is its penetrating insight that religion itself can be the means to disobedience. Aaron, who is representative of the cult, is left squirming as a dubious ally. He has no word from God, and yet he tries to adjust to the situation by throwing the mantle of religion over their programme for change. What was proposed as a device to salvage the faith shortly produced a compromise which struck a blow at the very heart of the divine human relationship.'[20]

As someone who has been intimately concerned with the performing arts in outreach and renewal, I am very conscious of the awesome task of holding fast to the truth, and yet having to be all things to all people in all places at all times.

The focus underlying the preceding discussion not only highlights the potentially unlawful and idolatrous nature of dance as a form of religious expression but reinforces the nature and fundamental importance of disciplined spiritual leadership and support for such ventures. All too easily and all too frequently, alas, it is my experience of working in the normal everyday commercial market, and in the main non-Christian market, that one becomes very much conditioned by the values and norms of that market. However right and proper the original motives and actions it is not long, because of the nature of the ungodly market, and the rightful concern to 'be all things to all people' as well as the need to survive economically that, like Aaron, we sometimes find ourselves having to compromise to the point of idolatrousness. To work efficiently and effectively within the market place of the secular world and not to be 'conformed to its patterns' (Rom. 12:2), is sometimes very difficult, especially for young and spiritually immature Christians. We must carefully and deliberately discipline our minds, 'transforming them and renewing them' in order to attain a conscious separateness. I cannot stress enough the importance of a good sound basic teaching rooted in scripture and surrounded by prayer.

Perhaps the most important and relevant single contemporary source of criticism about the Christian world of the performing arts comes from *Pop Goes the Gospel* by J. Blanchard,[21] 'A highly provocative, hard hitting examination of the pop scene and the use of rock music in evangelism . . . a devastating exposure of pop music . . . riveting, illuminating and sobering.' Although this is concerned primarily with the pop music scene, there is much that can legitimately be levelled at drama and dance groups, in theory at least, if not in practice, with regard to idolatry. A more recent and equally provocative book on the same subject is *Shall We Dance?* by B. Edwards.

(i) Some Christian musicians seem excessively concerned with fame and with their image: some record companies seem profit-orientated at the expense of the artists' ministries, and since their 'package' is wrapped up in pseudo-evangelical language and justification, few people have realised what is happening. (T. M. Morton)[22]

(ii) The main emphasis on pop music in British evangelism, especially among young people, is almost overpowering with its advertisements for music events, 'happenings', celebrations, festivals, concerts, and 'gigs' cramming the pages of the popular Christian press. (J. Blanchard)[23]

(iii) One of the subtlest ways of flattering man is to communicate the gospel in a way he wants rather than the way he needs. (P. Bassett)[24]

The criticisms of the performing arts in outreach and evangelism are sometimes posed in question form. These questions will, I am sure, be helpful in our coming to know and understand something of the unlawful nature of worship and dance.

Does it focus on man	or God?
Does it glorify man	or God?
Is it man-centred – either in its intention or reception	or God centred?
Is the focus on the 'singer'	or the song?
Is the focus on the 'star'	or God the son?
Is the artist and artifact the master	or the servant?
Is it primarily sensual	or spiritual?
Is it rooted in the 'flesh'	or the spirit?
Is it an end in itself	or a means to the gospel?
Is it 'worshipping' the art or the artist	or God?
Is it nothing more than a palatable religious entertainment, giving what is emotionally and commercially wanted	Is it a genuine, deliberate attempt at communicating the faith?

These critical questions usually levelled at the so-called 'liturgical circus' and 'evangelical roadshow' are equally applicable to the local performing arts group.

There is much, then, from this study of dance in Exodus 32 that is still highly relevant today. It applies to *all* who are involved in the ministry of the Word. The problem of idolatry has existed for every Christian everywhere since the beginning of time. Dance is no more and no less potentially idolatrous than anything else in our lives and worship. But the theatre encourages the focus to be on the stage and all that that implies, and almost by definition 'upstages' the Word if we are not very careful. However, the performing arts and dance particularly, when used lawfully, can constitute a most powerful and effective form of religious communication.

Example 3   Judges 21:21, 23
The annual feast at Shiloh

'"Go and hide in the vineyards and watch. When the girls of Shiloh come out to join in the dancing, then rush from the vineyard and each of you seize a wife from the girls of Shiloh and go to the land of Benjamin.". . .

'While the girls were dancing, each man caught one and carried her off to be his wife.'

Who danced?

The women of Shiloh danced.

Why did they dance? What was the occasion?

It was one of their annual religious festivals, a time when the community as a whole focused upon special religious events both past and present, giving thanks and praise to the Lord.

Some have conjectured that the annual feast at Shiloh was in fact the Passover, and that the dancing particularly commemorated the rejoicing of Miriam and the women of Israel after crossing the Red Sea (Exod. 15:21). 'More plausible,' argues the *Tyndale Commentary*, 'in the light of the mention of vineyards, is that it was the feast of tabernacles.'[25] J. D. Martin[26] sees the occasion as both a historical and a contemporary celebration. He writes: 'This dancing in the vineyards is most probably some kind of vintage festival celebrated at the end of the agricultural year. Such agricultural feasts were usually adopted by the Israelites when they entered Canaan and took up the life of settled farmers. Usually they related these events to their own sacred history.' In the case of the Autumn Feast of Booths, it recalled on that occasion how their God had brought them out of Egypt (Lev. 23:39, 43). In this way the festivals became festivals of honour of the Lord. But in this narrative, the Shiloh festival is still agricultural and still Canaanite.

Encyclopaedia Judaica provides perhaps the most positive and revealing insight into the extraordinary behaviour of the Benjaminites towards the maidens of Shiloh. 'The story of the capture of brides by the surviving Benjaminites indicates that choosing brides during vineyard dances was a recognised practice of Israel.' And according to the Mishnah, Rabbi Gsimeon ben Gamaliel declared, 'There were no holidays for Israel like the fifteenth of Av and the Day of Atonement, on which the daughters of Jerusalem went out in white dresses which were borrowed so that none need be ashamed of she who had none. And the daughters of Jerusalem went forth and danced in a circle in the vineyards. And what spake they? "youth lift up thine eyes and behold her whom thou wouldst choose"' (Ta'an 4:8).[27]

The annual feast at Shiloh, then, can best be seen as a celebration in both historic and contemporary terms:

  (i) It was an annual harvest celebration.
 (ii) It was a historic commemoration.
(iii) It was a traditional wooing and courting event.
(iv) It was a religious festival giving thanks and praise to their God – a time of rejoicing and enjoying God.

But above all, it was the Lord's appointed feast, a sacred assembly (Lev. 23:4), possibly one of three times a year when all men appeared before 'the Sovereign Lord, the God of Israel' (Exod. 34:23), where 'young and old, with sons and daughters, and with flocks and herds . . . went to celebrate a festival of the Lord' (Exod. 10:9).

What form did the dance take?

There are no specific details of the dance itself, but scripture affords many insights into its nature and conditions from descriptions of 'feasts' and also from general scriptural principles about worship. These together will give a fairly good idea of the social and emotional content of the event, even if not the actual steps and that is the more important and more relevant. What the women of Shiloh did is not nearly so important as why they did it, and what biblical principles underlie such an activity.

It is clear that the festival was a communal one and that although only the women of Shiloh are mentioned in this text, the whole community danced in some form either separately or together. We know this from the Bible and also from our studies of anthropology and social history. 'Maidens will dance and be glad, young men and old as well' (Jer. 31:13). One only has to think of the contemporary community celebrations in the Mediterranean and the Middle East, to gain a glimpse of the sort of occasion this might be. I am particularly conscious of such events in Greece where, although the actual physical sequence of events might be different from the women of Shiloh, the emotional and social community event is not dissimilar.

It was a time for rejoicing, giving thanks for the many goodnesses and mercies bestowed upon them. The people of Israel enjoyed their faith and enjoyed their God (Deut. 16:14, 10:12, 30:6, Jer 31:4, 31:12, 13, Is. 30:29, 12:5, 6). The feast or celebration involved shouting, singing, playing musical instruments, dancing, eating and drinking. The festivals were never mere formality or empty ritual, but essentially glad and joyful, communal expressions of their faith and anything less than this was strongly rebuked by the prophets (Is. 29:13).

What do we know about the dancer(s)?

We know very little about these dancers, except that they were women, and came from the Shiloh community. If the dancing at Shiloh was, in part at least, a traditional wooing or courting dance, then it seems likely that the dancers were young and unmarried. Probably the most significant point is that the dancers were not anything special at all. They were simply members of the community who danced to express something of this special and essentially religious occasion.

What do we know about the occasion in general biblical terms?

The feast of Shiloh was firstly a feast or festival and there-fore almost by definition involved dance. As already pointed out, the chief Hebrew word for dance is *hag*, and it is significant that the three major annual feasts are prefaced with the term *hag*: *Hag ha-Pesach, Hag ha-Sukkot, Hag ha-Shavuot*.

Dance may not always be mentioned specifically with references to feasts (as it is with the Shiloh festival), but 'It is clear that dancing was a prominent feature in religious *feasts* and may be implicit in the Hebrew word for "festival" or "pilgrimage".'[28] We know that ancient religion was joyous, and the sanctuaries were the scenes and the festivals the occasions of rejoicing before God, so that dancing would be an inevitable and normal part of worship.[29]

The words 'feast' or 'festival' denote a day or a season of religious celebration. To the Israelite the physical world in which he worked and lived was part of God's creation, made for the benefit of man. The seasons were part of this conception. 'By the feasts man not only acknowledged God as his Creator and Provider, but recorded the Lord's un-bounded and free favour to a chosen people whom he delivered.'[30] These were essentially occasions of joy, praise and thanksgiving where people were not only allowed but were *positively encouraged* to express their heartfelt thanks, 'Be joyful at your feasts' (Deut. 4:16, 6:3–4, Lev. 23:40, Is. 30:29, 12:5–6). Judaism was, and is, predominantly social and joyful.

What is the significance of this passage with regard to dance and the Christian faith today?

We seem to have identified at least five major scriptural principles from this dance reference. All five are perfectly applicable, if not essential, to contemporary Christian faith and worship and offer a potential, reliable and valid reason for dance. Underlying all this is the scriptural conception of 'celebration', of 'feasting' and 'rejoicing'. Let us take each of these five scriptural principles identified in this example of the feast at Shiloh and consider the same within the context of contemporary worship.

(i) *Celebration of the physical creation generally and harvest thanksgiving particularly.* The autumn harvest festival traditionally focuses on the Lord's great physical creation, when we remember the 'harvest' of our contemporary society. Although in the past the emphasis has been on agriculture, 'harvest' implies much more within our contemporary social understanding. 'Harvest' includes anything and every good thing that comes from all the many and varied complex developments within science and industry, art, education, medicine and agriculture etc.

Look for a moment at some of the following extracts from our great English hymnal tradition. Consider as you read and digest them in both your mind and heart, how you might give expression to the principles implicit in them, in terms of your church fellowship.

> Come, ye thankful people come,
> Raise the song of harvest-home:
> All is safely gathered in,
> Ere the winter storms begin:
> God our maker doth provide
> For our wants to be supplied:
> Come to God's own temple, come;
> Raise the song of harvest-home.
> (H. Alford *et al.*, 1844)

> Glory to our bounteous King;
> Glory let creation sing:
> Glory to the father, son,
> And blest spirit, Three in One.
> (Sir H. W. Baker)

> O Lord of heaven and earth and sea,
> To thee all praise and glory be!
> How shall we show our love to thee,
> *Who givest all?*

The golden sunshine, vernal air,
Sweet flowers and fruit, thy love declare;
When harvest ripen, thou art there,
Who givest all?

For peaceful homes, and healthful days
For all the blessings earth displays,
We owe thee thankfulness and praise
Who givest all?

(Bishop Wordsworth)

We thank thee then, O father,
For all things bright and good,
The seed time and the harvest,
Our life, our health, our food.
Accept the gifts we offer
For all thy love imparts,
And what thou most desirest,
Our humble, thankful hearts.

All good gifts around us are sent from heaven above;
Then thank the Lord, O thank the Lord,
For all his love.

(M. Claudius)

Such a focus is surely sufficient reason for us within our church fellowship to organise a 'feast', to 'celebrate' and 'rejoice'. Consider the possibility of imitating something of the Shiloh feast. Is this biblical example so out of place today? Would organising a parish supper with singing and dancing, feasting and merrymaking and generally rejoicing in God's bountiful goodness be inappropriate within our contemporary worship? Consider also the possibility of various church members 'offering' some of their God-given talents to the fellowship during the harvest festival weekend, and the climax of worship on the Sunday where all the fellowship are singing, and, maybe, dancing something of their heartfelt praise and thanksgiving to the Lord.

(ii) *Celebrations of great historical events within the Church.* In the specific reference to dance of the Shiloh festival, we recognise that at one level it is an annual harvest thanksgiving festival, but at another level it is a commemoration of great biblical events. Harvest festival is but one of many festivals that the contemporary Church celebrates each year. Other great celebrations include: Advent, Christmas, Epiphany, Lent, Palm Sunday, Good Friday, Easter Sunday, Ascensiontide, Whitsun, Trinity, All Saints' Day.

All these historic events are focuses for special celebration and a legitimate and potential expression in the dance. In the same way as our great Christian poets sought to express something of the great truths through poetry rather than the literal word so we, in dance, seek to express something of the heartfelt expression of those same great truths. Let us return to some of the festival hymns.

Advent

'It is high time to awake out of our sleep' (Rom. 13:11).

> Hark! a thrilling voice is sounding,
> 'Christ is nigh', it seems to say;
> Cast away the dreams of darkness,
> O ye children of the day!
>
> Lo! the lamb, so long expected,
> Comes with pardon down from heaven;
> Let us haste, with tears of sorrow,
> One and all to be forgiven.
> (Latin sixteenth century tr. E. Caswall, 1848)

Christmas

'Unto us a child is born – unto us a son is given' (Isa. 9:6).

> Hark! the herald angels sing
> Glory to the new born King,
> Peace on earth and mercy mild,
> God and sinners reconciled.
> Joyful all ye nations rise,
> Join the triumph of the skies
> With the angelic hosts proclaim,
> 'Christ is born in Bethlehem':
> Hark the herald angels sing
> Glory to the new born King.
>
> (C. Wesley *et al.*, 1739)

Epiphany

'A light to lighten the Gentiles' (Luke 2:32).

> Once far off, but now invited,
> We approach Thy sacred throne;
> In Thy covenant united,
> Reconciled, redeemed, made one
> Now revealed to eastern sages,
> See the star of mercy shine,
> Mystery hid in former ages,
> Mystery great of love divine.
>
> (B. Wood, 1810)

Lent

'In that he . . . suffered being tempted, he is able to succour them that are tempted' (Heb. 2:18)

> Lord, who throughout these forty days
> For us didst fast and pray,
> Teach us with Thee to mourn our sins,
> And at Thy side to stay.

The Passion

'Who his own self bare our sins in his own body on the tree' (1 Pet. 2:24).

> Ah, holy Jesus, how hast Thou offended,
> That a man to judge Thee hath in hate pretended?
> By foes derided, by Thine own rejected,
> O most afflicted.
>
> > (R. Bridges, 1899)

Palm Sunday

'Hosanna to the Son of David' (Matt. 21:9).

> All glory, laud and honour,
> To thee, Redeemer, King,
> To whom the lips of children
> Made sweet hosannas ring!
> > (J. M. Neale *et al.*, 1854)

Good Friday

'My God, my God, why hast thou forsaken me?' (Mark 15:34).

> Throned upon the awful tree,
> King of grief, I watch with Thee;
> Darkness veils Thine anguished face,
> None its lines of woe can trace,
> None can tell what pangs unknown
> Hold Thee silent and alone.
>
> (J. Ellerton, 1875)

Easter

'O sing unto the Lord a new song; for he hath done marvellous things' (Ps. 98:1).

> The strife is o'er, the battle done;
> Now is the victor's triumph won;
> O let the song of praise be sung;
> Alleluia!
>
> (Pott, 1859)

> Good Christian men, rejoice and sing!
> Now is the triumph of our King!
> To all the world glad news we bring:
> 'Alleluia! Alleluia!'
>
> (C. A. Alington 1931)

> This joyful Eastertide,
> Away with sin and sorrow,
> My love, the Crucified,
> Hath sprung to life this morrow;
> Had Christ, that once was slain,
> Ne'er burst His three-day prison
> Our faith had been in vain:
> But now hath Christ arisen,
> Arisen, arisen, arisen.
>
> (G. R. Woodward, 1902)

Ascension

'God is gone up with merry noise, and the Lord with the sound of the trumpet' (Ps. 47:5).

> God is ascended up on high,
> With merry noise of trumpets sound,
> And princely seated in the sky
> Rules over all the world Alleluia!
> (H. More, 1668)

'Rejoice in the Lord always' (Phil. 4:4).

> Rejoice the Lord is King,
> Your Lord and King adore,
> Mortals give thanks and sing,
> And triumph evermore:
>
> Lift up your hearts, lift up your voice;
> Rejoice, again I say, rejoice!
> (C. Wesley, 1746)

Whitsun

'The fruit of the spirit is in all goodness and righteousness and truth' (Eph. 5:9).

> Come holy Ghost, our souls inspire
> And lighten with celestial fire.
> (J. Cosin, 1627)

> Come, Thou Holy Spirit come;
> And from thy celestial home
> Shed a ray of light divine;
> Come, Thou Father of the poor
> Come, Thou source of all our store,
> Come, within our bosoms shine.
> (E. Caswall *et al.*, 1849)

(iii) and (iv) *Celebration of the Lord's unbounded goodness and mercy to us and to all men. Celebration essentially of the heart – an expression rooted in and arising out of scripture and related to the real world of everyday living and loving.* Although, as we shall see later, dance is in no sense necessarily limited to expressing joy, in the Bible at least, it is almost invariably associated.

I was watching *May I have the Pleasure,* a television series on the history of popular dancing. I remember vividly festive scenes in front of Buckingham Palace following the announcement of peace, where many hundreds of people, mostly dressed in service uniform, had gathered to celebrate. They held hands, walked, skipped and jumped in lines and circle formations, giving communal, physical and emotional expression to their deliverance. Similarly social dance generally in the form of ballroom, disco dance and folk dance, is an expression of communal joy. When I go on holiday to Greece, and join in the dancing at the local taverna, it is an act of communal enjoyment. Dance as an expression of communal rejoicing is not peculiar to the Old Testament Jews, nor does it belong to the past. The difference is that whereas in the Old Testament dance was necessarily a part of the communal religious expression which was intimately related to everyday life, today little communal dance is deliberately religious in its expression. But that does not mean that it could not be so, and within the church fellowship dance forms of this kind constitute a perfectly legitimate and potentially appropriate form of rejoicing.

(v) *Celebration of a special love for each other in the form of wooing and courting.* This last focus on dance arising out of our discussion of Judges 21:21–3, with its extraordinary, if not rather crude and primitive form of wooing and courting, seems on the face of it to be the least significant and relevant to our knowledge and understanding of dance within contemporary faith. But this may not be so. Leaving aside the extraordinary expression in the text and the Benjaminite and Israeli cultural tradition, I want to focus on one of the most important and yet within the contemporary Church, least recognised or understood aspects of popular social dance throughout its history – that of its courting and wooing function. Either in the couple dances or the group dances, sometimes quite directly and explicitly, and at other times much more subtly and discreetly, men and women have met in the popular social dance to find a partner, and legitimately so.

The form of the relationship is varied and by no means all dance is concerned with finding a partner, but this is an important element. Social dance allows and encourages human beings to meet and relate efficiently and effectively. From the earliest estampie, branle and farandoles, through the sixteenth-century pavane and galliard, the seventeenth-century courante, the eighteenth-century minuet and country dances, the nineteenth-century waltz and quadrille and the many and varied dances of the twentieth century, one of the prime reasons or functions was that of socialising. The social structures and procedures of wooing and courting may not be quite so crude and primitive as the Shiloh festivities, but they remain in principle basically the same. Some young girls I know referred quite recently to the 'cattlemarket', meaning the local disco dance where there is an element of wooing and courting. Until the sixties at least, it is a well-known sociological fact that the majority of marriages were made at the local ballroom.

Within the context of the Church, I can remember with affection the church socials and dances which encouraged members of the youth club or the general congregation to relate to each other. In this way, the dance – be it a waltz, quick step, jive, rock 'n roll, or more recently the disco – was a means whereby people could meet informally and come to know both themselves and other people.

This scriptural focus, then, may not be quite so unimportant as it first appeared. Social dance still constitutes a valid form of communal recreation and expression both within the Church and without. At the moment, it tends to be more without, but there is nothing to stop us considering how it may contribute to the Church within. Barn dances and folk dance are still very popular with both young and old and an effective way for the congregation to meet in festive spirit.

Example 4   2 Samuel 6:1–6, 15
Dancing before the ark

'David again brought together out of Israel chosen men, thirty thousand in all. He and all his men set out from Baalah of Judah to bring up from there the ark of God . . . They set the ark of God on a new cart and brought it from the house of Abinadab . . . David and the whole house of Israel were celebrating with all their might before the Lord, with songs and with harps, lyres, tambourines, sistrums and cymbals. . . . The entire house of Israel brought up the ark of the Lord with shouts and the sound of trumpets.'

'David, wearing a linen ephod, danced before the Lord with all his might' (2 Sam. 6:14).

'As the ark of the Lord was entering the city of David, Michal daughter of Saul, watched from a window. And when she saw King David, leaping and dancing before the Lord, she despised him in her heart' (2 Sam. 6:16).

In what is perhaps one of the most famous and most frequently quoted examples of sacred dance, we see at least three major discussion focuses: processional dance, solo-ecstatic dance and critique of dance.

Processional dance

Who danced?

David and the whole house of Israel.

What was the occasion?

They danced to celebrate the bringing of the ark, a symbol of the holy God, to Jerusalem.

What form did the dance take?

This celebration took the form of a procession, a vast gathering of people. David and all his men set out from Baalah of Judah to bring up from there the ark of God. They set it on a new cart and brought it from the house of Abinadab. Uzzah and Ahio, sons of Abinadab, were guiding the cart and Ahio was walking in front of it. David and the whole house of Israel were celebrating with all their might before the Lord, praising God with songs, and with harps, lyres, tambourines, sistrums, cymbals and since celebration and tambourine invariably implied dancing we can assume that much of this heartfelt expression of praise and thanksgiving was accompanied by the sacred dance.

The great religious processions that characterise church life in the Mediterranean lands are modern equivalents of the sort of event this must have been. Those who witnessed the wedding celebration and procession of Prince Charles and Lady Diana, both on the route to St. Paul's Cathedral and also in the cathedral itself, with its many bands of musical instruments playing, its choirs, its symphony orchestra and the spontaneous singing, shouting, clapping, waving and dancing of the many thousands of people will have a clearer idea of this procession of the ark. Similarly, those who witnessed the visit of Pope John Paul II have an example of a very real religious celebration. Such major communal processions involve various expressions of praise and thanksgiving although not all constitute the religious nature of the ark being brought to Jerusalem.

What do we know about the dancers?

We know that the procession was led by David, a great and highly respected prophetic leader (1 Sam. 18:6), therefore we can reliably assume that the expression was a legitimate and appropriate one. We know that David brought together out of Israel 30,000 chosen men. We know that at one point at least, probably at the actual entry into Jerusalem with the ark, if not continuously or at many points along the route, the whole house of Israel was celebrating. The whole house means, surely, precisely that . . . everyone, including young and old, men, women and children.

What do we know about the occasion in general biblical terms?

The procession of David and the whole house of Israel bringing the ark to Jerusalem is perhaps best seen within the context of processions generally; there is no better place to look than the psalms which in many cases were written specifically as processional proclamations or as poetic expressions related to celebrations of this kind. Psalms 149 and 150 come to mind immediately. We will be discussing these two great hymns of praise later but in them we see the sort of praise and thanksgiving that must have formed a part of this great and momentous procession into Jerusalem. There are many psalms which although they do not mention the ark or dance, nevertheless give us a good idea of the nature and conditions of such a celebration. In Psalm 24:7–10, we are told to 'lift up your heads, O you gates: be lifted up, you ancient doors, that the King of Glory may come in.' What gates? 'The gates of entrenched evil in society; the gates of pain and death; and above all the gates of human hearts barred against God' (G. H. Davies).[31] Davies draws our attention to many other processional psalms. Psalms 24:7–10, 26:6–7, 29:2, 42:4, 45:14–15, 47:5, 48:12–14, 84:4–7, 89:15, 95:1–2, 100:2–4, 109:30, 118:19–29, 122:1–5, 132:8–10, 149:1–4, 150 include the most obvious passages, he argues, though by no means exhaust the possible references. Such processions being mainly occasions of joy, would inevitably have included acts of dancing and rhythmic religious movement. Doug Adams in *Congregational Dancing*[32] has some interesting ideas about these movements.

Oesterley in *The Sacred Dance* adds Psalm 68:25–6. He also provides fairly convincing evidence for an important religious circling dance referred to in Psalms 26:6 and 118:27.[33]

David and the entire house of Israel brought the ark of the
Lord with shouts and sounds of trumpets and:

> 'the multitude, leading the procession to the house of
> God with shouts of joy and thanksgiving among the
> festive throng' (Ps. 42:4).
> 'with your priests clothed in righteousness; may your
> saints sing for joy' (Ps. 132:9).
> 'lifting up your heads' (Ps. 24:7).
> 'proclaiming aloud your praise' (Ps. 26:7).
> 'sacrifice with shouts of joy; singing and making music to
> the Lord' (Ps. 27:6).
> 'ascribing to the Lord the glory due to his name; worship-
> ping the Lord in the splendour of his holiness' (Ps.
> 29:2).
> 'to God, my joy and my delight' (Ps. 43:4).
> 'clap your hands, all you nations; shout to God with cries
> of joy. . . . God has ascended amid shouts of joy, the
> Lord amidst the sounding trumpets' (Ps. 47:1, 5).
> 'Let us praise his name with dancing and make music to
> him with tambourine and harp . . . with sounding
> trumpets, with harp and lyre, tambourine, strings,
> flute, cymbal . . . let everything that hath breath
> "Praise the Lord".'

Are there not events in today's church calendar that warrant such a heartfelt communal expression of our praise and
thanksgiving to God? It is surely a loss in the modern
Church that we ignore these biblical principles and biblical
expressions of the Old Testament Church with their wholeness of approach involving not only the mind but the
emotions and the body.

*What is the significance of this passage with regard
to dance and the Christian faith today?*

The first and most obvious significant point is the nature
and condition of religious processions. I do not mean
necessarily the sort of large-scale procession that we see

here in relation to the ark, although there are surely events within our Church that warrant such spectacle, but procession within our own fellowship. The procession is one of the oldest and simplest expressive forms available to all in the Church today. It is a well-established means whereby communal expression, be it joy, awesomeness, fear and wonder, mourning, praising, beseeching, thanking and crying, etc. may be symbolised, through the processing church body.

How does the body move? Obviously 'dancing' and 'mourning' in the metaphoric sense will involve two very different ways of actually moving as a body. Similarly, with the fear and awesomeness that accompany such prayers as the Prayer of Humble Access as we approach the Lord's table to receive the gift of his life in the guise of bread and wine. How the body moves has an expressive significance of its own, e.g. Lent and Palm Sunday?

Who processes? All the church body processes, church officials, children, families, women, men. Who processes and how they process represents a very different series of significant meanings?

Where do they process? To the altar, to the back of the church, to the baptismal font, away from the altar? The path they take in the procession represents a significant expression in itself?

Who leads the procession and who follows the procession? The elders of the Church, the Priest, the Dancers, the Choir, the Bishop?

What accompanies the procession? The cross, banners, music, dance, speech, prayers, shouting, clapping etc.?

The procession represents one of the most traditional and, in its rightful setting, a most effective and efficient form of religious expression. (See Dance Projects No. 1 and No. 3 in Section III of this book and also Appendix.)

In the history of social ritual the procession occupies an important place. The most cultured and the most primitive societies known to us all stress what is at first instance merely the act of moving a body of the people from one place to another . . . a social mobilization or route march, conducted with solemnity or in accordance with the *emotion expressed* by the purpose of the movement. Similarly, the return home has a ceremonial character – a recession. Using the term 'worship' in the widest sense of all solemn social action, we may regard social processions as being in itself an act of 'worship' (worthship). Besides the primary use of procession as a means to an end – the celebration of a particular ceremony – procession may have virtue in itself, an expression of a particular emotion or idea. (*Encyclopaedia of Religion and Ethics*)[34]

Let us return to our last discussion where I identified many of our great English hymns of praise and focused on some of the major annual church celebrations. Think of the following two potential processions as communal expressions of the sort we are now describing:

Lent

> Lord, who throughout these forty days
> For us didst fast and pray
> Teach us with Thee to mourn our sins
> And at Thy side to stay.

Palm Sunday

> All glory, laud and honour,
> To thee, Redeemer, King,
> To whom the lips of children,
> Made sweet hosannas ring!

Solo – ecstatic dance

David danced before the Lord with all his might.

Who danced?

David danced.

Why did he dance? What was the occasion?

He danced to give heartfelt expression in response to a great and glorious celebration, that of bringing the ark to Jerusalem.

What form did the dance take?

It was a spectacular, ecstatic, essentially spontaneous, religious dance, involving dance in the ordinary sense of the word *sahek*; rotating with all his might, *karker*; jumping, *pazes*; and skipping, *rakad*.[8] 'The feelings of the king were wonderfully wrought up and he gave free expression to the joy of his heart. He sacrificed, he played, he sang, he leapt and danced before the Lord with all his might; there are occasions of great rejoicing when all ceremony is forgotten, and no forms or appearances are suffered to stem the tide of enthusiasm as it gushes right from the heart. It was an occasion of the kind for David' (W. G. Blackie).[35]

What do we know about the dancer?

As already mentioned in our discussion of the procession of the ark into Jerusalem, David was a great and highly respected prophetic leader (1 Sam 18:6). Whatever Michal thought of his dancing, history is quite consistent on this point, so it seems unlikely that such an act by such a person could be seen as unlawful. Moreover, significantly he dances dressed in priestly clothing – a linen ephod.

What do we know about the occasion in general biblical terms?

See the previous discussion about the procession of the ark.

What is the significance of this passage with regard to dance and the Christian faith today?

In this example of ecstatic dancing, we see one of the most important justifications, forms and functions of sacred dance today. Much more will be said about this in Section II, but for the moment, let me share with you briefly what is to become my core justification for dance within the Christian faith, that of dance being 'a form of knowing' both in the *ex*pressive and *im*pressive sense of the term. That is, it is a way of making meaningful what we already know ineffably in our hearts, and a way of coming to know via our hearts that which we do not yet know. We live in an age which is dominated by the written and spoken word, yet much of our knowing and experience cannot be expressed or understood in such a way. This knowledge which dominates our everyday thought is not only frequently very inadequate to coming to know, but is also frequently totally inappropriate. This sort of traditional knowledge constitutes an effective and efficient means of everyday public communication, but in other contexts it constitutes quite the opposite and may even be a barrier to come to know! Discursive and propositional knowledge with regard to religion and art, for example, is essentially abstract knowledge *about* art and religion. It is not knowledge *of* art and religion. However fundamental knowledge *about* art and religion is, it can never by itself lead us to a true knowledge and understanding of them. Knowledge *of* art and religion is essentially lived-in knowledge. It is a personal experiential knowledge 'of' and not 'about'. In this example of David dancing before the ark, the Holy God, we see an example of a man of God trying to express the ineffable in terms that words will not allow.

Let me make it quite clear that I am not talking about what is sometimes referred to as 'dancing in the spirit' or 'dancing in tongues'. I am not talking about some of the more extreme forms of educational 'expressive' or 'creative' dance symbolised by such expressions as, 'Now then children, I want you to listen to this music, then express yourselves all over the floor'! I am not talking about mere uninhibited hip swinging or writhing ecstatically on the floor in some vague, unconscious or intuitive way. The expression I have in mind is not symptomatic but symbolic.

'Dance is not a symptom of how a dancer happens to feel but a symbolic expression of its composer's or performer's knowledge of many feelings. A dance like any other work of art is a perceptible form that gives concrete expression to the nature of human feeling – the rhythms and connections, crises and breaks, the complexity and richness of what is sometimes called man's inner life. It is an objectification of one's inner life' (Susan Langer).[36]

I am most anxious to retain something of the spontaneity and intuitiveness which seems to characterise David's dancing and yet I do not want to allow the vague, undisciplined symptomatic expression that has for some time been a part of both education dance and religious dance. This will be discussed in depth within our educational justification of Section II.

In arguing for dance as a form of knowing, I have in mind something much more than the ecstatic joyfulness expressed in David's dance before the Lord. Dance is a means whereby we can give shape and form to a whole range of human emotions and feelings. Worship, since it involves our whole being, necessarily involves every nuance of feeling that comes from the heart's response to the faith. We can come as the psalmists did 'bowed down' with 'groans of an anguished heart', 'thrusting and panting'. We can come, because we are human and fallible, with a 'cold and hardened heart, O God'. We can come with a sense of fear, reverence and awe 'into his sanctuary and beauty of his holiness, blessed in the fear of the Lord'. We can come following such traditional prayers of the Church as:

'Almighty God, unto whom all hearts be opened and all
desires known and from whom no secrets are hid,
cleanse the thoughts of our hearts by the inspiration of
thy holy spirit . . .'

'We do not presume to come to this thy table, O merciful
Lord, trusting in our own righteousness . . . we are not
worthy so much as to gather up the crumbs under thy
table . . .' (Prayer of Humble Access)[37]

'Holy, Holy, Holy Lord'.

We can come as David did and as the psalmists in Psalms
95 and 100, 'singing unto the Lord; heartily rejoicing in the
strength of his salvation, coming before him with thanksgiving; and showing ourselves glad in him with psalms'
(Ps. 95); 'Joyful, serving the Lord with gladness' (Ps. 100).
As the *Book of Common Prayer* states 'it is very meet, right,
and our bounden duty, that we should at all times, and in
all places, give thanks unto him'. There is much surely to be
enthusiastic about, but how often do we worship with our
lips, not our hearts and lives?

The last act of worship (in our Sunday morning service) is
traditionally a great encouragement to our faith. When
the peace of God which passeth all understanding or the
blessing of God the Father, Son, and Holy Spirit, or the
grace of our Lord Jesus Christ are evoked over our heads,
it is to assure you that if you will but accept of them
through Jesus Christ, these blessings are actually yours!
True, there is no part of our services more frequently
spoilt by formality: but there is no part more rich with the
blessing of the faith. So when David blessed the people, it
was an assurance it was theirs if they would only take it.
How strange that any hearts should be callous under
such an announcement: that any should fail to leap to it,
as it were, and rejoice in it, as glad tidings of great joy.
(W. G. Blackie)[38]

Religious dance, either yesterday or today, is not the exclusive province of women. It is often deduced that because most biblical accounts of dance refer to women, men are necessarily excluded and that David's dancing is an extraordinary exception to this. This is not so from my reading of the relevant literature.

(i) Wedding dance. Dancing in honour of the bride was considered an act of religious devotion! This account refers to Rabbi's dancing (*Encyclopaedia Judaica*).[39]

(ii) Feast of Tabernacles. A dance performed by the chief men of the city was a special incident of the feast of the Tabernacles. At the close of the first day, men of piety and repute, singing hymns, danced with torches in their hands. 'No one who has seen this joy', said the Proverbs, 'has seen true joy' (Succa 5:1–4).

(iii) David and the *whole house* of Israel celebrated with all their might (2 Sam. 6:1–6).

(iv) Then maidens will dance and be glad, *young men and old as well* (Jer. 31:13).

(v) Let them praise his name in dancing (Ps. 149). How could communal dance be communal if the men did not in some sense join in the dance? It may be that men and women danced separately, in some instances, as is the case in the Mediterranean lands today, but they danced.

I do recognise that within our contemporary society there are still many situations where for historical reasons it is sometimes thought unseemly for a man to dance, especially in church. This male inhibition has little to do with the intrinsic nature of dance itself and is, moreover, one that belongs to our culture. In many Mediterranean lands, e.g. Greece, it is considered particularly manly to dance – and like David, dance an improvised solo or lead a male procession.

Critique of dance

'And when she saw King David leaping and dancing before the Lord, she despised him in her heart . . .

Michal, daughter of Saul, came out to meet him and said, "How the King of Israel has distinguished himself today, disrobing in the sight of the slave girls of his servants as any vulgar fellow would"' (2 Sam. 6:16, 20).

Michal is clearly very critical of David's dancing. She despised him in her heart perhaps because of the unseemliness – as she saw it – of the King breaking through conventional decorum to dance wildly in front of the religious procession? She compares him with a sort of buffoon who strips himself to dance and play the fool. Perhaps she despises the event as being too frivolous, indecent, unfitting, disorderly, a dancing of the flesh rather than the spirit, glorifying himself rather than the Lord, entertaining rather than worshipping? Perhaps she thought the whole to be more of a circus than a service? Perhaps she thought that he 'upstaged' the worship of God and that the dancers, the dance, its costume and its accompaniment tended towards the idolatrous? We do not know exactly why Michal despised David's dancing. Whether her criticisms are valid or not is another question, but the various commentaries on this passage are without exception on the side of David and very critical of Michal. They point out, for example, that, 'Michal's character could not but act like an icicle on the spiritual life of the household. She belonged to a class that cannot tolerate enthusiasm in religion' (W. G. Blackie)[40] and that, 'When Michal describes David as empty headed, she may in fact be revealing herself as the one who has no proper insight'. I, like most who believe in the dance, want to say that we should stop judging by mere appearances (John 7:24), that everything is good that comes from God, or if all these criticisms are reliable and valid, then be careful that we do not equate misuse with non-use. Nevertheless, while it *is* true that nothing is unclean in itself, if it is unclean for a Christian brother or sister, then initially at least, we must carefully consider what we are doing. However right dance is in itself, and right for us as Christian dancers, if it is a stumbling block for others, if it undermines the faith, then in that sense of truth, the dance becomes wrong.

The example of David dancing before the Lord with all his might is, for me, the most marvellous and telling example of what the sacred dance should be, and I have no doubt that David was right and Michal was wrong. But taking into account all those possible criticisms concerning Michal's rejection, we see today's criticisms of dance in worship and must, out of respect for the faith and the fellowship, recognise that for some dance is 'unclean'. We must also recognise that dance within worship is never an end in itself, but always a means to worship. Worship must be our first priority. Of course, for those who believe that dance has a rightful place, and contributes to worship, not to dance is also a stumbling block. What any of us do in worship must be firstly and fundamentally negotiated within the fellowship. As dance propagators, we have to recognise sensitively and lovingly that for many, dance is not helpful within the context of worship. We must accommodate this fact and also, educate our brothers and sisters, helping them to 'judge not by appearances' and the uncleanliness that may be in their hearts, since that is essentially where uncleanness lies, and to 'make a right judgment'. When we have done this and have reached the point where all can be built up by the dance in worship, then we have a right and proper foundation from which to dance.

Example 5   Psalms 149 and 150
Praise him with dancing

'Let them praise his name with dancing
And make music to him with tambourine and harp'
(Ps. 149:3).

'Praise him with tambourine and dancing,
Praise him with the strings and flute'
(Ps. 150:4).

Who is to dance?

We are *all* exhorted to dance. Everything that hath breath is exhorted to dance.

Why are we to dance?

To give thanks and praise to the Lord.
To rejoice in our Maker.
To be glad in our King.
To praise him for his mighty heavens.
To praise him for his acts of power.
To praise him for his surpassing greatness.
To rejoice in his honour.
To sing for joy.
To praise him because the Lord takes delight in his people.

What form did the dance take?

We are encouraged to use everything in our praise and above all our whole being – mind, heart and body. We are encouraged to make music, to sing and to dance in his sanctuary, in the assembly of the saints. The expression here is above all one of rejoicing, giving thanks and praise, exalting in his goodness and mercy towards us. What is important is not the precise nature of the steps, postures and gestures that the dancers may have performed, but rather that we recognise the biblical command to give thanks and praise, and that dance constitutes one of many legitimate ways of doing this. The occasion was a great feast and time for celebration, for 'making merry' and being glad.

What do we know about the dancers?

The dancers were the people of Israel, God's chosen and redeemed people. The songs or psalms they sang and danced to were 'new songs' of a new redemption and of a restored people ('Old Song' Exod. 15).

Are we so very different from these people? Are we not also a redeemed people following Christ's death upon the cross? Are the scriptural principles behind the function and form of expression of the Israelites so inappropriate to us today?

What do we know about the occasion in general biblical terms?

It is in the psalms, that glorious collection of hymns used in the liturgical worship of the temple, that we perhaps gain the most vivid insight into the nature and conditions of worship, and the worship in which Jesus Christ took part since the Psalter was very much the hymn book of the times. It became, perhaps, the most popular book among the Jews and even today it still constitutes one of the most readable and most identifiable books of worship.

In Psalms 149 and 150, we have two of three specific references to dance in the Psalter. Psalm 30, the third reference, is discussed within the context of Eccles. 3:4 (Example 6). In all three cases, we see the common practice of associating dancing with rejoicing. The last two form a magnificent climax to what is sometimes referred to as the Halleluya Psalms (Psalms 146–50) where each begins and ends with Halleluya – 'Praise the Lord'. These two psalms should be seen within the context of the whole and the last five are a positive affirmation of faith in God's mercy and love. It is, significantly, with 'dancing' rather than 'mourning' (Eccles. 3:4) that the final psalms are concerned, thus affirming the scriptural teaching that 'weeping may remain for the night, but rejoicing comes in the morning' (Ps. 30, Deut. 32:39, 1 Sam. 2:6). These final psalms, marvellously jubilant, breathe a spirit of intense hope and eager joy.

In the psalms we experience the whole range of human feelings within the continuum of 'mourning and dancing', but 'joyful praise' dominates all other feeling. Although 149 and 150 represent the climax, other examples include Psalms 147:7, 138:1, 92:1, 47:1, 6, 66:1, 33:1–3.

*What is the significance of this passage with regard
to dance and the Christian faith today?*

Firstly, in these two psalms we have everything concerning
the nature and conditions of worship generally: *Where* do
we worship? *Why* do we worship? *How* do we worship?
Whom do we worship?

Secondly, the psalms are above all human documents,
and the human feelings to which they owe their origin are
very much the same in every age. In these religious expressions, especially in the last two psalms, is recorded an
essential part of all men, in all places and at all times. I find
this both a sobering thought and a comforting one. We
sometimes think that twentieth-century man is very different from historic man, but although in this century man *may*
have made material advances far beyond those of any other
time and place, to us today man appears much as he did to
the psalmist. These religious expressions record the whole
range of human feeling in an open, honest and uninhibited
manner, typical of the Eastern way of life. There is surely a
need for honesty and openness within our contemporary
religious life. While it may not always be appropriate to
express these feelings in terms of dance and in such an
uninhibited way, we cannot dismiss totally this universal
and unchanging essential nature of man.

Thirdly, there is very little in these psalms that is not
relevant to contemporary worship and much that is highly
relevant. My experience of Anglican worship at least, suggests we have lost a great deal of the essential nature of our
faith, both in terms of content and form.

Spurgeon in his commentaries on the psalms reminds us
that these

psalms are associated with the deliverance at the Red
Sea, and that this form of worship set forth the most
jubilant and exultant of worship. The hands and feet
were employed and the entire body moved in sympathy
with the members. Are there not periods in our life when
we feel so glad we would fain dance for joy? Let not such

exhilarations be spent upon common themes, but let the name of God stir us to ecstasy. There is enough in our holy faith to create and to justify the utmost degree of rapturous delight. If men are dull in the worship of the Lord our God, they are not acting consistently with the character of their religion.[41]

J. Stott in *The Canticles and Selected Psalms*[42] writes: 'Christians are redeemed people of God. Their hearts should be so brimful of praise to God who has stooped to seek and to save them, that it spills out of their mouths in singing.' Indeed, one of the sure signs of the fullness of the holy spirit is 'singing and making melody to the Lord with all our hearts' (Eph. 5:19).

These two psalms are addressed to everyone at all times and in all places. 'Let everything that hath breath, Praise the Lord.'

Once again, I ask the question, 'When we are exhorted to rejoice and be glad, to give thanks and praise, what do we do?' And again, 'Is it not possible that dance might legitimately and appropriately constitute a means whereby we realise this exhortation?'

Example 6   Ecclesiastes 3:1 and 4
A time to mourn and a time to dance

'There is a time for everything, and a season for every
    activity under heaven:
A time to weep and a time to laugh
A time to mourn and a time to dance.'

With the previous references to dance we have focused our discussion within the framework of six basic questions. In this example we see the term 'dance' used in a very different way. All the other references have been concerned with literal, practical dance events. In this case, it is used in a metaphorical sense and the previous discussion framework does not apply.

The use of dance as a metaphor for the 'laughing and

rejoicing' side of life is a common occurrence in scripture. This association with rejoicing and being glad, with praising and being joyful, with feasting and celebrating constitutes the most significant fact in our coming to know and understand the nature and conditions of dance within contemporary Christian culture. In all cultures throughout the ages dance has been closely associated with such an expressive context and has been used both in its forms and its content as a means of individual or communal expression.

The theme of the passage is two-fold:

(i) The nature of life is such that it inevitably and necessarily involves both weeping and laughing. This is something that every human being has to come to terms with and for the Christian particularly, it is the paradox of the core of our faith – loving. Loving, as with life, necessarily involves 'weeping' in order to 'laugh'.

(ii) This paradox of life is, in part at least, properly and divinely ordained. Everything comes from God, and his timing is perfect; 'weeping' and 'mourning', 'laughing' and 'dancing' come from God and should be seen as an act of his unique love for us. There is a season for every activity under heaven.

These themes are fairly common throughout the Bible; underlying each example is the requirement to see it as God's will and also to rejoice in our sufferings – having faith in his mercy and love for us. (Deut. 32:39, 1 Sam. 2:6, Ps. 30:6, Job 5:7, Job 14:1, Jer. 31:4, Luke 6:21, John 16:22.)

Paired opposites occur in the various examples of mourning and dancing:

Mourning		*Dancing*
wailing	Ps. 30:11	dancing
sackcloth	Ps. 30:11	joycloth
weeping	Ps. 30:5	rejoicing
night	Ps. 30:5	morning
sorrow and sighing	Ps. 35:10	gladness and joy

mourning	Job 31:13	gladness
death	Deut. 32:39	life
wounded	Deut. 32:39	healed
poverty	1 Sam. 2:7	wealth
humble	1 Sam. 2:7	exalt
torn to pieces	Hosea 6:1	healed
weeping	Luke 6:21	laughing
dirge	Matt. 11:17	flute
grief	John 16:20	joy

We know from our discussion so far that dancing in the Bible is consistently synonymous with 'dancing' as described above. All the references are associated with the 'dancing' end of the mourning/dancing comparison. In this particular context the term is used metaphorically, but there is no logical reason why the emotions listed under 'dancing' of the paired opposites should not be articulated and made meaningful within dance in the literal sense of the term.

We should recognise also that dance has proved to be a most effective and efficient means by which 'mourning' can be accommodated and 'dancing' restored. The therapeutic aspect of dance has long been recognised by anthropologists and dancers, but not, perhaps, by the public generally nor the Church. Dance, like music, is a marvellous restorer or tonic. When dance and music are combined, we have a very special therapy for many of the ineffable sicknesses and tirednesses of the soul. Most of our discussion about dance so far has been on the expressive aspect; we express or 'say' through the dance something of our knowledge and understanding of ourselves and our lives. It should be recognised that there is an impressive aspect of equal importance which comes through the activity, the 'doing', and this effects our already existing inner knowing and understanding. Time and time again, I have gone into the dance 'sick' and come out 'healed' – physically, intellectually, emotionally and socially. When we dance, we involve our whole personality, both in the expressive and impressive sense of the term. It has been very much the theme of dance educators in this century. Rudolph Laban, one of the great twentieth-century dance education innovators used to say, 'Dance is like a swim, it refreshes and cleanses'.

Dancing, then, has both an *expressive* and *impressive* aspect. Moreover, it is not exclusive to 'dancing' but includes also the 'mourning' side of our lives. Not only do we individually invest something of ourselves in the dance, but equally something arising out of the dance experience impresses upon us. These impressions, like expressions, can be emotional, intellectual, physical, social or spiritual. It can be, and probably is, a combination of all five. Dance is a unique form of expression involving the whole man.

Example 7   Matthew 11:16
We played the flute for you but you did not dance

'To what can I compare this generation? They are like children sitting in the market place and calling out to others:
"We played the flute for you, and you did not dance;
We sang a dirge to you, and you did not mourn."'

As with our previous discussion of Ecclesiastes 3:4, we need to approach this reference within a similar open format rather than the six-question structure that formed the basis of our other discussions. Here, too, the term 'dance' is used not so much in a literal as a metaphorical sense. There are several metaphors within this one parable, and we will need to translate them before we can reliably discuss dance in the literal sense of the term. Irrespective of the metaphorical meanings, however, we can see that:

(i) dance is a normal, everyday part of life, so well-understood, that Christ uses it to make a powerful point!
(ii) dance is still very much associated with rejoicing and within the context of this metaphor is a synonym for 'the good news'.

'this generation' – is likened to children playing. What is important here is not so much the games as the character-istics of children playing them – their butterfly minds, their fickleness, petty squabbling and short attention span, al-ways looking for something new to do, and in the end, any squabble as one game or another is not important at all. So the generation that Jesus is referring to is rather like these children.

'the games' – I suggest represent the squabble within the Church with regard to what is 'true'. Truth is symbolised by the forms of two games:

(i) The singer of the dirge symbolises John's procla-mation of coming judgment; the mourning represents repentance that the proclamation was designed to elicit. The singer, i.e. John, was one who 'came neither eating nor drinking', and 'who had a demon'. His presentation was grave, reproving, threatening, solemn, and severe with its emphasis on self-denial.

(ii) The flute playing represents Jesus preaching the good news and dance symbolises the joy that salvation brings. The Son of Man came eating and drinking, and they said, 'Here is a glutton and a drunkard, a friend of tax collectors and sinners.' Jesus spoke in tones of joy, cheerful and quickening, as he declared God's love.

The gospel as preached by John and Jesus is symbolised in these two very different and, on the face of it, incompatible games. The children in the market are members of the Church arguing like children about which is right and which is wrong and in the end neither is accepted. Both are misunderstood and both are rejected. Both are seen as opposites and irreconcilable.

What is the significance of this passage with regard to dance and the contemporary Christian faith?

Firstly, the two very different approaches to the faith as represented in the life and styles of John and Jesus, appear to be totally opposite and irreconcilable but are two sides of the same coin. 'It takes both sides to make the gospel and involves John's call to repentance and Jesus' offer of salvation. If we do not receive the grave truths of the gospel, we will not receive the joyful ones: if we do not receive the joyful ones, we will not receive the grave. Those who mock John the Baptist's call for repentance slight all the hopes of the rise and joy of calvary' (R. Glover).[43]

Here we identify a very important truth about our faith, about dance, and especially perhaps about dance within evangelism. All too often the gospel is presented within 'flute playing and dance', terms neglecting the equally important 'dirge and mourning'. J. Blanchard[44] and J. White[45] make much of this and similar points, arguing that the 'evangelical roadshow', 'the liturgical circus' with its frequently emphasised 'sugar and spice and all things nice' approach to the gospel, its oh-so-joyful singing and dancing and sense of fun and entertainment-like atmosphere sometimes cause us to forget the fundamental prerequisite of receiving such good news – repentance. Moreover, we soon learn that the Lord is approached not with the informal intimacy of a circus entertainment, but rather with fear, awe, and a great sense of mystery and wonder. It is from this approach that love and praise emerge.

Equally, of course, there are many churches which emphasise the other side of the gospel and ignore the good news. Some of the more traditional conservative churches, some of the more extreme fundamentalists can, by their emphasis, forget the good news of salvation, because they over-emphasise man's sinful nature and the threat of eternal damnation.

A healthy church, a healthy evangelism, and a healthy dance group is one that sees the gospel in terms of John and Jesus. In the sacred dance, we embrace a full gospel of repented faith and new birth.

A second point concerns the teaching styles that metaphorically the children were squabbling over. One should recognise that there is no one teaching style, no one exclusive way of presenting the gospel. No one person, or one mode of communication and expression has *the* way of transmitting the truths of the gospel. Traditionally we have seen communication within the Church dominated by discursive thought based upon traditional, academic, analytical thinking and disciplined propositional knowledge. One does not doubt the truth underlying such communication, but one must sometimes question its effectiveness and efficiency within our contemporary multicultural and multimedia society. The problem for the Church today is not truth, but rather communicating truth in such a way that man is encouraged to attend to it, understand it and accommodate and accept it. The 'language' of dance, music and drama – popular and effective contemporary forms of communication in society in general and evangelism in particular – are as reliable and valid as the traditional sermons provided that, like the sermon, all communication is rooted in scripture and relevant to today, and is effective in communicating the *truth*.

Example 8   Matthew 14:6–8
Herodias's daughter

'On Herod's birthday, the daughter of Herodias danced for them and pleased Herod so much that he promised with an oath to give her whatever she asked. Prompted by her mother, she said, "Give me here on a platter the head of John the Baptist."'

Who danced?

The daughter of Herodias, Salome.

Why did she dance? What was the occasion?

The occasion was King Herod's birthday and Salome, Herodias's daughter, danced before the King with the result, if not the deliberate intention, of seducing him.

What form did the dance take?

This was a secular, solo, artistic form of dance, a deliberately seductive and erotic after-dinner entertainment celebrating the King's birthday. The 'entertainment' pleased the King so much that he promised with an oath to give the dancer whatever she asked.

The thinking generally about this dance is that it was influenced more by the Roman and Greek conceptions of dance and entertainment than the traditional sacred dance of the Jews. To the Jews, not only was this dance unlawful, it was, I suggest, alien although probably not unknown to them. This certainly was not sacred dance. The idolatrous dancing at the golden calf, although unlawful was at least religious dance, however misguided the expression and context. This dance of Salome has no associations with religion whatsoever, except that it brought about the execution of one of the great religious men, John the Baptist.

The Catholic Encyclopaedia[46] tells us that,

> Dancing as after-dinner entertainment, although known among Egyptians, developed more directly from the Greek symposium, at which professional dancers were featured in artistic performance. (**Xenophon, Symposium** 2–9). In later phases scantily clad courtesans, professional male dancers, and dwarfs provided lewd and flamboyant spectacles. The most popular dance entertainment in the first centuries A.D. was the pantomimus, a solo enactment of a popular story theme in stylised mimicry, often with dramatic and sensual movements and postures. It has been suggested that Salome's dance for Herod's birthday guests was in this tradition. The performance of Herodias's daughter, and the pleasure it afforded to Herod and his guests showed how Greek and Roman corruption had, about the time of Christ, made headway among the higher classes of Palestine.

This last sentence provides us with a possible clue as to why there is such a paucity of material related to the sacred dance in the New Testament.

What do we know about the dancer?

We do not know very much about Salome except that she was the daughter of an evil and perverted woman. It is not clear just how much involved she was in this treacherous act. The Bible tells us that King Herod's response to her dancing was the promise to give whatever she asked. She was prompted by her mother to ask for the head of John the Baptist! But whether the dancer was innocent, the dance and dancing were certainly not; this was a shameless dance which brought about the execution of John.

In one sense, of course, this example of dance has no place within this discussion of the sacred dance. There is nothing here that can possibly be seen as sacred, or help to justify a place for it within contemporary worship. But in another sense there is every good reason for focusing on this example, for it will help us in identifying just what religious dance is not.

What do we know about the occasion in general biblical terms?

All we said about idolatry in the worship of the golden calf can be applied to this example of dance with the added dimension that this is in no way a religious or a communal dance. It is a secular, deliberately erotic after-dinner entertainment. It may be seen as an example of something good that God created being turned into something bad by man.

What is the significance of this passage with regard to dance and the Christian faith today?

This is an example of what dance in the Christian faith today should not be. It was a form of dance which was becoming increasingly popular within the Greek/Roman culture of Christ's time and is as popular today within the mass media. But it is not the only dance expression, nor is it necessarily the most popular. Alas, within the Church at least, it seems that criticisms and rejections of dance within the faith stem more from this and the golden calf notions of dance than any other. Some find it very difficult to distinguish between the different types of dance expressions and refuse to allow that a misuse of something is not necessarily a reason for its non-use. This is both wrong and sad for we know that everything that is good comes from God, and that nothing is unclean in itself, nor should we allow anyone to make it unclean, or say that it is.

G. Horner in his *Commentary of the Psalms*[47] writes,

It may be added, that there is no better method of combating the mischievous effects flowing from the abuse of music [dance, my insertion], than by applying it to its true and proper use. If the worshippers of Baal join in a chorus to celebrate the praises of their idol, the servants of the Lord should drown it, by one that is stronger and more powerful, in praise of him who made heaven and earth. If the men of the world rejoice in the object of their adoration, let the children of Zion be joyful in their King.

Let me reiterate on what is 'clean' and 'unclean' in dance. The dance itself, its steps, postures and gestures, are neither clean nor unclean in themselves. I sometimes receive letters asking for 'religious steps'! There is no such thing: what makes the step religious or not, clean or unclean, is what each one of us – dancer and spectator alike – invests in the steps, and this investment comes from our hearts! It is our hearts which make a dance clean or unclean (Matt. 15).

The church fathers writing to justify dance in Christian celebration often contrasted the dancing of David with that of Herodias's daughter: '. . . If you wish to dance in devotion at this happy ceremony and festival, then dance, but not the shameless dance of the daughter of Herodias, which accompanied the execution of the Baptist, but dance the Dance of David to the true refreshment of the ark which I consider to be the approach to God, the swift encircling steps in the manner of the mysteries' (St. Gregory of Nazianzus).[48]

Let us bring together this discussion by comparing the dance of David with the dance of Herodias's daughter in the hope of highlighting what religious dance should and should not be.

David 2 Samuel 6:12–16	*Salome* Matthew 14:6–8
(i) solo dance	solo dance
(ii) religious celebration	secular entertainment
(iii) praise and worship	wining and dining – revelry
(iv) lawful	unlawful
(v) a spontaneous, heartfelt expression of the ineffable	a deliberate, mindful expression of an evil, cunning mind
(vi) dance of the spirit	dance of the 'flesh'
(vii) a dance to God	a dance to Herod
(viii) dance as a means to the end of praise and thanksgiving	dance as a means to evil ends
(ix) an ecstatic dance	an erotic dance
(x) performed by a highly respected prophetic leader	performed by a dancer entertainer
(xi) danced in priestly robe	danced in provocative dress
(xii) encouraged and advised by sacred dance tradition	encouraged and advised by an evil and cunning mind
(xiii) motivated out of an intense love	motivated out of an intense jealousy and hatred (on the part of the mother)
(xiv) danced in glory and honour of God	danced to the personal satisfaction of the dancer

(xv)	dance rooted in scripture	dance rooted in the world
(xvi)	focus of the dance of God	focus of the dance on the dancer
(xvii)	glory given to God	glory given to the dancer
(xviii)	focus on the 'Son' of God	focus on the 'star'

Example 9   Luke 15:25–7
The Prodigal Son

'Meanwhile, the older son was in the field. When he came near the house, he heard music and dancing. So he called one of the servants and asked him what was going on. "Your brother has come," he replied, "and your father has killed the fattened calf because he has him back safe and sound."'

Who danced?

The father, family friends, and servants – the family and friends of the Prodigal Son.

Why did they dance? What was the occasion?

They danced to celebrate the return of a beloved son, a son 'who was dead and is alive again; he was lost and is found'.

What form did the dance take?

The dance has to be seen within the context of feasting and celebrating, giving praise and thanksgiving for the return of the lost son. No doubt there was eating and drinking, music making and dancing of a communal nature. Above all, it was a time of rejoicing and being glad. The dance was a means to that end.

What do we know about the dancers?

We know that the father's reaction was one of uninhibited and unconditional joy and 'that when the lost son was a long way off, he saw him and was filled with compassion and ran to meet him, throwing his arms around him and kissing him.' We know that immediately he ordered the bringing of the best robe to put on the lost son, a ring on his finger, and sandals on his feet. He ordered a feast and the killing of the fatted calf. Such was his joy on the son's return and no doubt the rest of the family rejoiced also, although we are told that the elder brother was not pleased at the attention given to his brother.

What do we know about the occasion in general biblical terms?

This reference is perhaps best seen within the context of the whole of chapter 15 which consists of three separate parables united by a single theme spoken essentially in defence of Christ's ministry to tax collectors and sinners. The three stories illustrate from everyday life God's attitude towards the repentant sinner who returns to him.

(i) Parable of the lost sheep – illustrating the seeking shepherd and his joy on recovering a lost sheep.
(ii) Parable of the lost coin – which reinforces the first parable of seeking and finding.
(iii) Parable of the lost son – the climax and the ultimate focus of the three stories in which God is illustrated as a father rejoicing at the return of a long lost son.

However glad we are over the finding of a lost sheep and a lost coin no emotion can possibly equal that at the return of a long lost son! The pardoning and rehabilitating love of

God is available to all (Rev. 3:20) at all times, and in all places, but expecially to outcasts, both within the Church and without. In a sense, we are all lost sheep. We have all 'erred and strayed from the paths of righteousness' as lost sheep, and if we say that we have no sin, the truth is not in us and we deceive ourselves. We all need to be 'found', 'recovered', and 'saved'.

What is the significance of this passage with regard to dance and the Christian faith today?

The most obvious significance of this passage is that when a brother or sister within the Church or outside 'comes home' then we as a church, receive him or her with the joyous, uninhibited and unconditional love of our Father in heaven. Is it any wonder that at times such as missions and renewals and various outreach events there is frequently a joyous atmosphere of feasting and celebrating, singing and dancing, making merry and being glad and especially towards the climax of the evening when many of the lost sons of God have been introduced or reintroduced to their Father? A communal dance as an element in joyful celebrating over the return of a lost sheep represents valid contemporary religious expression.

From our discussion of biblical dance, we can say that:

(i) Dance and religion were intimately related and that, in the main, the sort of religious/secular distinctions common to western society did not exist in the Jewish culture.

(ii) Dance was predominantly communal, and was rarely an end in itself.

(iii) Dance functioned as a means of: worship, expressing heartfelt praise and thanksgiving, honouring a welcoming hero, celebrating victory, celebrating and commemorating a historic or religious event, welcoming a loved one, celebrating the harvest or a feast and in wooing and courting.

(iv) It appears to have been predominantly spontaneous

or interpretative rather than codified, but we must not rule out the possibility of a formulated dance pattern and steps, taking different structural forms. In the main, dance constituted a heartfelt expression of exalting the Lord and celebrating God's goodness, mercy, wonder, power, surpassing greatness, steadfastness, redemption, forgiveness and love. Its vocabulary of expression was extremely varied. It involved skill, good order, all one's might, one's whole being and strength.

(v) The dance expression was all that was the opposite to what was implied by 'mourning': it was joyful, spontaneous, full of grace and beauty.

(vi) It was accompanied by a variety of vocal expressions and music and could be performed by the whole people: old and young, rich and poor, the expert and the amateur.

It is abundantly clear from the evidence so far gathered from the Bible, from Talmudic literature, and from historical and ethnic studies that sacred dance was a normal and intimate part of everyday Jewish life. Moreover, there is not one reference in the Bible where there is even the hint of disapproval, let alone the prohibition of dance itself. Whilst there may be no specific biblical commands to dance, equally, there is no biblical command that we should not. However, there are any number of biblical principles by which we can both justify and criticise dance and it is to these that we should attend to with regard to the sacred dance and the contemporary Christian faith. For those who argue against dance on the basis of the golden calf and Herodias's daughter, let us remind each other once again that the misuse of a good thing is not reason for its non use. Indeed, it is every reason to show its proper use, since everything good comes from God. God created the media of expression – dance, the instrument of expression – body and the focus of expression – life. So; 'Come – let us praise his name in dancing!' (Psalm 149).

SECTION I
DANCE AND SCRIPTURE

Part II

Dance implicit in biblical principles

1. THE BIBLICAL USE OF THE TERM 'WORD'

I want to begin our discussion of biblical principles by returning to the concept of the Word. I have already pointed out that all too often the word is seen predominantly in terms of writing and verbal utterances. The written word, moreover, is expressed in a highly elaborate, theological, linguistic tradition and in some extreme evangelical traditions is worshipped almost to the point of biblical idolatry. I argued that revelation is not the exclusive concern of any one particular language tradition. Propositional knowledge and discursive thought, which in the main characterise the language of words, is undoubtedly a proven, efficient and effective public system of communication, but it is only *one* of many 'languages' through which man comes to know and understand the world – through which the Word is revealed. I use the term 'language' in the extended sense to mean any symbolic system of thought through which we construct reality, articulate, give meaning to and make sense of the world – and the Word. The language of words, music, dance, science, etc. are all means whereby we can come to know the Word. Not all languages are verbal or rational in the scientific sense of the term, but they are all in their own way meaningful systems of thought.

I recognise that this is a very provocative position. Let me make it quite clear that I am *not* wanting to undermine the fundamental importance of the written word – especially in terms of scripture. Nor am I proposing that we substitute the performing arts for the written word. I have already argued that dance as a form of religious expression must be rooted in scripture. Music, dance and art must arise from the written word. What I want to do is put the written word within the proper context of the Word (John 1:1), i.e. God. I want to question the exclusiveness and sometimes naïve literalism that not infrequently accompanies the written word.

My argument is essentially this: the Bible – the written word – however fundamental and important it is in our coming to know God, is *not* knowledge 'of' God, but rather knowledge 'about' God. True knowledge of God involves knowing 'about' and knowing 'of'. It involves more than this as we shall see shortly, but for the moment, let us recognise that the written word by itself is only a means whereby we come to know God; it is not the end.

It is in St. John's gospel that we see most clearly some of the important meanings and uses of the term 'word'.

The Word

'In the beginning was the Word, and the Word was with God, and the Word was God' (John 1:1). The use of the term 'Word' is a metaphorical expression clearly equated with God himself. It does not point to a reality of which it is only an intellectual expression: it is reality itself. That is why the reality of the word in the literal sense of the term is in no way exhausted by its verbal expression.

This conception of God as the Logos or eternal Word is peculiar to the gospel of St. John, but is by no means exclusive to it. It is implied, for example, in Col. 1:15–18, Heb. 1:2–4 and Rev. 19:13 as well as many other places.

The Word made 'flesh' – the Word incarnate

'The Word became flesh and dwelt among us' (John 1:14).

The use of the term here is synonymous with God in Christ. Jesus Christ was God manifest in the flesh. He came, not just to point the way, the truth and the life. He was and *is* the way, the truth and the life.

It was by men that God gave himself to men, till, in the fullness of time he came for good and all, in the God-man, Christ – the living *Word*: in whom God is present in him, reconciling the world to himself, not merely acting through him, but present in him, reconciling and not speaking of reconciliation or merely offering it to us. (R. Abba)[1]

It is of the highest importance that Jesus Christ himself, the one in whom God imparts himself to us, is called '*the Word*'. It is therefore he, this person who is really the *Word*. He himself is the communication, the self communication of God; it is he himself in whom God proclaims and realises his will to lordship and his will to fellowship. The new point of view in the New Testament in contrast to the Old is that God offers his word no longer only in the words of the prophets, but in the Word become flesh. *It is thus unmistakenly clear that what God wills to give us cannot really be given in words*, but only in manifestations; Jesus Christ. God himself in person is the real gift. The word of god in its ultimate meaning is thus precisely not 'a word from God', but god in person, God himself speaking, himself present, Immanuel. (E. Brunner)[2]

The Word made flesh. The words and actions of Jesus are inseparable. Already then, we recognise that the written word by itself cannot lead us to a true knowledge of God. The Word is as much a verb as it is a noun! The Word is not given as something distinct from Jesus, but is manifested in his person – he *is* the Word. In him the fundamental unity of word and action is realised. In him the Word has all its dynamic force and the action, all its proper power of eloquence.

The first chapter of St. John's gospel is an echo of the first chapter of Genesis and 'provides a living key to the Creator of the world by the *Word*. For in fact, it is in Christ that all things were created: everything was created by him, and in him, all things hold together (Col. 1:16)' (J. J. von Allmen).[3]

'I bring you good news of great joy that will be for all men'
(Luke 2:10). 'Emmanuel. God is with us' (Matt. 1:23).

'The Word became flesh and dwelt among us' (John 1:14).
'Let us praise his name with dancing' (Ps. 149).

The written word

'The words I have spoken to you' (John 6:63).

The term 'word' is used here in its literal and common
meaning of either verbal utterances to communicate
thought or thought communicated through signs and symbols, which we call writing. The 'word' here refers to the
intellect (Deut. 4:36), scripture which is 'God-breathed and
is useful for teaching, rebuking, correcting and training in
righteousness so that the man of God may be thoroughly
equipped for every good work' (2 Tim. 3:16). Here we use
the term in the sense of being a means whereby the
'thought' of God is mediated to the human mind. 'In the
literal sense the Bible consists of the words of men expressed in terms of visible signs and symbols. It is not the
utterances of God in the sense in which it is the utterances
of man. The importance of this fairly obvious and
elementary discussion is that it exposes the fallacy of
arguing from an admission that the Bible is "the word of
God" to the conclusion that it must possess God's own
infallibility' (C. H. Dodd).[4]
   It remains more or less true, of course, that it is essentially
by means of words that we arrive at the testimony rendered
to the Word and set down in the Old and New Testament.
But these words, which are thoroughly human, are nothing
in themselves and have no authority. The ministry of the
Word has been entrusted to the Church to whom grace was
given to receive the Word, to bear it, to give it to the world.
Announced by the prophets and having come among us in
the person of Jesus Christ, the word has been passed on by
prophets and apostles (Eph. 2:20) built on the foundation of
Christ himself as the chief cornerstone. In him the whole
building is joined together and rises to become his holy
temple of the Word. 'Preaching of the Church consists not
so much in recalling and declaring the words of Jesus as in
proclaiming Jesus himself who *is* the *Word*. To preach the
Word is to preach Jesus' (J. J. von Allmen).[5] In order that
these words become a source of knowledge and acquire the
potency of the event, it is necessary that the Holy Spirit

should illumine them and 'read' them in such a way that the Word of God resounds through the human word to become the Saviour, sacrifice and King in whom the whole history of salvation is located. *Then* the written word becomes in its turn the Word of God.

The written word, then, by itself is not necessarily synonymous with the Word, i.e. God, but rather a potential means whereby God is made known. The written word is knowledge *about* God and not *of* God. It undoubtedly constitutes, within western society at least, one of the most powerful public means whereby the Word is communicated but it remains, but one of many means through which man can come to know the Word – God. The problem for religion today is not Truth, i.e. God, or the Word, but rather with *communicating* Truth. Truth, as expressed in the Word, is universal, absolute and unchanging. The problem for each generation of Christians, and Christian preachers and teachers especially, is that of communicating these unchanging truths in such a way that they can firstly be attended to, secondly made intelligible and thirdly accommodated and accepted.

The use of the written word which has traditionally dominated Protestant teaching and thinking since the Reformation, almost to the point of exclusiveness in some cases, is a serious mistake and represents a negation of scriptural truths about how we come to know God and also contemporary truths concerning empirical knowledge and research with regard to perception and truth. With the growth of outreach and renewal and the many mass missions throughout the country there has been considerable criticism recently of dance and the performing arts generally. 'The written word as recorded in scripture, it is argued, is of paramount importance; nothing must distract from the word.' 'The word cannot be expressed in terms of music, dance and drama.' 'The sort of depth concepts that are implicit in the written word cannot be understood in terms of choreography.' There is, of course, much more behind these criticisms than just the problem of the exclusiveness of the written word. Much of the criticism arises because all too often the performing arts are not rooted in scripture, they tend to 'upstage' the message or even become a substitute for the good news. As one writer puts it, 'It is sometimes difficult to distinguish between the stars and the Son.'

While I accept that the performing arts can upstage and become more meaningful and entertaining than the Word in its written and verbal form, I do not accept that the Word cannot be expressed through such non-verbal 'languages'. The performing arts are as rooted in the Word as is the language of the written word. The problem for both remains the same: communicating to gain attention, understanding and acceptance. My experience is that when the Word is expressed exclusively in terms of the written word and especially within the highly elaborate, linguistic code of theology, the Word is frequently lost! The sad fact is that sometimes this 'speaking in tongues', i.e. a foreign or unintelligible language, can also upstage the Word and can undermine it, too! When I go into a comprehensive school in East London, my problem is not the Word, but how to express and communicate it. This can be done in a wide variety of ways, and in a society dominated by the visual media, it may be that visual communication has an important part to play.

I am not trying to undermine the fundamental importance of the Word as expressed in scripture. Scripture *must* be at the root of all evangelical communication, be it language in the literal sense, or dance, heavy metal, clowning, mime and puppets. As Luis Palau said recently in TV broadcasts, 'Back to the Bible, or back to the jungle.' I adhere strongly to the principle that the written word as expressed in scripture is fundamental in every sense of the term and that all 'languages' within evangelical communication specifically and the Church generally, must be rooted in it. As J. G. Ryle[6] says, 'I can find no record of church assemblies in the New Testament in which preaching and teaching orally does not occupy a most prominent position. It seems to me to be the chief instrument by which the Holy Ghost not only awakens sinners but also leads on and establishes saints.'

Many contemporary writers stress that the Word is not

the exclusive concern of one medium of communication. 'The evangelical witness with its emphasis on the power of the Word in scripture and in preaching . . . is very much a valid emphasis, but if it is isolated and left to itself, it is in danger of being reduced to mere cerebral moralism, powerful in its challenge, but failing to reach the heart and therefore to charge the affections and challenge the will' (M. Marshall).[7]

J. F. White[8] discusses the various 'languages' through which the Word can be understood and expressed. He asks, 'Just how explicit must the contents of the Christian message be, and just how explicit must our awareness of the Word – God, be defined?' He argues that it seems increasingly apparent within the current media that there is less need to rely exclusively on verbal symbols to communicate the awareness of God.

Today there is widespread experimenting with alternative forms of worship within liturgical innovation. One reason for the developing use of non-verbal language such as music and dance is the recognition which allows for and indeed encourages a less specific and more 'open' experience of the message than propositional knowledge allows. There are many aspects about our faith that simply cannot and should not be expressed in verbal terms although they may still be rooted in scripture.

J. F. White again, distinguishes between what he calls 'high definition media' and 'low definition media'. In the former, there is little left to the interpreter's imagination, as for example in the ideal of science, whereas in 'low definition media' there is the demand for a much higher degree of audience participation. In the former the audience is seen essentially as a passive recipient of information, whereas in the latter it is seen as an active participator in the information. In the former the message is spelt out more or less explicitly, whereas in the latter a higher degree of participation is encouraged as the individual is allowed to supply much of the content from his or her own knowledge and experience. The rector of the church from which the dance ministry of Springs grew once said, 'The problem with dance, like all the arts is that meaning is open to more than one interpretation.' But that is its strength. The nature of art is that it is an essentially contested concept in the sense that there is never *one* meaning.

We have a dance in the company's repertoire called *The Wondrous Cross*, which is based upon the hymn of that name. It explores in dance/movement terms something of the paradox of the cross both in literal terms, of Mary at the foot of the cross, and in metaphorical terms of our everyday Christian lives. It is a dance which is deliberately open to many interpretations. There is 'layer upon layer of meaning', depending upon who dances it, where it is danced, how one feels at the time, the choreographer's intention, the dancer's interpretation, the context of which the dance is performed and so on. The same applies to music, e.g. Bach's *St. Matthew Passion*. This is the nature of art. There is never any ONE meaning.

We sometimes use as a criteria of 'good art' the notion that it *is* open to many meanings. But, of course, the meaning does not lie in the dance or music *per se*, but rather in the meanings that we each bring to the artifact from our unique knowledge and understanding of scripture. The root of the dance remains faithfully in scripture, but the nature of its expression and perception as interpreted by the audience or congregation is infinite. This non-specificity is its strength and characteristic. The scriptural focus of *The Wondrous Cross* remains absolute and unchanging; the way we express this truth is open to a wide variety of media expressions. In the past we have been brought up to rely on words for worship and in doing so diminished it to the wordy! An interesting and significant point is made by Marshall McLuhan who argues that modern man is post-literate, that he has gone beyond dependence on the medium of the printed page as his prime means of communicating information.

There is a renewed stress on the non-verbal characteristic of early and medieval Christianity. Protestantism turned its back on such forms in the sixteenth century in favour of the then new form of communication especially the real word.

There is no reason to limit ourselves to any one form of communication and understanding. All forms of com-

munication or 'languages' in the general sense of the term
have their place within the faith as they do in everyday life.

2. KNOWING THE WORD – KNOWING GOD

I want now to move our discussion slightly from the term
'word' to the question of how we come to know the Word,
i.e. God. How do we come to understand, communicate,
express and make meaningful our knowledge and understanding of the Word? How do we come to know, understand, communicate and express our knowledge and love
of God?

Coming to know God involves several species of knowing and no one of these species by itself can lead to a full
knowledge and understanding of the Word. These different species although conceptually distinct are in reality
intimately related. I shall refer to them as 'co-ordinate
species of knowing' to emphasise their interdependence.

Three co-ordinate species of knowing

To *know* the Word, to *know* God, means to know him in four
different ways at least, not separately, but interdepen-
dently. To know God means to know him with our minds,
with our practical lives and with our hearts – all surrounded by his Holy Spirit.

Knowing 'that' is essentially revelation or knowing of the
'mind'; it is theoretical knowledge *about* God; it is objective
and publicly verifiable knowledge obtained, expressed and
validated in discursive and propositional terms.

Knowing 'how' is essentially revelation or knowing of the
'body'; it is empirical knowledge rooted in the Word,
knowledge attained, expressed, communicated and validated in practical and procedural life terms.

Knowing 'of' is essentially revelation or knowing of the heart; it is existential knowledge *of* the Word; it is subjective knowledge attained, expressed and validated in terms of first-hand, inner, heartfelt experience of the Word.

Spiritual knowing is essentially revelation of knowing independent of man. This knowledge is not of man's making and not of man's initiative. This is knowledge of the spirit which comes to man by the grace of God.

Knowing 'that'

We see the first kind of revelation or coming to know God expressed in such passages in scripture as:

Rom. 10:17	'faith comes from hearing the message, and the message is heard through the word of Christ'.
Luke 4:4, 8, 12	'it is written'.
Luke 21:33	'heaven and earth will pass away but my words will never'.
Rom. 12:2	'be transformed by the renewing of your mind'.
1 Pet. 1:13	'prepare your minds for action'.
2 Tim. 3:16	'scripture instructs, enlightens, informs, rebukes'.
Heb 5:12	'it nourishes and it promotes growth'.
Ps. 19:10	'they are sweeter than honey'.
Heb. 4:12	it is 'sharper than any double-edged sword'.

Although this mind or intellectual knowing is fundamental in coming to know God or the Word, our minds unaided are insufficient. There are many scriptural truths that simply cannot be grasped by the intellect. Paul particularly reminds us that our mind alone cannot reach through to God (1 Cor. 1:21, Job 11:7). He tells us (1 Cor. 3:18–19) that we are unable to understand the gospel because the human intellect is too proud. As A. W. Tozer[9] says, 'God gave us spirit to apprehend himself, and intellect to apprehend the-

'Teach me, O Lord, the way of thy statutes; and I will keep it to the end' (Ps. 119:33). 'Create in me a pure heart, O God and renew a steadfast spirit within me' (Ps. 51:10). 'Open my lips and my mouth shall declare your praise' (Ps. 51:15).

ology – there is a difference.' The domination of scientific categories and categories of conceptual thinking can easily blind us to the fact that some kinds of truth have to be lived into and not just thought into. There is a strong predisposition within western thinking generally towards the critical and analytical. 'Knowing facts is an intellectual process. Knowing people involves emotional and volitional interactions. You may read the Bible to know certain facts but this is only the beginning. Your real aim is to know Christ. Bible study should be conducted not with the view of knowing *about* Christ, but to knowing him personally' (J. F. White).[10]

We can know *about* God, but not *of* God. Knowledge 'that' does not by itself bring an encounter with God. Although intellectual knowledge may be fundamental, there is an inner emotional knowledge that is ultimately essential for a full knowledge of God. 'If I speak with the tongues of men and angels, but have not love, I am only a resounding gong or a clanging cymbal' (1 Cor 13:1).

Knowing 'how'

We see the second form of revelation of knowing the Word expressed in such passages as:

1 John 3:18	'Dear children, let us not love with words or tongue, but with actions and in truth'.
Jas. 2:17	'faith by itself if it is not accompanied by actions is dead'.
Jas. 1:22	'Do not merely listen to the word, and so deceive yourselves. Do what it says'.
John 8:32	'If you hold to my teaching, you are really my disciples. Then you will know the truth'.
Jas. 2:14	'What good is it, my brothers, if a man claims to have faith, but has no deeds?'
Heb. 4:12	'the word of God is living and active'.
Matt. 7:24	'Therefore everyone who hears these words of mine and puts them into practice, is like a wise man who built his house upon the rock'.

All biblical truths are essentially practical. As the Anglican prayer of general thanksgiving states, 'we show forth our praise *not only with our lips, but in our lives*'. The word becomes known and expressed, i.e. knowledge is realised through our flesh and it is an essential part of coming to know the Word. As Tozer once said, 'Truth that is not experienced is no better than error, and maybe fully as dangerous.'[11] There is a knowing that can only come from experience. Martha Graham, one of the great contemporary dancers and choreographers, once said, 'Dance is first of all a verb.' No amount of thinking, reading or romanticising about getting your leg up will get it up. Either it is up in practical and physical terms or it is not. Only when you have practised it in that verb sense of the term does dance become a noun. So it is with our faith. The Christian faith is firstly a verb and then a noun. The real can never be fully understood as purely rational. It requires a practical realisation and has to be lived into. 'Revelation is not found in words but deeds' (L. Morris).[12]

But we must recognise that actions by themselves, rather like intellectual knowledge by itself, does not lead necessarily to knowing God. What we do must firstly be rooted in scripture, secondly in practical, everyday life.

'Sad to say, many religious people make the same mistake today. They think that these good works and religious deeds will save them, when actually these practices are keeping them from being saved' (Warren W. Wiersbe).[13] The law cannot give righteousness: it can only lead the sinner to the Saviour who alone can give righteousness. What we do must always be underpinned by scripture. All too often we are so involved in doing things that we lose sight of 'why' or 'how' and frequently go astray (Mark 12:24, Eph. 2:8). Furthermore there is much emphasis these days on what is sometimes referred to as relational theology where personal relationships and experiences tend to take precedence over the Word. Christian life must be an interplay of both experience and truth and must be accompanied by the heart since an action may be materially good and right within the written word, but wrong if it proceeds from a sinful heart. The right action for the right reasons must be accompanied by the right heart.

'Show me your ways, O Lord, teach me your paths. Guide me in your truth and teach me' (Ps. 25:4, 5).

'I will instruct you and teach you in the way you should go; I will counsel you and watch over you' (Ps. 32:8).

Knowing 'of'

We see the third kind of revelation and knowing God expressed in such passages as:

Mark 7:6 'These people honour me with their lips, but their hearts are far from me'.

Rom. 2:28 'A man is not a Jew if he is only one outwardly, nor is circumcision merely outward and physical. No, a man is a Jew if he is one inwardly: and circumcision is circumcision of the heart, by the spirit, not by the written code'.

1 Cor. 13:1	'If I speak in tongues of men and angels but have not love, I am only a resounding gong or a clanging cymbal'.
Jer. 29:13	'You shall seek me and find me when you shall seek for me with your whole heart'.
2 Cor. 3:3	the new covenant is written 'not on tablets of stone, but on human hearts'.
Rom. 10:9	'If you confess with your mouth, "Jesus is Lord", and believe in your heart that God . . . for it is with your heart that you believe and are justified.'

Referring to the last passage in Romans, J. Blanchard writes, 'Here faith becomes intensely personal and not just abstract knowledge of the truth.'[14] If we do not see ourselves as being called into a personal relationship with God the Father, our conception will certainly be sub-Christian. 'The question of truth is always for the Christian, as Kierkegaard insisted, an existential one. It is not simply Pilate's question "What is truth?", but "What is my relation to the truth, what is true for me?"' (J. A. Robinson).[15] We cannot know a person, and certainly not God, purely in 'that' term – in a cold, neutral, objective, unemotional 'I – it' relationship. We can only know a person, and God particularly, in personal, intimate, subjective, involved 'I – thou' terms. 'His [God's] relationship was not based upon a cold-hearted logic, but a warm-hearted love. He was challenged to retain a relationship, not to judge God's reasonableness.' (Jean Darnell)[16] The conviction that God exists, or even the knowledge about who he is, is not enough. We have to know him, to be acquainted with him in a personal way. To know 'that' is to know him second-hand, and at a distance, but to know 'of' is to know him first-hand as a person. There is no substitute for this personal encounter.

This is sometimes the most difficult aspect of knowing and coming to understand the Word. We so often know what is right and wrong and what we must do in practical, everyday terms, but to accompany this with the right heart is the most difficult experience and communication of the

'My ears had heard of you but now my eyes have seen you'
(Job 42:5). 'You have filled my heart with great joy' (Ps. 4:7).

truth. Yet it is a fundamental one upon which all the other
truths depend. In Luke 22:50, Jesus could not automatically
change Peter's heart and remove the hatred and violence
that was in it. 'Sometimes outwardly we are one person,
but inwardly we are quite another. Outwardly we are
perhaps theologically correct and sound, but inwardly we
are far away from God' (A. Redpath).[17] One of the most
difficult aspects of coming to know the Word lies within our
heart. It is within this aspect of knowing, perhaps more
than any other, that we need the help and support of the
Holy Spirit, that form of knowing which is beyond man's
initiative.

To know God, to know the Word, means to know him in
three different but interdependent ways. We must come to
know and understand him through our intellects, through
the practical, everyday working of our lives and through a
personal encounter of him via our inner being. If we ignore
any one aspect of these three dimensions we undermine
the whole. A healthy religious life necessarily involves a
daily exercising of the three.

We see these three-fold truths expressed in that most profound of simple prayers, the prayer of St. Richard of Chichester:

'May we know thee more clearly,	('that')
Love thee more dearly,	('of')
And follow thee more nearly, day by day.	('how')

To know the Lord, to come to love him, serve him, and to worship him, involves our whole being, minds, hearts and bodies.

Knowing of the spirit

These three forms of knowing, however fundamental, do not and cannot bring us to a true knowledge and understanding of God and the Word by themselves. There is yet a fourth dimension to our knowing that is perhaps most important of all – spiritual knowing. 'Spiritual knowing comes not by man's achievement or man's initiative, but by the grace and mercy of God alone. Of itself, scripture is nothing but the dead letter, like any other historical document. Before we can find the living word of God in it and have assurance that this is personally addressed to each one of us, there must be an intervention of the Holy Spirit' (F. Wendal).[18] We see this fourth dimension expressed in such passages as:

1 Cor. 2:11	'No man can know God except by the Holy Spirit'.
1 Cor. 2:14	'The man without the Spirit does not accept the things that come from the Spirit of God, for they are foolishness to him and he cannot understand them, because they are spiritually discerned'.
John 16:13	'When the Spirit of truth comes he will guide you into all truth'.
John 4:24	'Then he opens their minds so they could understand the scripture, God is Spirit, and

he that worships him must worship him in
spirit and truth'.

The realm of the spirit is closed to the intellect. 'The
gospel gives light but it cannot give sight' (A. W. Tozer).[19]
True understanding is not natural to us; an act of enlighten-
ment wrought by the Holy Spirit is essential for true understanding of the Word. 'Bible study does not, by itself, lift
the veil or penetrate it. The word does not say, "No man
knoweth the things of God except the man who studies his
bible." It does say that no man knows the things of God
except by the Holy Spirit' (A. W. Tozer).[20] As Paul said to
Corinth, 'And I, brethren, when I came to you, came not
with excellence of speech or wisdom, but in demonstration
of the spirit and of the power.' 'A man may think he knows
the truth because his intellect has been taught but he really
knows the things of God only when the Holy Spirit reveals
them to his heart' (A. Redpath).[21] The heart coincides in
scripture with the Holy Spirit so that it is almost synonymous with it at times.

Our relationship with God then, 'is not something into
which we entered in our own right and on our own terms; it
is something given us solely and completely on the initiative and in the grace of God' (Jock Anderson).[22] 'The
Church today has had much experience of the word, a
growing experience of "deed", but all too little experience
of the power of the Holy Spirit' (D. Watson).[23]

The teaching of the New Testament is that God and
spiritual things can be known finally only by a direct
encounter of God within the soul. The pure understanding
of God must be by personal spiritual awareness. The Holy
Spirit is indispensable. But the spirit of the human heart is
not unconscious or automatic. Human will and intelli-
gence, human hearts and human bodies must all yield to
and co-operate together with the benign intentions of God.
To know the Word, to know God, through our Lord Jesus
Christ is to know him with our whole being, mind, body,
heart and spirit.

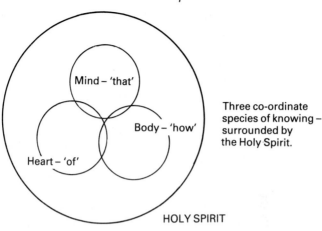

Three co-ordinate
species of knowing –
surrounded by
the Holy Spirit.

*The significance of the four dimensions of knowing to
religious dance*

Firstly, the religious knowledge of the performer(s) and
choreographer should be rooted in this four-fold conception of understanding and truth.

Secondly, the dances and the dancing should be an
expression of this four-fold understanding and truth.

Thirdly, although the dance and dancing must necessarily be rooted in this full four-fold dimension of truth and
understanding, it is perhaps within the third and fourth
dimensions of knowing that this unique non-verbal form of
expression comes into its own. While I do not want to give
the impression that religious dance is essentially a language
of tongues, I believe that more often than not it functions in
a very similar way by giving expression to the ineffable, the
mystical and unutterable. Dance is essentially a language of
the heart and the spirit. Through this non-verbal and
non-rational (N.B. *not* irrational) 'language' we are able to
come to know and express that which is beyond the everyday verbal and rational. Although dance is rooted in theoretical ('that') and practical ('how') knowledge, it is a unique
means to knowledge 'of' the inner psyche – the heart and
spirit.

3. **WORSHIP AND THE WORD**

The four-fold dimension of knowledge is built into New Testament conceptions of true worship. We are exhorted to 'worship in spirit and in truth' (John 4:24). Truth implies a three-fold involvement of mind, body, and heart surrounded by the Holy Spirit. True worship includes our whole being, and if we neglect any aspect of our being, then the truth of our worship will be seriously undermined.

Worship and the whole person

(i) *Mind* 'When our eyes are good so also will be our hearts and bodies' (Matt. 6:22–23). (Our bodies and hearts are expressions, in part at least, of our mind.)

(ii) *Body* 'If you are offering your gift at the altar and there remember that your brother has something against you, leave your gift there in front of the altar. First go and be reconciled to your brother; then come and offer your gift' (Matt. 5:23). (Our worship must be accompanied by a rightful mind and a rightful heart. Equally our hearts and minds must be accompanied by rightful actions.)

(iii) *Heart* 'If our hearts are hard then we worship in vain' (Matt. 15:9). 'Without the heart we will ever be hearing but not understanding, seeing but never perceiving' (Matt. 13:14).

(iv) *Spirit* Spiritual worship may be interpreted in two ways, human and divine. The human notion of spirit is very much related to man's spiritual nature as felt and known in the heart. It is an inner, ineffable knowing and understanding of something more than everyday human feeling and emotion. It is no accident that so often in Scripture we see spirit and heart associated together.

The divine notion of spirit, the Holy Spirit, is expressed quite specifically, and particularly in worship, as being within our bodies. When scripture urges us to offer our bodies as living sacrifices of praise and thanksgiving, it means firstly our whole beings and our life generally but, within the context of this discussion of dance, it surely means present our bodies literally, i.e. our physical bodies, 'God's temple' (1 Cor. 3:16). The sacrifices of the Old Covenant were of bulls and goats whereas the sacrifices of the New Covenant are expressed in terms of ourselves. We are told that this *is* our spiritual worship which 'is holy and pleasing to God'. For those who still see the body as sinful, let us remember that, firstly, we should not call anything unclean which comes from God, especially since our sinful bodies have been washed pure by his saving passion and blood, we having been called 'out of darkness into his wonderful light' (1 Pet. 2:9); and secondly, 'Do you not know that you are temples of the Holy Spirit, who is in you, whom you have received from God? You are not your own; you were bought at a price' (1 Cor. 6:19). We should honour God with our bodies in every possible sense of the term. 'Let us continually offer to God a sacrifice of praise', as we are commanded to and because 'with such sacrifices God is pleased' (Heb. 13:15, 16).

Spiritual worship involves our bodies as whole beings – 'living sacrifices of praise and thanksgiving'. It is difficult to see how the body at least, if not dance, can honestly be left out of our worship. As Christians we do not *have* a body: we *are* our body. When we are exhorted to worship with our whole selves this must necessarily be the body not *as a part* of something, but ourselves.

With this scriptural concern for wholeness in mind, is there any other form of expression which involves our whole self – intellectual, physical, social, emotional and spiritual – in such a comprehensive way as dance? Is there any other as close to the human personality as dance? Most expressive forms are based upon extensions of the body. The instrument of expression in dance *is* the body. We *are* the body.

'This is the day the Lord has made. Let us rejoice and be glad in it' (Ps. 118:24).

Worship and the New Covenant

Let us now examine the New Covenant's *expression* of worship. In the Old Testament we saw that dance was synonymous with praise and thanksgiving which were always characteristic of Israelite worship, and was associated with rejoicing. When we come to the New Testament, we see very little difference in this aspect of worship. In fact, rejoicing and being glad takes on an extended meaning since not only are we exhorted to rejoice always (Phil. 3:1, 4:4, 1 Thess. 5:16), we are also told that these expressions are 'fruits of the spirit'.

'Time to dance . . .' (Eccles. 3:4)

'In Genesis we see a picture of God enjoying and delighting in what he made – his creation. In Revelation we catch a glimpse of man enjoying and delighting in the one who made him – his Creator. The Bible, from cover to cover, is the story of worship and how people in the Old Testament and New Testament alike are worshipping people' (M. Marshall)[24] and that the core of all this worship is heartfelt praise and thanksgiving. Celebration is at the very heart of the way of Christ. He entered the world on a high note of jubilation, 'Behold I bring you good news of great joy that will be for all people' (Luke 2:10), and 'he will be a joy and delight to you' (Luke 1:14).

He left the world on a similar 'high', bequeathing his joy to the disciples saying, 'These things I have spoken to you that my joy may be in you and that your joy may be full' (John 15:11).

The procession of the good news as recorded in the New Testament is frequently presented in terms synonymous with celebrating and feasting. It is likened to a marriage (Matt. 9:15) and a great wedding banquet (Luke 14:16, 12:36). It was likened to a hidden treasure and pearl.

The characteristic of worship, praise and thanksgiving in the New Testament is no different from that of the Old in its basic motivation and heartfelt emotional response. It is as applicable to us today as it was yesterday, and can be responded to naturally by dance. Within the Christian faith dance represents a potential means of expressing our whole selves in an act of praise and thanksgiving. Not only is this a legitimate religious expression on the part of a loving and grateful people, but it is also a manifestation of spiritual fruits. We should remember that Jesus had some very strong words for those who reject enthusiasm of this kind. When the Pharisees tried to curb the enthusiasm of crowds as he entered Jerusalem, they said, 'Teacher, rebuke your disciples!' 'I tell you,' Jesus replied, 'if they keep quiet, the stones will cry out' (Luke 19:40). We read elsewhere that 'the whole crowd of disciples began joyfully to praise God

in loud voices' (Luke 19:37). Other biblical references include Gal. 5:22, Heb. 13:15, Jas. 5:13 and Eph. 5:19.

Michael Green[25] writes, 'We cannot doubt that heartfelt praise was one of the most striking characteristics of the early Church . . . to be honest, we do not know much of heartfelt praise today.' I can remember David Watson making a similar point at a cathedral where he was preaching. He described the 'spiritual' atmosphere as being so cold that it was possible to skate down the aisle on the ice!

For many of us in the Church today, could it be that although we know God, we neither glorify him as God, nor give him thanks? (Rom. 1:21). Do we, in fact, worship with our lips, but our hearts are far from him? (Mark 7:6). Is it possible that the structures of yesterday's worship have become strictures for today's, and as a consequence hardened our hearts? (Heb. 3:8). Worship which is not rendered heartily is not true worship. Suddenly, the inward spiritual attitude of the worshipper begins to come to the front as an important factor in worship. Many of us, of course, are very shy of allowing our emotions to be expressed in public (and in private, too, perhaps!). Any overt expression of grief or joy is sometimes frowned upon, within our rather inhibited and emotionally restrained society. But commitment to Christ, and to life itself, is not based on intellectual understanding alone, but rather on an intimate, feeling encounter. As this necessarily involves an opening up and exposing of our true selves we inevitably become vulnerable. Loving is a risky business and remains so all our lives. David Watson told a vivid story about love, likening it to two porcupines living in sub zero temperatures. To keep warm they have to get close together, but in doing so, of course, they prick each other. Loving is rather like this. Inevitably, we are 'pricked' but that is the price to be paid for loving. Frequently, when we have been 'pricked' we do not again allow ourselves to open up and be loved. Many of us are hesitant in expressing our emotions. Maybe we fear the Pharisees' criticism? Maybe we should fear the Lord's answer! (Luke 19:37–40).

There are times when hosannas should be on our lips and exuberant joy on our faces, and everything else that goes with the proper celebration of the coming of the King of Kings. Delight yourselves in the Lord. Ps. 37:4 is not the idealistic dream of the psalmist, but a specific instruction to 'rejoice in the Lord always' Phil. 4:4. (J. Young)[26]

Worship and feelings

The great obstacle to personal involvement is fear of emotion. Everything that is truly personal to us, everything that involves us as persons raises a wind if not a storm of emotion: love, guilt, faith, grief, joy, success, failure, rejection and creativity. But notice that it is not so much the emotion that we are afraid of, but letting it show, revealing ourselves in the heat of emotion, betraying ourselves. Emotion is bound up with life itself, in animals as with man, it cannot be eliminated. The expression of emotion is repressed in our society. (Paul Tournier)[27]

There is nothing wrong with emotion. We used to learn to express and enjoy our emotions much more than we do, especially with regard to our fellowship with God. What could be more wonderful, or emotionally stirring, than feeling the presence of God. (D. and R. Bennett)[28]

Worship is the submission of *all* our nature to God: the quickening of conscience by his holiness, the nourishment of our mind with his truth, the purifying of our imagination by his beauty, the opening of our hearts to his love, the surrender of will to his purpose and all in adoration. (William Temple)[29]

Christ set us free (Gal. 5), 'where the spirit of the Lord is, there is freedom' (2 Cor. 3:17). Sometimes we do not experience his freedom because we feel a measure of security in our bondage: it is what we are used to and we may be reluctant to step out of it into the unknown.

Our justification of dance so far has been mainly within the *dancing* aspect of the 'dancing-mourning' continuum (Eccles. 3:4), concentrating on feasting and celebrating *communally and publicly* within the context of *everyday, worldly living*. The 'mourning' consciousness as opposed to 'dancing' consciousness, the 'private' and 'personal' consciousness as opposed to 'communal' and 'public' consciousness, the mystical consciousness as opposed to world consciousness have hardly been touched. I want now to extend our thinking by looking beyond this seemingly exclusive 'communal-worldly-praise' focus to a more 'personal-mystical-mourning' focus, for I believe that dance can accommodate both.

'Come unto me, all you who are weary and burdened, and I will give you rest' (Matt. 11:28). 'I stand at the door and knock. If anyone hears my voice and opens the door, I will come in and eat with him, and he with me' (Rev. 3:20). 'You will know the truth, and the truth will set you free' (John 8:32). 'Blessed is the man who makes the Lord his trust' (Ps. 40:4).

'Time to mourn' (Eccles. 3:4)

We recognise the fears and inhibitions which have traditionally surrounded the expression of 'mourning'. *Expressing* one's feelings and opening up oneself to *impressions* of feelings is not normally considered healthy or acceptable in our society. Classical objectivity and emotional restraint combined with a stiff upper lip is more the norm within our everyday living and particularly within our faith.

But we recognise also that loving, especially loving God, involves a commitment of the heart and an opening of ourselves in order that we may be loved, and may love in turn. As with all forms of knowing, loving includes both impressive and expressive experiences. We receive (impressions) and we give (expressions). Feelings have traditionally been seen as uncomfortable intrusions in our lives, yet they are an important part of our human make-up given to us by God and created for our use. They are fundamental to knowing and understanding God, ourselves and the world. Feelings are a part of our identity as a person. It is vital that we affirm them, and affirm them in gratitude to God. 'God created you as a person; created you and redeemed you. In view of God's mercy the only fitting response is to offer yourself and all that you are' (J. Young).[30] Feelings and emotions are important in the Bible. Above all they are basic to a proper, heartfelt knowledge and understanding of life. 'My mouth will speak words of wisdom; the utterance from my heart will give understanding' (Ps. 49:3).

We are told to worship with all our being. We can come with a joyful and grateful heart, but we can also come with a heart 'travailed and heavy laden' (Matt. 11:28). We can come as we are knowing our Father in heaven will receive us in love. All human feelings and emotions are valid legitimate concerns within worship. The performing arts generally, but dance and music specifically, can accommodate such heartfelt expressions, both in the impressive and expressive sense of the term. The dance in its many and varied expressive movement forms, can help heal and

'He heals the broken-hearted and binds up their wounds'
(Ps. 147:3). 'Cast all your anxiety on him because he cares for
you' (1 Pet. 5:7). 'I tell you the truth, anyone who will not
receive the kingdom of God like a child will never enter it'
(Luke 18:17). 'Let us then approach the throne of grace with
confidence, that we may receive mercy and find grace to help
us in our time of need' (Heb. 4:16). 'The fear of the Lord is the
beginning of knowledge' (Prov. 1:7).

restore, articulate and make meaningful the nature of the inner self as it struggles to know and understand itself, the world and God.

God created us to respond to life with our hearts as well as our minds. His own life and the life of the apostles show this and Christ's feelings and sufferings are recorded in the Bible.

'Feelings' are an important topic not just because they are fundamental to healthy growth and development but also because it is ultimately within this focus that I propose to offer a justification for the performing arts generally and dance specifically as a non-verbal, disciplined means of coming to know and to express our world.

Time for mystery, fear and awe . . . 'Holy, Holy, Holy is the Lord Almighty' (Isa. 6:3).

Our discussion of the 'mourning' consciousness within the 'dance-mourning' continuum has shown that dance is a legitimate expressive form of the 'mourning' aspect of our hearts as well as of praise and thanksgiving.

I want to extend the conception of dance further by looking critically at yet another continuum, that of the 'natural-supernatural'. The Bible is quite clear that while our faith must be rooted and worked out in horizontal terms of everyday life, at the same time we must remain separate from it. Equally we know that the Word is both immanent and transcendent. He is immanent in the sense that his spirit dwells within each one of us, but he is transcendent in the sense that he is spirit and beyond our natural consciousness. We can never 'see' him.

By 'natural consciousness', I mean a reality rooted in the direct, concrete, physical world of everyday life dominated by man. By 'supernatural' I mean a consciousness that is more intuitive, metaphysical, spiritual and mystical to which we all as Christians, in the sense that God is transcendent, aspire. This supernatural or 'ideal' world, which is beyond us and beyond our achievement and initiative, while in some sense related to us, is nevertheless 'separate

'Holy, Holy, Holy' (Rev. 4:8). 'You are awesome, O God' (Ps. 68:35).

from' and 'more than' our everyday worldly consciousness.

God as *immanent* is recorded in Luke 17:21, John 15:4, Matt. 18:20, Phil. 1:20, Gal. 2:20.

God as *transcendent* is recorded in 1 Cor. 2:9–12, John 16:13, 14:6, Luke 2:14, Matt. 13:14, Is. 6:3, Acts 9:3, 1 Tim. 6:16.

G. Harkness[31] argues that, 'the supernatural and mystical are found in every great religion. It is the very life of religion, for it centres in the communion of the Holy Spirit with the ultimate ground of reality upon which existence rests.' Whether this is wholly accurate or not it is a reminder of a characteristic common and basic to many religions.

The Christian faith is essentially and fundamentally a mystical and supernatural faith (1 Tim. 3:16, Col. 1:27). It is a faith bound up with the belief that there is a transcendent reality – the Word – and the implicit knowledge that man is meaningfully related to that reality as to the end to which he aspires. God is separate from all beings; he alone is immortal and lives in unapproachable light.

> The title 'holy one of Israel' occurs no less than twenty-six times within the book of Isaiah. It was this experience of the holiness of God that was the foundation of Isaiah's message. It is this understanding of the holiness of God that stands at the heart of all the Old Testament has to say about God. It is this holiness of God that is revealed above all in the life and teaching of Jesus. (R. Gordon)[32]

> No Christians need draw back from the word 'transcendental' for at the very root of the holy faith is a belief in a transcendent world. A world above nature, different from and lying beyond matter and space and time, into which science cannot pry and at whose mortal uncomprehending reason can do no other than reverently kneel and adore. Nor should he shrink from the word 'supernatural' for it quite accurately describes an important tenet in his Christian creed. (A. W. Tozer)[33]

Mystical knowledge is *separate from* and *beyond* man's initiative and achievement. It stands outside the range of man's possibilities and is clearly related to spiritual knowledge. It is a knowledge dependent upon God; man does not possess the faculties to achieve this union with God on his own. 'It is a startling disclosure, to be made with awe and thankfulness. Expressions like "the mystery of faith", "the

'Serve the Lord with fear and rejoice with trembling'
(Ps. 2:11).

mystery of religion'' (1 Tim. 3:9,16) are affirmations that the
essential teaching of Christianity are truths made known by
revelation, not worked out by the unaided mind' (L.
Morris).[34] W. Jonstone[35] reminds us that mystical knowledge is not knowledge in the ordinary, everyday, consciousness sense of the term. It calls for a different consciousness: 'mystical knowledge arises from a deep level of
the psyche which is ordinarily dormant. It is a different
kind of knowledge from that which we ordinarily enjoy.
Mysticism does not mean that we learn new things so much
as learn to know in a new way which belongs to a different

level of consciousness and for this reason it is ineffable and can never adequately be described or talked about. It is an affair of the heart rather than the head.'

Michael Marshall[36] reinforces this plea for a different kind of consciousness and extension of every perception in coming to experience the holy and ineffable.

> Perhaps the place in the Old Testament where we see the richest and fullest agenda of all the implications of worship is the well known passage of Isaiah 6 in the story of the prophet's vision. It begins, as all worship must, when the prophet enters into a realisation of the presence of the presence, the holiness of the glory of God. That moment is the given moment of the numinous with all the power that is latent within such religious experience. It is a moment of vision and insight. It is a moment when the doors of perception, normally closed by man's cerebral censorship are flung wide open. Ears which had previously seemed deaf, begin at last to hear. Eyes which must have been blind in the past, are opened at last.

This concern for extending consciousness and freeing ourselves from the almost exclusiveness of traditional analytic and discursive thought in order to realise the holy, the spiritual, the numinous and ineffable is not beyond man's perception even though it is 'separated'.

> There is a realm of the spirit which is related to the material world, but is not identical with it. Whatever this may mean about its wider existence beyond man, this realm of the spirit is within man, the *human* spirit has the capacity to discern some kinds of channels other than the ordinary ones of sensation and rational education. It uses these channels, to be sure, but finds in their use a deeper meaning. (G. Harkness)[37]

Dance remains the natural and physical 'language' through which we come to know something of this mystical and spiritual knowledge, but known from within a different worldly consciousness.

This 'separateness from' and 'extension of' normal every-day living and thinking is a key concept within this area of consciousness. William James[38] reinforces the fact that,

> There are states and insights into depths of truth un-plumbed by the discursive intellect. In short, mystical experiences adds to the subject's grasp of reality by an intuitive rather than logical approach. It is not sensory experience, scientific verification, or logical deduction that the mystic's knowledge is dependent, but by a clearer vision and a depth of feeling that seems to come from a source beyond itself.

> Theology was once defined by P. Tillich as taking rational trouble about mystery. But there are thousands today who cannot recognise the mystery (theos) because of the logos. (J. A. Robinson)[39]

Ralph Vaughan Williams, one of the great English musical mystics, argued that the function of art was not to represent reality, but rather to go beyond it. The position that he was taking up was one which sees art not as *re*presentation, i.e. expressing what already exists, but rather going beyond what already exists. It is the position that Susan Langer[40] takes up when she argues for what she terms the *'presentational'* nature of dance as art, rather than the *'representational'*. Dance and music are unique forms of coming to know rather than merely representing, in sound or movement, something of what we already know.

Mystical and spiritual consciousness is concerned with a different mode of being, a different degree of reality, free from the normal, everyday, conditioned responses. C. S. Lewis[41] remarks, 'That the range and scope of our rational faculties are very limited. Our thinking is only the thinnest possible film on the surface of the vast deep.' No wonder the faithful have always struggled to understand and express the ineffable, using, for example, the following 'agonising' and 'ecstatic' terms. In the Bible generally, and the Psalms particularly, we find many expressions of the agony and the ecstasy of the mystical and ineffable.

The agony and the ecstasy of the mystical Word

AGONY
deep inner longing
groaning inwardly
sighing
yearning
panting and fainting
with the inmost being
'As the deer pants for streams of water, so my soul pants for
     you, O God' (Ps. 42:1–2).
'My soul yearns, even faints for the courts of the Lord; my
     heart and flesh cry out for the living God' (Ps. 84:2).
fearful (Heb. 10:31).
overwhelmed (Ps. 143:4).

ECSTASY
'Ah, Lord God, behold I cannot speak' (Jer. 1:6).
'overflowing with thankfulness' (Col. 2:6).
'inexpressible and glorious joy' (1 Pet. 1:8).
depths of ineffable love (Ps. 28:7).
love so amazing, so divine ('When I survey the wondrous
     cross').
We are told that frequently people were amazed, fearful,
     awed, astonished, wondrous.
We are told that this area is ineffable, unutterable and too
     great for words, a 'thing that cannot be uttered' (2 Cor.
     12:4).
It is mysterious, strange and wondrous.
It is Holy, Holy, Holy.
It causes man to fall down, to worship, in fear and awe, in
     wonder, reverence and praise.
It brings about a peace of mind which is 'beyond all under-
     standing'.

The mystical consciousness is keenly aware of the inad-
equacy of words, and that, 'No eye has seen, no ear has
heard, no mind has conceived what God has prepared for
those who love him' (1 Cor. 2:9), but it is also aware that
God has revealed himself by his Holy Spirit and that 'the

spirit searches all things, even the deep things of God' (1 Cor. 2:10). On the one hand, there is the yearning to know the Word, to know God in the sense of communion with him which is expressed in utterances of 'agony', and on the other there is the struggle to express this ineffable mystery in terms of 'ecstasy'.

The mystic may seek for knowledge and expression within languages other than words, sometimes strange and unfamiliar 'languages'. By 'language' I mean any form of communication which makes meaningful both our inner and outer world of experience. There are simply some things that cannot and should not be put into words, and these are often our most important and meaningful experiences. Words, in the non poetic sense, although constituting the supreme means of public communication, may be inappropriate and even form barriers to understanding when expressing the spiritual, mystical and transcendental world.

When we are 'lost in wonder, love and praise', when we 'cannot speak', when 'we hear things that cannot be told' and 'cannot be uttered', 'when our soul yearns and even faints and our flesh cries out', *then* . . . the spirit of the Lord intercedes for us, and maybe through dance and music, in a way that words cannot express. As David Watson[42] says:

Language is basically a series of sounds or syllables that we understand. But why should my spirit not communicate with God, who is spirit, with sounds or syllables which I may not understand, but which are still vehicles of communication? Tongues are not irrational, but transrational or supernatural. God is not limited to rational thought, important though that is. There are many forms of communication between the believer and God; silence, 'sighs too deep for words', intelligible words, songs, shouts, movement, dance and so on. When my spirit wants to worship God or pray to him, a wide variety of meaningful expressions may be called upon.

Worship and movement – the psychophysical manifestations of worship recorded in scripture

Before bringing this section on the Bible's holistic concern for true worship to a close, I should like to return briefly to the body aspect of worship. It is interesting to note that while very little is said specifically in scripture about the dance vocabulary, there is considerable information about the movement vocabulary of body expression in worship.

The root meaning for the Hebrew word we translate as 'worship' is 'to prostrate'. The word 'bless' means 'to kneel'. 'Thanksgiving' refers to 'an extension of the hand'. Throughout scripture we find a variety of physical postures and gestures related to worship and incidentally, a potentially rich movement vocabulary for dance. For example: lying prostrate, standing, bowing down, kissing, lifting up one's hands, shouting, bowing the head, stamping, lifting one's eyes, stretching out one's hands, trembling, groaning, leaping.

We are invited to worship with our bodies and all these actions, although not by themselves constituting dance, form a good basic raw material for much of what we call religious dance. They are what dancers call 'poses'. I hasten to add however that whilst the pose does form a part of dance, the dance is not made up of poses so much as actions which occur between those poses. How we move, for example, between kneeling with our heads on the ground to standing with our arms held high above our heads and moving towards the altar alone or with each other is essentially where the dance lies, not so much in the positions that we are going to as how to get into and out of those positions.

The physical expressions are a combination of both literal and metaphoric meanings but the notion of movement is very clear in the following quotations: 'Therefore *lift* your *drooping hands* and *stretch* your *weaknesses,* and *make* straight *paths* for your *feet*' (Heb. 12:12–13). 'The twenty-four elders, who were seated on their thrones before God, *fell* on their *faces* and worshipped God' (Rev. 11:16). 'Rejoice . . . and *leap for joy,* because great is your reward in heaven' (Luke 6:23).

Dance – a form of knowing

Dance constitutes a unique non-verbal means whereby something of the deeply spiritual, mystical, ineffable and unutterable can be made known and made meaningful. 'The function of art is to obtain revelation of that which is beyond human senses and faculties – of that which is spiritual . . . the human, visible, audible and intelligible media which artists (of all kinds) use, are symbols not of the visible and audible things, but what lies beyond senses and knowledge' (Vaughan Williams).[43]

Dance comprises the artist's felt conception of reality – his feelings, ideas, fantasies, mysteries, anxieties. It is not ornamentation or distraction but is a way of giving form and meaning to life – to express emotional meaning in organised patterns of movements and stillness.

Susan Langer,[44] one of the most international and articulate of dance philosophers, writes:

> Art may be defined as the practice of creating perceptible forms expressive of human feeling. I say 'perceptible' rather than sensuous forms because some works of art are given to imagination rather than to outward senses. Feeling covers much more than it does in the technical vocabulary of psychology. It takes in all possible meanings: it applies to everything that can be felt. The word expression has two principal meanings: in one sense, it means self expression, giving vent to one's feelings. In this sense it refers to a symptom of what we feel. In another sense, however, it means the presentation of an idea in the symbolic perceptible sense of the term.

Much more will be said about the nature and conditions of dance as a form of knowing in Section II, Dance and Education.

Dancing and 'tongues'

The question of 'speaking in tongues', whether in the sense of 1 Cor. 14 specifically or 'foreign languages' more generally, is an important one within the context of contemporary thinking about the sacred dance. Scripture is quite unequivocal that speaking in tongues is good and to be encouraged. It is certainly not forbidden in itself. What is forbidden, of course, is speaking in a 'tongue' or a 'language', or any expressive form which is unintelligible and which makes the listener a 'foreigner'. This can be applied to some of the more literal expressions of tongues as well as the foreign or unintelligible expressions of dance and drama. It can also be applied to the unintelligible, elaborate, linguistic codes of some of the Church's preaching! The Bible reminds us that, 'Unless you speak intelligible words with your tongue, how will anyone know what you are saying? You will just be speaking into the air. Undoubtedly there are all sorts of languages in the world, yet none of them is without meaning. If then I do not grasp the meaning of what someone is saying, I am a foreigner to the speaker and he is a foreigner to me' (1 Cor. 14:9–11).

Clearly if a 'language' is to communicate, there must be a deliberate and sensitive attempt to come to know and understand the 'listener'. It is amazing how frequently this basic fact is forgotten, especially in forms of religious expression. Perhaps it is a confusion between education and communication on the one hand, and the scriptural nature of 'tongues' on the other. Within the context of this study, I am using the term 'tongues' in the more general sense of 'foreign languages'. In this sense of the term 'tongue' and 'language' are synonymous with 'form of knowing'. The problem for dance within our contemporary Christian faith is less a scriptural than an educational one. So few people within the Church really understand the nature of dance, either as art or religion. This is as much the fault of dance as it is of the Church and education.

My experience is that as dancers we sometimes display an extraordinary insensitivity to the need for dance education and dance perception. This is probably because we have been with the body and dance for so long that we find it difficult to put ourselves in the shoes of the non-dancer. We take both the body and the language for granted. I know from my own experience how reluctant dancers are to talk about their art form, and also how notoriously inarticulate they can be since their 'language' is body rather than words.

People sometimes accuse me of exaggerating the need for education in sacred dance. They argue that it is impossible to talk about something which is essentially non-verbal. My reply is that whilst no amount of talking will ever equal the true nature of dance, that does not mean to say that we cannot say a lot *about* dance and in doing so greatly refine and extend our knowledge and understanding of the expressive form.

For dance to become an established language within the faith there is a very serious need for education. Another interesting point I have noticed about the many youthful and enthusiastic dance companies, both amateur and professional, religious and secular, coming on to the market during the present dance explosion is how so often they pursue their own artistic needs rather than meeting the needs of the community.

There has been considerable criticism recently of the way the Arts Council gives money to avant-garde groups, sometimes at the expense of the community which the money should be supporting. I accept the need to encourage the extension of art but there is also the fundamental need and obligation to communicate in such a way that the community, and in our case the Christian community, can understand and enjoy this expressive form. Misunderstandings and insensitivities have resulted in many within the Church rejecting or at best being very sceptical of this 'language' or 'tongue'.

Because of this scepticism and lack of dance education within the faith, we should heed scripture which reminds us that 'the man who speaks in tongues should pray that he may interpret what he says. For if I pray in a tongue, my spirit prays, but my mind is unfruitful.' It must be understood that the function of dance within the faith is not an end in itself, but rather a means to an end. Only if dance contributes to worship and through worship to building up the church body, does it have a place.

Briefly, a word about dancing in the spirit. Earlier I distinguished between public/communal dance and private/individual dance. I believe that 'dancing in the spirit', which is probably the equivalent of the 'spiritual use of tongues', is perfectly acceptable and pleasing to God. I am anxious not to undermine it as a means of coming to 'speak' to the Lord and of him speaking to us personally through our dancing. In this private situation, I *know* that dance is perfectly acceptable. I *know* from my own experience that there are some things that can only be known or expressed in terms of dance, and usually without music. The problem arises when this sort of dance is made into a public form of worship and the congregation is asked to use it as a means to *their* worship. My experience is that this has not always been very helpful, and for many it represents an embarrassment at best, and self-indulgence at worst. The vocation of the Christian dancer is to share the unique ministry of dance so that 'we built up the body of the Church'.

For dance to take up its rightful place within worship it is important that education takes place between the dance and the Church, that there is a disciplined dialogue between the two so that all parties can attain a positive understanding of the nature and conditions of what is intended. The obligation of any communicator is in fact to bring about communication. The art of communication is always something 'more than' and 'separate from' the expressive form itself. In the case of dance much more needs to be done in the education of both the dancers who purport to be communicators and the Church body generally.

'All things were created by him and for him' (Col. 1:16).
'From whom all things come and from whom we live' (1 Cor.
8:6). 'God created man in his own image; in the image of God
he created him' (Gen. 1:27). 'God saw all that He had made,
and it was very good' (Gen. 1:31).

4. THE BODY AND DANCE

And now, in seeking biblical principles to justify dance, we come to one of the more difficult topics within the Church: the body. The body is often the main reason for rejecting dance. As an expression of the body, dance is intimately related to the physical body, and by association takes on all the negative, conditioned, socio-historical responses that we have inherited. Until we understand and accommodate a disciplined scriptural notion of the body, and develop a biblical attitude towards it no amount of argument, however skilled and justified, will persuade us to accept dance as a normal and legitimate part of worship. 'Praise the Lord' that within contemporary society there is a growing positive, healthy and honest attitude towards dance. Certainly there are signs of an opening of minds and a relaxing of puritanical fears and attitudes which hopefully will help restore the body to its rightful and lawful place within God's creation.

The body in creation

Let us recognise firstly that God 'made the world and everything in it' (Acts 17:24), 'through him all things were made' (John 1:3), 'all things were created by him and for him' (Col. 1:16), 'from whom all things came and for whom we live' (1 Cor. 8:6). Secondly, that 'God created man in his own image; in the image of God he created him; male and female' (Gen. 1:27). And thirdly, that God looked at his handiwork and 'saw that it was good' (Gen. 1:12), 'very good' (Gen. 1:31).

The body is a part of God's creation. 'Everything God created is good and nothing is to be rejected if it is received with thanksgiving because it is consecrated by the word of

God and prayer' (1 Tim. 4:4,5). Our bodies, the basic instrument of expression in dance, are a part of and an expression of God's handiwork.

'Clean' and 'unclean'

Scripture tells us that we should 'not call anything impure that God has made clean' (Acts 10:15). Like Peter we have to learn that nothing is unclean that comes from God. As Paul says, 'nothing is unclean in itself' and, 'as one who is in the Lord Jesus, I am fully convinced that no food is unclean in itself' (Rom. 14:14). 'Understand this. Nothing outside a man [be it his body, dance or food] can make him unclean by going into him. *Rather it is what comes out of a man that makes him unclean*' (Mark 7:14,15).

It is important to recognise that the body, and the dance by association, is not unclean in itself. It is good since it was created by God and he said that it was good. What makes the body 'unclean', and frequently by association dance unclean, is more to do with how we come to perceive it than what it is in itself. Because of the complex deeply ingrained conditioned negative attitudes towards the body inherited, in part at least, from the past, we tend to find it difficult accommodating the body with a 'clean' and proper healthy perception.

If we accept that the body in itself is good, then we must ensure that it is used in a rightful and lawful way, and that we perceive it in this way. Once again, the abuse or misuse of the body is not a reason for its non-use, but a reason for its proper use. It is a fact, of course, that much of the dance we see in the mass media is quite deliberately and explicitly a misuse, in the Christian sense of the term at least, of both the dance and the dancer. While recognising this misuse, let us also recognise the basic goodness of both and 'let us draw near to God with our bodies and the dance, with a sincere heart, a full assurance of faith, having our hearts sprinkled to cleanse us from a guilty conscience and having our bodies washed with pure water' (Heb. 10:22). 'If we hold to his teaching, we will be one of his disciples. Then we will know the truth and the truth will set us free' (John 8:31). In these two passages we see the true context of freedom in worship.

'Thinking stirs feeling and feeling triggers action. While our thoughts stir our feelings and this strongly influences our will, it is yet true that the will can and should be pastor of our thoughts. Every moral person can determine what he will think about and what he will not' (A. W. Tozer).[45] Every talent may be used for good or evil, but every talent nevertheless comes from God. 'Blessed are the pure in *heart* for they shall see God' (Matt. 5:8). When there is a pure heart with regard to the body and dance, there we shall see true dance in worship. Let us rid ourselves of all that is impure, cleanse ourselves of the traditional uncleanliness that has been, and in some cases still is, associated with dance. Let us 'stop judging by mere appearances and make a right judgment' by trying to understand the purity of intent behind the dance (John 7:24).

'In the records of the Lord's life and teaching and whole revelation, we find the dignity and claims of the body as an integral part of human nature constantly recognised. The gospel gives no support to the philosophic tendency, so often reflected in certain types of religious teaching, to treat the body with disparagement. Jesus accords full rights to the corporal side of our being' (*Dictionary of Christ and the Gospels*).[46]

In emphasising the basic goodness and cleanliness of the body, and by association dance, I am not implying that dance should therefore necessarily be an intimate part of worship. If to some dance is unclean then, for the moment at least, let us not distress them by using it. Education may be needed to restore dance to its rightful and lawful place. Dance and dancers will have to be very patient and sensitive to the needs of such an education but equally there must be a loving on the other side. For some, it should be recognised, *not* to dance may be equally a stumbling block to worship!

PSALM 8

'You have set your glory above the heavens'

'When I consider your heavens, the work of your fingers, the moon and the stars'

'What is man that you are mindful of him?'

'O Lord, our Lord. How majestic is your name in all the earth'

The body – and the Holy Spirit

The body in scripture is given a very special place. Scripture is surprisingly explicit in stating that 'our bodies are temples of the Holy Spirit'. 'We are his house' (Heb. 3:6), 'the temple of the living God' (2 Cor. 6:16), 'Christ is in you' (Rom. 8:10). God's temple is sacred, and you are that temple!

The New Testament has at least thirty passages saying with stark clarity that every child of God is the indwelling place of the Holy Spirit. 'Your body is a temple of the Holy Spirit, who is in you and whom you have received from God . . . You were bought at a price. Therefore, honour your God with your body' (1 Cor. 6:19, 20).

The body – and Platonic dualism

One of the traditional stumbling blocks with regard to the body is based on the frequently made assumption arising out of the Platonic dualistic notion of man.

> Platonic dualism may be understood as seeing human beings as both body and soul but the latter being far superior to the former. But not only is the body inferior to the soul it encumbered and defiled the soul. The soul aspired to the spiritual purity of another world and the body was envisaged not as windows for seeing out of, but barrier or impediment to seeing the true world. Death was seen as the happy release from the prison-house or tomb of the body. Much of this disparagement – indeed almost hatred – of the body was absorbed into Christianity as it sought to come to terms with the thought world of the Graeco-Roman culture. (J. G. Davies)[47]

It is sometimes assumed that St. Paul's doctrine of man is formed under Hellenistic influences and that he sets up a rigid dualism between body and soul, matter and spirit.

It is true that he makes use of contrasting terms 'flesh' and 'spirit', but notwithstanding his use of these terms, St. Paul's doctrine of man is firmly rooted in the soul of the Old Testament teaching and anything like the great dualistic antithesis between body and soul was far from his thoughts. For him, as for other Old Testament writers, the psychophysical unit of the person was the fundamental feature in the conception of man. The body, no less than the soul, was essentially human nature and its completeness. (J. Hastings)[48]

The writings of Paul, argues J. G. Davies,[49] are very much concerned with man as a whole being. 'Not only do we *have* bodies, we *are* bodies. There is nothing more of the Platonic dualism – quite the opposite. So far from there being a hatred of the body, there is, if anything, a paean of praise for God's creation.'

When we realise the true nature of the body in God's creation, and it is clear that God is as much concerned with our bodies as any other part of our selves, then maybe we will begin to see it and all that surrounds it in a very different light. 'In him we live and move and have our being' . . . 'We are his offspring' (Acts 17:28). 'There are also heavenly bodies and there are earthly bodies; but the splendour of the heavenly bodies is one kind, and the splendour of the earthly bodies is another' (1 Cor. 15:40).

The attitude that regards the body as a servant of God has no difficulty in expressing worship through the body. 'We are told that "the body is for the Lord and the Lord for the body". Dancing then in this sense of the meaning constitutes a unique unity of body and spirit, it expresses and intensifies their unity' (J. G. Davies).[50] Our bodies are made as an integral part of our nature, the physical expression of our life on earth. 'We cannot be separated into different compartments of body, mind, and emotions etc. Rather we are whole people and as we allow spiritual truths to be worked out in our bodies they become real and dynamic' (Liz Attwood and Joy Potter).[51]

To return to dance as one of the primary means of self-expression, we recognise that like everything else which comes from God and is good, it can be abused and misused. Throughout its history there has been almost constant association with the carnal, wantonness and lasciviousness and this has been one of the main reasons for its rejection within the Church. As Christians, we have the obligation to see that it is used rightfully (see Rom. 6:12, 13). If the attitude of the mass media is unlawful, then do not let us accept it simply because the majority do, but rather let us restore both the body and dance to its lawful place. Although we belong to the world of the 'flesh' we must also be separate from this world. Above all, whatever the past, let us not allow anything to be called evil 'by holding on to the traditions of men' (Mark 7:8).

In all true worship there is a living link between heaven and earth, sacred and secular, spirit and flesh – the link is Jesus Christ. The flesh is the vehicle of the spirit and spiritual worship is always clothed in matter. Artists, architects, musicians and dancers have seen the raw material of their craft immeasurably enhanced through worship. The inevitable result is that since the very beginning of the Church's life, an offering which is spiritual in its goal has never been ashamed to pick up and shape the raw material that is at hand on the way, bending it exclusively to the glory of the spiritual and unseen God. (M. Marshall)[52]

'Let your light so shine before men that they may see your good deeds and praise your father in heaven' (Matt. 5:16). 'We are therefore Christ's ambassadors, as though God were making his appeal through us' (2 Cor. 5:20). 'My soul doth magnify the Lord' (Luke 1:46). 'Offer your bodies as living sacrifices, holy and pleasing to God' (Rom. 12:1). 'Christ will be exalted in my body' (Phil. 1:20).

The body – and sexuality

Human sexuality is a difficult subject for many Christians. It is a topic that all too often is ignored or pushed under the carpet, and yet it is so intimately and necessarily related to the body and dance that it cannot be ignored. Not only is this unhealthy, it is untruthful both in general terms and dance terms particularly. 'If dance is to be introduced into worship, then the question of sexuality can no longer be put aside.' (J. G. Davies).[53] It is a fact that dance is, potentially at least, sexual and erotic whatever form it may take and however chaste and pure its intentions may be. Dance throughout the ages has always been associated either explicitly or implicitly with this aspect of our beings. It has also, in the main, been seen as a perpetual problem by our society in general.

The 'body', and by implication dance, is not meant for sexual immorality (Rom. 6:12), 'but for the Lord, and the Lord for the body'. In addition, as we saw in our discussion of the body, of feelings, and the whole realm of God's creation which he saw was good, *so too* with our sexual and erotic natures. These are as God given as anything else and by definition are, in themselves, 'good', very good.

'And nothing so liberates a man from the grip of sin as the intoxicating discovery that he is freely accepted and for-given' (J. White).[54] Anything that was unclean has now been washed clean by his most precious blood. Whatever man's behaviour, his sexual nature is basically and orig-inally good, and a gift from God. Again, we have to remind ourselves that the misuse of a good thing is not a reason for its non-use.

In our discussion of the sexual nature of the body and dance this 'positive consciousness' and 'acceptance' of our God-given sexuality must be our starting point and what-ever the misuse and abuse of this gift Christians must not be ruled, blinded or conditioned by mere tradition. Let us by all means respect and learn from tradition, but let us also not be bound by it. Instead of denying the sexuality of dance, as is usually the case, I want to affirm it. Whatever form dance may take, including religious dance, although it may not be deliberately or explicitly sexual and erotic (and this is surely the case with the majority of dance in our society) it is, by its nature, implicitly so. This is not to say that dance is necessarily immoral.

To say that everything that comes from God is good is not to say that man, by his fallen nature, does not make 'unclean' what was in its origin 'clean'. I am all too well aware of the way dance has been abused, and abused deliberately.

'The first step then, is to recognise our sexual natures and thank our loving Creator that we do experience sexual desire. For not only is sex itself ordained by God, so also are the physical pleasures associated with it. Your body has the capacity to be stimulated because God made it so!' (J. Young).[55] 'Pleasure,' as C. S. Lewis pointed out, 'is God's invention, not the devil's.'[56] Sexuality is a part of our identity as persons. 'Not only did he make you; he has made provision to make you whole. If you are a Christian, you are not only doubly precious, you are beautiful in his eyes. He sees you in Christ' (J. White).[57] Accordingly it is vital that we both affirm our own sexuality in gratitude to God and also learn to relate to those of both sexes.

Admitting and acknowledging our sexuality as good and lawful is a vital step towards a positive and healthy recovery, in our attitude towards sex generally and the dance specifically. It is amazing and also a little sad to see the reaction of some audiences after I have encouraged them to free their hearts and minds and to recognise the rightful place of dance, the body and sexuality. For many it is difficult even to look at another body, and especially a dancer's body with all its deliberately exposed beauty and skill. For the dancer not to give back to God what has surely been given to her or him by God is to make nonsense of both the body and worship. We give thanks and praise to the Lord for the beauty of the dance and the dancer, the instrument of expression – the body, the choreographic structure and form of expression – movement, and for the content of expression itself. We marvel at this exquisite and wonderfully made creation in mind, body, heart and spirit. We admire the extraordinary physical skill, the almost infinite number of possibilities in terms of dance patterns, shapes, designs and forms. We enjoy above all the exquisite sensual beauty that underlies all these psychophysical expressions and we recognise that it is good.

For one of the most positive and enlightening critical discussions into the area of sexuality and worship generally as well as dance, I would draw the reader's attention to J. G. Davies' book *New Forms of Worship Today*,[58] and also J. White's *Eros Undefiled*.[59] Both represent healthy, disciplined discussions on this sensitive subject. In the chapter entitled 'Sexuality and Worship' J. G. Davies writes:

> If the desire aroused by an attractive man or woman passes over into a desire to have sexual relations with that person then the result is either lust or infidelity to one's partner. But if the desire aroused is no more, though no less than a pleasurable and enjoyable sensation, it is difficult to see why it should be condemned. What is more natural than that the beauty of a human being should arouse sexual feelings? Is not the natural given by God, according to the doctrine of creation? There need be no infidelity here when a person is not contemplating intercourse, but simply experiencing some sexual pleasure. What the reasonable enjoyment of food is to gluttony, the controlled enjoyment of sexual sensations is to lust. It must be admitted that such an approach has its dangers and that some people would rather avoid the risks involved by either, by in the case of alcohol embracing teetotalism or in the case of eroticism by rejecting such feelings entirely. In the latter case they simply come back as guilt. But the exercise of human freedom always involves risks. The acknowledgment of the sexual element in dance and, through it, worship does not necessarily lead to indulgence in provocative sexiness which itself is a hang-up stemming from the body-mind dichotomy. It is not 'lack of control' that turns sensuousness into lust or sensuality, but the subordination of human bodily spontaneity to the egocentric drive of the human mind. It can be said further that lust is the product of sensuality which is what happens when the body is

driven by the mind and used as an instrument of pleasure for reasons found in man's mental and spiritual state. The roots of sensuality are not in bodily impulses, but in man's mind. In contrast, erotic feelings are a pleasurable sensation located in the sexual organs and are usually the accompaniment of genuine love for another person.

J. White remarks:

Our obsession with sexual purity is out of all proportion to our concern for other Christian virtues. We have strained at gnats and swallowed camels. For though it is true that neither a gnat nor a camel is meant to be swallowed our failure to condemn with greater zeal, sins like avarice, malice, resentment, pride and lying, all of which are found among us, has made our obsession with sexual purity suspect.

5. The church body and truth

Truth involves something more than propositional statements as reflected in the written word. It has to be translated and negotiated in everyday worldly terms within the Church. While on the one hand there seems from our discussion so far to be sufficient scriptural justification for dance within worship, we have to recognise that there is another truth which exists within the body of the Church, as that unique local church sees it.

Another important fundamental truth is that related to the building up or edification of the church body. All that we do within the Church must be seen in terms of how it contributes to the edification of the body. Whatever does not lead to the building up of the body must be questioned. And whatever leads to the undermining of the body, must be seriously questioned. So we must ask, 'Does dance contribute to the edification of the body?'

If our 'tongue' or 'language' of expression alienates members of the body and is unintelligible and 'foreign' to them, then we must seriously question the nature of what we are doing.

The church body

Firstly, the church body, like the physical body, is made up of a wide and complex variety of different parts, conceptually distinct but in reality intimately related and interdependent. For such a body to function effectively and efficiently each part needs to be accommodated within the whole and work in a harmonious relationship to the whole.

Secondly, the church body, like the physical body, is made up of a complex variety of specialist parts each of which has its appointed function. No one part is any more or less important than another, since all work for the whole and each is dependent upon the other. If one part suffers then all parts suffer.

A church body is made up from a variety of personalities with a wide diversity of gifts. All these personalities and gifts constitute a part of God's creation and a part of Christ's body, the Church; they are all, in their different ways, legitimate and lawful elements of the body and as such cannot and must not be ignored since they all serve the same purpose. 'To each one the manifestation of the spirit is given for the common good' (1 Cor. 12:7) 'in order that the church may be edified' (Eph. 4:12). 'In Christ we who are many form one body, and each member belongs to all the others. We have different gifts, according to the grace given us' (Rom. 12:5, 6).

What are these gifts of the church body?

In Rom. 12:6–8 we read of prophesying, serving, teaching, encouraging, contributing to others' needs and leadership.

In 1 Cor. 12:8–10 we read of wisdom, knowledge, faith, healing, miraculous powers, prophecy, an ability to distinguish between spirits, speaking in different tongues and interpreting tongues.

In Eph. 4:11 we read of apostles, prophets, evangelists, pastors and teachers.

It is clear that these are not a once-and-for-all exclusive list of possible gifts, but are examples. Within the church body today we can all call to mind many gifts not listed, and yet we would not want to exclude them from our understanding of the term 'gift'.

Each member of the church body, and this must surely include the dancer, should use whatever gift he or she has been given faithfully to administer God's grace in its various forms. If anyone speaks, he should do so as one speaking the very words of God; if anyone serves, he should do so with the strength God provides, so that in all things God may be praised through Jesus Christ. The gifts represented by the three lists are representative. The biblical principle for us here is that there are many gifts and each has an important place in the body for, 'The eye cannot say to the hand, "I don't need you!" And the head cannot say to the feet, "I don't need you!" On the contrary' (1 Cor. 12:21). Each is dependent upon the other.

To dance or not to dance – that is the question

In the sense that God created the world and all that is in it, and saw that it was good, then dance and all that surrounds it, is good and acceptable. These are scriptural truths. But as we have seen, there are many other truths that have also to be considered alongside these truths. Scriptural truths have to be interpreted and negotiated, and worked out with that family. It may be that, initially at least, dance is not accepted as a valid and legitimate form of expression for some in the church. It may represent a stumbling block and may for some represent a foreign language or be unintelligible. Dance is never an end in itself, but one of many ways through which we can worship. When it leads towards the edification of the fellowship then it is most acceptable, but if it undermines the worship then until such times as there is an acceptability, an intelligibility and the congregation are not 'foreigners' to the language, we must carefully and prayerfully negotiate and educate our fellow Christians. Hopefully, they will allow us to help them to understand this gift from God and to move from apprehension to comprehension. We must think and work in this way in order to 'keep the unity of the spirit in the bond of peace'.

The church body and the dance

The question about dance is firstly a scriptural one and secondly one of interpretation, revelation and negotiation on the part of the unique and local church body. Each church body has the authority and responsibility for the interpretation and realisation of the faith and it is within these canons, logics and truths that the question of dance has to be answered.

(i) 'All scripture is God-breathed and is useful for teaching, rebuking, correcting and training in righteousness, so that the man of God may be thoroughly equipped for every good work' (2 Tim. 3:16). 'Faith comes from hearing the message, and the message is heard through the word' (Rom. 10:17).

(ii) 'Remind the people to be subject to rulers and authorities, to be obedient, to be ready to do whatever is good' (Titus 3:1).

Fundamental to all that we do, whether it is a question of dance or any of the many other questions about the nature and conditions of the faith and worship, is 'the entire law' summed up by the command, 'Love your neighbour as yourself' (Gal. 5:14). The kingdom of God, as we have already seen, is not a matter of eating and drinking (or dancing) but of righteousness, peace and joy in the Holy Spirit. 'Keeping God's commandments is what counts' (1 Cor. 7:19). This summary of the law has to be worked out and made real in practical congregational terms, led by responsible, mature Christians – 'Deacons are to be men worthy of respect, sincere, not indulging in much wine, and not pursuing dishonest gain. They must keep hold of the deep truths of the faith with a clear conscience' (1 Tim. 3:8). Everything should be submitted to the church body for the Lord's sake (1 Pet. 2:13) and 'out of reverence for Christ' (Eph. 5:21), 'be completely humble and gentle, be patient, bearing with one another in love. Make every effort to keep the unity of the spirit through the bond of peace' (Eph. 4:2, 3), 'warn those who are idle, encourage the timid, help the weak, be patient with everyone' (1 Thess. 5:14), 'Get rid of all bitterness, rage and anger, brawling and slander along with every other form of malice. Be kind and compassionate to one another, forgiving each other' (Eph. 4:31).

'In quietness and in trust is your strength' (Isa. 30:15). 'The Lord is my shepherd. I shall not want' (Ps. 23:1).

We recognise in this fundamental law that however right and lawful our actions may be, they are never ends in themselves. For the Christian, *how* we act and *why* we act is as important, if not more so, than the act itself. *The means whereby we achieve our ends ARE in fact ends in themselves*. In terms of the sacred dance group, *how* we respond to all the ingredients of this basic law outlined above is, in the end, what the dance is about. How we live out our Christian lives is what we are. I have emphasised this point many times within the dance team. Matthew 5:23 says, 'if you are offering your gift at the altar and there remember that your brother has something against you, leave the gift there in front of the altar. *First* go and be reconciled to your brother; *then* come and offer your gift.'

To accept that dance must always be seen as a means to the end of the faith and especially 'love thy neighbour' and all that this implies within the body of the Church, can sometimes be very difficult, especially if you are a trained dancer or with a very real skill and love for this expressive form. The sacred dance company Springs grew out of a famous City church in London. The church loved us, prayed for us, taught us and looked after our general spiritual well-being. They gave us all that we needed as members of the church body and yet, during the four years that we were church members, we never once danced in worship. We were all fully trained, professional dancers with a unique commitment to propagating dance and the Christian faith within the Church generally, education and community, both in this country and abroad. And yet we never danced within our own church worship. It was out of that church's love and respect for us as members of the church body that they encouraged us in every possible way – except by allowing us to dance within worship. It was out of our love and respect for the church body that we accepted this decision of the elders. Both sides made every effort to keep the unity of the spirit in the bond of peace.

Some prerequisites of a sacred dance group – scriptural/dynamic

I want now to focus on the dance group itself, whatever its form and function within the Church, be it professional or amateur, full time or part time, exclusively home church based or travelling and performing widely, adults or children.

Fundamental support of the Church

The first and most important prerequisite is for the group to have its roots within the church fellowship. The sacred dance group cannot and should not attempt to survive, let alone grow and develop, without this basic infrastructure. The many complex and awesome responsibilities implicit in such a ministry and the many pitfalls open to such a (usually) young and vulnerable group are rarely understood either by the group or the Church. Out of an act of attractive, energetic, youthful enthusiasm, and an innocent love for the Lord and the dance, these groups are usually allowed to form and grow on their own without mature, responsible back-up and support. The result, more often than not, is their eventual collapse, with the ensuing hurt, disappointment and resentment, both within the group and the Church.

The responsibility for such a basically worthwhile venture must be the Church's. The foundations of such a group should be built on the sure and firm 'rock foundations' (Matt. 7:24) of the Church, rather than the loose 'sand foundations' of youthful enthusiasm, however attractive and convincing they may appear. And the sacred dance group, in turn, must be prepared to submit to the authority and responsibility of the church body, for the Lord's sake as well as their own. They must humbly, patiently and lovingly respond to the elders (1 Pet. 2:13). From such a foundation the group will have a good chance to grow both as Christian dancers and as Christians. The fellowship, hopefully, will be made up from a mature, disciplined, encouraging and supporting group who through regular prayer, teaching and guiding generally will enable the team to establish itself and become a positive member of the body. The sacred dance must belong to something bigger than itself and it must be answerable to some body outside itself. It must, above all, be looked after by a mature and committed group of Christians.

Fundamental support of scripture

The second prerequisite, closely related to the first, is the need for sound and regular teaching of scripture. Anyone who wants to know the Lord and seeks to communicate this knowledge to others will not only *want* but will *need* to know the scriptures. The Bible has much to say on the importance of studying scripture (Deut. 6:6–9, 2 Tim. 3:14). Some Christians who practise the performing arts appear at times to despise any kind of theoretical knowledge, either of their art or of God, insisting that all true knowledge comes from 'doing' and no amount of talking will equal 'real art' or 'real faith'. This position is a classical one that most artists and Christians have taken at some time or other.

It is true, as stated earlier, that no amount of talking can by itself equal the artistic or religious experience, but that does not mean we cannot express in words a great deal about both and so refine, deepen and extend our knowledge of art and our faith. In the case of the Christian faith, a disciplined and regular study of the written word together with regular prayer and fellowship is absolutely essential. Scripture is 'useful for teaching, rebuking, correcting and training in righteousness, so that the man of God (the sacred dancer) may be thoroughly equipped for every good work' 2 Tim. 3:16. Moreover, the word represents the rock upon which you can grow and defend yourselves against all that is unrighteous and unlawful.

In my experience, because of the nature of dance and of the young, immature Christians who, in the main, carry the burden and responsibility for religious communication in the arts, the commitment to such a ministry is usually emotional and social, rather than a disciplined commitment to scripture. The primary concern of sacred dance is faith. Whilst a disciplined understanding of dance *does* constitute an important focus, fundamental to the art must be a knowledge of what the dance is attempting to communicate. But more than that 'the sensuous Christian (i.e. the Christian whose faith is essentially, if not exclusively heart based) is someone who lives by his feelings primarily rather than through his understanding of the word. The sensuous

Christian cannot be moved to service, prayer and study unless he feels like it. His Christian life is only as effective as the intensity of present feeling. When he expresses spiritual euphoria, he is a whirlwind of Godly activity; when he is depressed, he is a spiritual incompetent'. This is faith without content. (Matt 8:24.) In the end, it is not the heart that gives us the will and the strength to go on running the great race – either in faith or dance, since both involve considerable struggle and heartache – but rather the objective, disciplined 'honey-sweet' (Ps. 19:10) word of assurance. When our hearts and bodies are sore and tired, then hopefully the rock-like discipline of scripture will guide us and support us in our work. Time and time again, in my ministry of travelling from place to place, performing, teaching, leading workshops in schools, missions, colleges, churches and communities, working often in very inadequate conditions and very trying circumstances, I have been grateful for this truth. And when in our dance fellowship we have become tired, rundown and perhaps a little frustrated and disappointed with ourselves, and the response to our work, and when, because of the sustained pressures and tensions of travelling and performing continuously we become impatient with one another and misinterpret and misunderstand each other, scripture has rescued us. There is a biblical principle to cover all circumstances. How, in the end, we work out our everyday life, is what fundamentally the dance ministry is about.

In the same way that a dancer returns to the barre for daily physical exercise, even though her heart is rarely in it, she does so because she knows from her training and experience that failure to do so will seriously undermine her dancing. So it is with the faith. Irrespective of whether our heart is in the daily, regular discipline of prayer and Bible reading, we observe them out of experience and disciplined respect. Just as for the dancer to miss a day will seriously undermine her dancing, so too with missing daily prayer and reading. The dancer becomes a dancer through the hard struggle and discipline of the barre. The Christian becomes a Christian similarly through the daily struggle and discipline of his prayer and teaching. Neither the dancer nor the Christian will receive the victor's crown unless he or she competes according to the rules (2 Tim. 2:5). Included in the rules of coming to know God and coming to be a sure and faithful minister of the WORD through the dance, is a knowledge and understanding of the mind. All scripture is God breathed and useful for teaching, rebuking, correcting and training in righteousness so that we may be thoroughly equipped for our ministry (of dance) (2 Tim. 3:16).

Scripture is pictured as food and as honey (Ps. 19:10, Rev. 10:9). 'When evangelism is not fed by, fertilised and controlled by theology, it becomes a stylised performance seeking its effect through manipulation skills rather than the power of vision and the focus of truth' (J. Packer).[60] Scripture must constitute the rock foundation and support for the sacred dance group.

'The joy of the Lord is your strength' (Neh. 8:10).

A ministry rooted in a personal encounter with the Word – Jesus Christ

However important and fundamental the truth and knowledge of the written word, it is not by itself sufficient. As we have already seen, there is a knowledge and truth both of the 'heart' and the 'body'. The third prerequisite focuses on knowledge and truth of the heart.

Truth 'about' the Word has to be 'lived in' before it can be fully known, understood and made manifest in our lives through our behaviour generally and our art form specifically. Truth that is not lived in is no better than error, and may be fully as dangerous. As David Watson says, 'Unless we have a clear inward experience of the living Christ, know his transforming power, and have experienced something of the joy of the Holy Spirit, our words [and our dancing] however true as propositions will strike others as pious platitudes.'[61]

It is out of the abundance of the heart that the mouth speaks and that our bodies in the dance speak. If the heart is not full of the love of Christ then the mouth or the body, however skilful, will not speak the truth. The problem for the Christian dancer is to express these heartfelt truths. As Margot Fonteyn says in her autobiography,[62] 'I learn the steps quickly, but it is a long time before I dance them.' So, too, for the Christian dancer. In terms of both art and personal faith, it takes time to know and understand these written expressions of truth. Steps or words by themselves do not make the dance religious or even true dance. I sometimes receive letters from newly formed Christian dance groups asking for 'religious steps'! There is no such thing. What makes a step religious is not the step itself, but rather what we invest in it. Part of this investment must arise from a heartfelt knowing and understanding of the Word.

A ministry realised from a personal, practical living of the faith

We have focused on the truth of the objective written word and the truth of the subjective, heartfelt knowledge of the Word. These two have now to be combined and then expressed and realised within practical and procedural terms of everyday living.

'Faith by itself, if not accompanied by action, is dead' (Jas. 2:17). Do not merely listen to the word or merely feel it in your heart, and so deceive yourselves, but express these elements of the faith in your everyday life (Jas. 1:22). Two very important points arise from this scriptural command. Firstly, there is a knowledge and truth that can only be gained from a practical working out of the written word. Hence the importance of living our knowledge and understanding of scripture. Secondly, there is a knowledge and understanding that comes from our dancing as Christians in that *who* we are and *how* we live is reflected in our dance.

This is difficult enough for any Christian but if we are Christian leaders (and we are if we set ourselves up as a performing group) then this is doubly a problem and all the more reason for having the sort of mature, loving and disciplined support from the Church which I spoke of earlier. If the communication of the word is in part at least dependent upon us as dancers, then suddenly our responsibility becomes quite awesome. When I first became involved in religious dance, the rector of our church questioned, 'the rightness of putting young and immature spiritual Christians up front'. I did not understand at the time what he meant. But I soon did! To whom much is given, much will be expected. Dancing for the Lord, whatever form it may take, must not be undertaken lightly or alone. This Christian, practical and procedural truth has to be learnt before it can be reliably and validly expressed. Those concerned with such groups should recognise the importance of Christian living and working together as much as of dance technique and choreography which so often dominate. In a very real sense Christian dancers *are* the message. From a proper, disciplined encouragement and support from the Church the dancers will become good trees, and bear good fruit (Matt. 7:17).

'Let the word of Christ dwell in you richly as you teach and admonish one another with all wisdom, as you sing [or dance] with gratitude in your hearts to God' (Col. 3:16) 'and put these words into practice like the wise man who built his house upon the rock' (Matt. 7:24). 'Be careful how you live, not unwise, but as wise, making the most of every opportunity, because the days are evil' (Eph. 5:15). 'Live in peace with one another. Warn those who are idle, encourage the timid, help the weak, be patient with everyone' (1 Thess. 5:13). 'Be kind and compassionate to each other, forgiving each other, just as Christ forgave you' (Eph. 4:32). 'Clothe yourselves with compassion, kindness, humility, gentleness and patience. Bear with each other and forgive whatever grievances (Col. 3:12). 'Submit to one another out of love for Christ' (Eph. 5:21). 'Love deeply from the heart' (1 Peter 1:22). 'Make every effort within the working out of your fellowship and ministry to live in peace with all men and be holy: without holiness no one will ever see God' (Heb. 12:14). Certainly people will not see God 'if you keep biting and devouring each other', as so often happens in small artistic groups! 'Watch out or you will surely destroy yourselves' (Gal. 5:15). 'Be humble and gentle, patiently bearing with one another in love' (Eph 4:2). 'If you are offering your gift of dance within worship of your church or sharing it with other churches, schools and colleges etc., and you remember that your brother or sister has something against you, leave your gift of dance at the foot of the altar and first go and be reconciled with your brother, then come and offer your gift' (Matt. 5:23).

For those who are fully trained professional dancers familiar with the secular world of theatrical dance (and all that that implies) 'see that none takes you captive through hollow and deceptive philosophy which depends upon human tradition and the basic principles of this world than the world of Christ' (Col. 2:8). Having worked hard and struggled for ten years or more, and been conditioned to expect to go into the Royal Ballet and join other professional companies, living the 'bright life', earning a 'fabulous wage', going to 'fantastic parties', doing the round of 'fun and pleasure', getting your 'Equity' and dancing in a *'proper* dance company' rather than a Christian company, I can sympathise with and understand the doubts, struggles and possible regrets. But, 'be transformed by the renewing of your mind'. Set your mind on what you know in your heart is right, since 'I am afraid that just as Eve was deceived by the serpent's cunning, your minds may somehow be led astray from your sincere and pure devotion to Christ' (2 Cor. 11:3).

In the working out of your fellowship and the dance, 'Be self controlled and alert. Your enemy the devil prowls around like a roaring lion looking for someone to devour' (1 Pet. 5:8). Especially when things are going well, or when you are very tired – this is when the devil gets in. 'Endure the hardship of the dance, of the working out of the fellowship' (Heb. 12:7), and 'rejoice in the hope of the glory of God . . . not only so because we rejoice in our sufferings, but because we know that suffering produces growth' (Rom. 5:2). There will be many times in your work when you will struggle hard, when you will be disappointed, hurt, let down, rejected, when you will fail. You may be injured, you may have insufficient money, there will be disputes and quarrels within the group over leadership and authority, personality clashes, the repertoire, who dances what, technique, rehearsals, money, solos, etc. All groups experience the same problems. Impossible as it may seem, try to see these as growth points and all the time ask yourself, 'What is the Lord trying to tell us?' 'Blessed is the man who perseveres under trial, because when he has stood the test, he will receive the crown of the life that God has promised to those who love him' (Jas. 1:12). Above all, submit to each other for the sake of love and peace.

There is no half-way in this venture. The Christian faith is all or nothing! Rather like the dance. You do not enter a ten-year dance training half-heartedly, if you want to re-ceive the crown. You start to dance in faith, never knowing if you will succeed, but not daring to look over your shoulder and doubt or certainly you will not make it. The great race must be run without quivering.

Performance and idolatry

Another stumbling block for many Christians with regard to the performing arts in the Christian faith is the feeling that all too often the performing art and the artist become ends in themselves rather than means. The result is idolatry which is reflected in such things as spectacularism, show biz presentation, sparkling personalities, costume, lighting, sound and the content of the presentation. Even at the purest level of intention it is argued that there is an inevitable element of idolatry because of the inherent nature and tradition of the art itself. I have to admit that this *is* a very real problem and that this sort of criticism is quite valid. Sometimes 'theatre' can become an end in itself. However, this is not an argument against the notion of 'performance', indeed quite the opposite. The sacred dance is and should be a performance. The notion of performance within theatre implies much more than theatricality and spectacle. It implies a professional objective, disciplined and skilful concern for expression based upon an intimate knowledge and understanding of the art form in question and the whole complex area of projection and communication. In this sense, dance *is* a performance. All too often many of the Christian performing arts groups are *not* professional in this sense of the term: they are frequently enthusiastic amateurs who have little or no disciplined knowledge and understanding of either the performing arts or stage skill. There is a serious need for mature guidance, encouragement and support from within both the Church and the performing arts. As much harm has been done by these untrained groups as by the professionals who have perhaps overdone the performance focus. To return to the problem of the performance becoming more important than the message, I hope that, as a professional performance artist, I have sufficient insight and skill to be able to submerge myself in the song in such a way that only the song is heard. Hopefully, when I go to see a professional actor or professional dancer in a performance, either within the secular theatre or the religious 'theatre', I will not see him or her *per se*, but rather the message, the expression or the word. As with iconography it is the icon and not the iconographer which should shine. The criticism of unlawful worship, and idolatry especially, is I believe a valid one at this time, and will probably always be.

The Christian artist walks a fine line between what is true and what is false. We do not want a sort of professionalism that is so spectacular that we see professionalism *per se*. Equally, we do not want amateurism so inadequate that we see, painfully, amateurism *per se*. We want to see an efficient and effective artistic means whereby the word is expressed and communicated. It is not my experience that Christian groups deliberately misuse or abuse their art. More often than not, it is simply spiritual and professional immaturity and lack of experience, guidance and support. Some of the criticism levelled at these groups must surely also be levelled at the Church, be it the local body or the Church as a whole. I cannot emphasise enough the fundamental importance of church support. The problem for Christian dancers, and Christian performing artists generally, is that whilst there has been a most extraordinary upsurge of interest and development within the religious communications media, there has not been a corresponding upsurge within the church body. Thus formal recognition on a scale necessary to make full use of these developments has not been forthcoming.

In political, theological and economic terms, the Church as a national institution has remained almost completely unmoved by the quiet revolution of the performing arts within the faith over the past twenty years. We have seen very little sustained formal encouragement and support for such a potentially powerful means of communication. The work by Christian performing arts groups within schools has been little less than spectacular in spreading the gospel, and for many children within the present state of religious education, the visit of such groups is probably the most significant and meaningful statement they will receive during their education. For a young black girl in a comprehensive school in London, 'Jesus Christ' was nothing more than a swear word until such groups as Springs informed her otherwise! The communication potential of the performing arts within the Church has hardly been touched, let alone formally recognised. Such groups constitute viable and credible means of outreach and renewal within society generally and religious education particularly. It is time that the Church nationally got together with credible performing arts agencies to work out a theology of the arts, a stable, political and economic base for establishing more formally guidance and development. Five years ago when I first started out with Springs, I was tactfully and gently reminded by a senior Church of England bishop that 'these groups don't last, of course'. The advice was well meant, but looking back I see that its implication was two-fold. Firstly, one should not take the idea of a dance ministry too seriously, and secondly, there is something inherent in the nature of such groups which prevents them from sustaining such a ministry. 'They all collapse in the end', I was told. The problem with the performing arts may in part be due to the fact that the Church has not taken such a ministry seriously enough.

The reason for many of the collapses may simply be that the Church would not support such ventures. My own experience of establishing a group is that there comes a point in its political and economic life when there is a serious need for a capital investment – what is sometimes called 'pump priming'. It is at this point that most groups go under, when they have established themselves as viable and credible concerns, having worked for three or four years at subsistence level. They need a financial boost to enable them to buy such basic capital requirements as transport, advertising pamphlets, sound, etc. The Church has for too long had the performing arts on the cheap! Most Christian artists receive willingly much less than a curate's salary! I recognise that many misuses and mistakes have occurred within the field of Christian art, and I accept that there have been many groups who should not have been allowed to work professionally. Nevertheless there remains a great deal of proven professional expertise, goodwill and potential in this country if only the Church would wake up to it, shake out some of the traditional, negative, political and economic strictures and support what many already recognise as being professionally reliable and valid. The Arts Centre Group (ACG), Christian Arts Trust, SEEDS, Music in Worship Trust (MWT), Christian Dance Ministries (CDM) are internationally established Christian performing arts associations with a very credible, respectable and viable base.

Performance and idolatry in evangelism

It is within present-day evangelism that we see the problem of 'performance and idolatry' most vividly. There has been considerable criticism in recent times about this special ministry. Here the concept 'entertainment' seems to be the critical focus rather than 'performance' or 'idolatry' but clearly the latter two are both implied by the former in such descriptions as: The evangelical roadshow, the liturgical circus, entertainment evangelism, holiday religion, the Christian nightclub show.

The following critical statements are also indicative of the same basic attitudes:

   (i) 'The business of preaching is not to entertain, but to lead to salvation, to teach them to find God.'
  (ii) 'Words are of paramount importance; nothing must distract from them in any way; any kind of psychological manipulation must be avoided.'
 (iii) 'We do not attract people to Jesus by entertaining them.'
 (iv) 'Evangelism can so easily reduce the gospel message to triviality.'
  (v) 'We bring in all roots of antiscriptural and unscriptural claptrap to keep people happy and keep them coming.'
 (vi) 'You don't have to run a church like a circus in order to attract people, nor import big names and speakers at fancy prices . . . lecturing in a classroom, exposition rightly delivered and doctrine rightly explained will satisfy the deepest cravings of Christian spirits for the truth.'

(vii) 'The life of Jesus was not a religious roadshow; he did not come to give a performance, but to give life . . . Jesus is not a pill needing sugar-coating.'

(viii) 'Much singing in certain types of meetings are designed to arouse the libidinous. The current vogue of physical beauty and sparkling personalities in religious promotion is a further manifestation of the influence of the romantic spirit in the Church. The rhythmic sway, the synthetic smile and the too, too cheerful voice betray the religious worldling.'

(ix) 'The heroes today for many contemporary Christians are guitar-toting stars rather than faith-walking saints.'

Irrespective of their validity and reliability such criticisms point unequivocally to potentially unlawful and idolatrous behaviour. And such behaviour within evangelism is surely the worst kind of idolatry. For such a ministry we are especially reminded that, 'It is written: worship the Lord your God and serve only' (Luke 4:8). J. Perry[63] reminds us that, 'In their insecurity, people look for props, and props become idols and idol worship is at its most subtle and most dangerous in the whole area of human relationships.'

There are several common prayers I frequently use when performing – the first is taken from the prayer of Humble Access which begins: 'We do not presume to dance in your name trusting in our own righteousness but in your manifold and great mercies. We are not worthy so much as to gather up the crumbs under your table'.[64] We cannot go up front trusting in ourselves. We need his spiritual support. We need his cleansing also as expressed in the Prayer of Confession: 'Almighty God, to whom all hearts are open, all desires known, and from whom no secrets are hid: cleanse the thoughts of our heart by the inspiration of your holy spirit that we may perfectly love you, and worthily magnify your holy name. May the words of our "mouths" (dance) and the meditation of each and every heart be acceptable in your sight. Amen.'[64]

And when we have finished performing and have returned to the dressing room we remind ourselves yet again of the source of our performance: 'Yours Lord, is the greatness, the praise and the glory, the splendour and the majesty; for everything in heaven and on earth is yours. All things come from you, and of your own do we give you. Amen.'[64]

These prayers are in our minds when we perform. They help us to accommodate the inevitable show biz response that is so frequently associated with such missions.

'Worship the Lord your God and serve him only' (Matt. 4:10). Be ever weary of being caught up with and affected by the worldly and idolatrous nature of the theatrical entertainment world and the advertising market – of flashy, worldly photographs, badges, balloons and T-shirts, etc. 'Whatever you do, whether in word or deed, do it all in the name of the Lord Jesus, giving thanks to God the Father through him' (Col. 3:17). 'To the King eternal, immortal and invisible, the only God, be honour and glory for ever and ever' (1 Tim. 1:17).

As Bishop Michael Marshall says in *Renewal and Worship*,[65] 'We are always to some extent in danger of mistaking the creature for the creator and we are always ready to turn the icon of creation, in all its forms, into an idol to which we will give our worship. Idolatry is never far below the surface whenever the instinct for worship is at its strongest; in art, music, poetry, in "high church" and beautiful ceremonial the confusion between the creature and his creation is however but one of many hazards facing the worshipper.'

We are reminded again and again, that scripture is fundamental. For the Christian performing artist 'active' in the ministry of evangelism this regular daily and disciplined teaching is essential food and nourishment and should form the base from which all his art comes. This applies as much to managers, promoters, agencies, record houses, advertisers, etc. as to performers.

Let us return to some of the criticisms already identified and see what more we can learn by them. They are strong stuff indeed, and pretty scathing in both their form and their content. They do represent valid and very real poten-

'If I glorify myself, my glory means nothing' (John 8:54). 'Whether you eat or drink or whatever you do, do it all for the glory of God' (1 Cor. 10:31). 'For we do not preach ourselves, but Jesus Christ as Lord, and ourselves as your servants for Jesus' sake' (2 Cor. 4:5). 'Not to us O Lord, not to us but to your name be the glory' (Ps. 115:1). 'Lord – you know that I love you' (John 21:17).

tial problems for the performing artist/evangelist as he or she carries the heavy, awesome and frequently lonely responsibility of spreading the 'good news' to ALL people, at ALL times and in ALL places. The Christian performing artist, like the evangelist, faces formidable problems with regard to being 'upfront' in the secular ungodly market. Whilst I respect the positions that such writers as J. Blanchard and J. White with regard to what they scathingly call 'The Evangelical Roadshow' and 'Liturgical Circus', there is at times an extraordinary naïvety and possibly ignorance about both the nature of performing arts evangelism and I would hope that this next discussion might bring about a more positive balance than hitherto critical literature has allowed.

As Christians generally and as evangelists particularly we are told to 'go into the world' (Mark 16:15), i.e. the secular, often unsupportive, ungodly and frequently quite explicitly alien world, where for some, as I have already pointed out, 'Jesus Christ' is nothing more than a swear word, where 'man without the spirit cannot accept things which come from the spirit of God' and, where on the face of it 'they are foolishness to him and he cannot understand them, because they are spiritually discerned' (1 Cor. 2:14). And yet, 'we must preach the word' (2 Tim. 4:2) 'plainly'! We must communicate in clear, everyday terms of communication, meaning and understanding 'day after day', all the time 'proclaiming the good news' (Acts 5:42). This is the world that the Christian performing artist/evangelist has to work within. Within this ungodly and alien world he has the responsibility to communicate the Word. What is the significance of this position? It lies in the fact that however true the message, the empirical, everyday, worldly fact is that this truth is dependent upon communication. Unless the truth, the Word – universal, absolute, unchanging and for all men, in all places – is communicated in such a way that it can be attended to, understood and then internalised and accepted, it will not be realised. The primary skill of preaching is not theology, but rather education and a good working knowledge and understanding of the nature and conditions of teaching and learning the psychology and sociology of perception and communication generally.

Truth and communication

We sometimes assume that because the 'Word' is truth, it will automatically be communicated and accepted as such. The problem for the preacher is not truth itself, but the communication of truth.

Firstly we have to encourage people to come to listen to the Word. That is to *attend physically* otherwise no word will be heard. The question then is, 'How can we get people to attend?' The so-called 'evangelical roadshow' may constitute an efficient and effective means of actually getting people to come to hear the Word.

Secondly, when you have persuaded people to attend physically, you then have the problem of their *attending with mind and heart*. I am thinking of the morning assemblies in schools, where much of our work is done in evangelism: you may have motivated a person to attend physically – sometimes voluntarily and sometimes against their will – but now you have the problem of presenting the Word in such a way that they are thirsty, i.e. they want to drink and actively attend in terms of their mind and heart. It may be that the performing arts constitute a legitimate and reliable way of establishing such a fundamental prerequisite.

Thirdly, the Word has to be presented in such a way that people not only stop and attend, but *understand* what is being 'said'. There is no point in getting people to stop if what we have to 'say' to them alienates them, is unintelligible or in some cases actually puts them off the Word. (And as a consequence of our poor communication never bother to attend again!) The Word *has* to be presented in such a way that it is appropriate and meaningful to the time, the place and the persons listening.

In this sense of 'preaching the word' we have to speak in a 'tongue' that is intelligible and meaningful to the listeners. We have to 'speak' in such a way that the individual, within that peculiar cultural setting we are 'preaching', feels 'at home' rather than a 'foreigner' (1 Cor.

14:9). There can be an extraordinary combination of arrogance and naïvety in the way preachers sometimes go into differing social settings with their highly elaborate and socially elitist linguistic code, not infrequently creating a situation where the listeners *are* foreigners, and this is especially so in schools.

Paul advised preachers to 'be all things to all people'. The middle-class language, for example, with its traditional emphasis on the written word, discursive knowledge and abstract theological truths, is not always the best way of bringing about understanding. In schools one must ask what are the predominant languages of expression within that particular adolescent culture and multicultural setting. When I go into a comprehensive school in south-east London with its multicultural society, or into one of the elite and expensive public schools, or to Ridley or Oakhill theological colleges, I am concerned with communicating truths in terms of dance and the Christian faith, but I recognise that I have to adopt a wide variety of social and

'Everyone who exults himself will be humbled and he who humbles himself will be exalted' (Luke 18:14). 'Jesus Christ is the same yesterday and today and for ever' (Heb. 13:8).

intellectual roles in order to communicate effectively.

In communicating the Word through dance, I have to ask myself, 'What is the young people's conception of dance?' Dance in itself is not sufficient, especially if, like our dancers' backgrounds, it is predominantly classical ballet. The Word has to be expressed within a dance form that the people can attend to and understand. Accordingly, our repertoire for schools includes at the time of writing, the style of *Fame*, *Hot Gossip* and *Top of the Pops*, as well as classical ballet and contemporary dance. We do this for the sake of the gospel and the hope that by all means some may be saved (1 Cor. 9:23).

Many of our dances may seem irreverent, like some of the marvellous *Riding Lights* drama sketches. We have one very 'entertaining' dance about 'three bovver boys' and the climax of this dance is a spitting competition! Another dance called *Nero Watching Video While Rome Begins to Burn* by Garth Hewit is a deliberately 'slick', spectacular dance in the style of *Fame*. In all cases the dances are rooted in scripture and although the message may not come across immediately, something comes across which is even more fundamental and that is we are attended to, we are listened to and people immediately begin to understand something of the message as expressed firstly in the dance and secondly in ourselves.

The fact is, we do, *quite deliberately*, entertain in the sense that I have been describing it. I wish that more preachers would entertain in this sense! At the time of writing, I have on my desk a copy of 'The Church Times' May 18th 1984. There is on the front cover a picture of Bishop Trevor Huddleston CR, sitting in a rickshaw about to be pulled or pedalled by Rev. Dr. Elliott, the Director of Christian Aid. The picture is taken in front of the House of Commons and we are told that they are about to deliver Christian Aid envelopes. Is this a mere publicity stunt, mere entertainment? Is it nothing more than a front page attraction, a stunt? Of course not. It represents a very clever and effective means whereby a fundamental scriptural message is communicated. It is entertainment and amusement designed as a means whereby the gospel is communicated.

The Rev. Dr. J. Watson speaking recently in defence of the performing arts in evangelism said, 'The New Testament is full of the fun and humour of Jesus in his pithy sayings and stories. It is not necessary to descend to the crude abuse of critics and talk about "sugar coating" to show that Jesus was a master story teller. Dance can tell stories, too. A few more stories in the barren wilderness of so-called doctrinal sermons might be more scriptural.' He went on to say that, 'Certainly the aim of the performing arts is not merely to entertain, but in the last hundred years of its history, many a sinner has stopped to listen to the Salvation Army band and stayed to receive the Saviour they were playing about.'

With regard to the performing arts in evangelism, let us 'not judge by mere appearances'. 'Let us make a right judgment'. By all means, let us be constantly critically aware of abuse and misunderstanding, but let us not reject out of hand the potential of such 'languages' of communication.

Art forms submitted to God's word and used for God's glory can greatly enhance the meaning of worship. They do not have to be condemned, but rather controlled. In criticising the performing arts within the faith generally and evangelism particularly, let us be very careful not to throw the baby out with the bathwater!

We recognise that dance in the secular world *is* entertainment and is seen predominantly as a performance for its own sake within the non-Christian market. How else could it be seen? The dance firstly and the dancers secondly *are*, for the non-Christian, the message. Faith is first of all communicated in terms of our art form and ourselves, but out of this form of communication we pray that something of the faith will be communicated, especially when we come to actually speaking about it. It is in the third stage that we actually begin to communicate more specifically in terms of the Bible, but even then, still very much in everyday terms of the listener. Any teacher supports the fact that one of the most effective ways of communicating a subject is to be good and to be enthusiastic about the subject. The PE teacher who is a skilful dancer and gymnast has a powerful argument in her favour for such activities. So too with the dance and the faith. Since dance is the first focus of the audience, the dance we use for communicating the faith must be the best possible in terms of its form, content and skill. So, too, with the dancer. Since it is essentially through the dancer as a person that people come to see the faith, the Christian dancer must be the best possible Christian.

There is a tradition that still exists within school evangelism that almost expects Christian performing arts groups to be inferior and second-best. Christian performing arts groups going into the schools must not only be as good as the secular equivalents, but better! Christian art, like its artists, must be the best possible for God. I reinforce my plea to the church body to encourage and support in every possible way good art and good artists, for the sake not of the groups, but the gospel.

So we praise and thank those contemporary critics of the performing arts in the Christian faith who have rightly in recent times written so clearly and forcefully about some of the ways in which the performing arts are being misused. Let us take and digest these questions and apply them to our own work wherever they are applicable.

There is little doubt in theological, theoretical and social empirical terms that the performing arts have a very important part to play within contemporary religious communication, both within the Church and outside it. David Watson, one of the leading British evangelists who did so much to foster the growth and development of the performing arts within the faith, writes in *My God Is Real*, 'The reason why I travel with a team (actors, musicians and dancers) is that they are able to communicate the gospel much more effectively than I can with words. I find that the team is effective almost anywhere and especially to those who are right outside the Church.'

Finally, from Rev. Dr. J. Watson: 'Saints in the long history of the Christian Church have varied from the near-mad to the intense intellectual. Playing a guitar, dancing or singing are not qualifications for sanctity, nor do they preclude it. Francis of Assisi, Martin Luther, Thomas

Cranmer, William Booth, Eric Liddell might find a meeting rather uncomfortable, but they were all saints.'

Criteria for the sacred dance

From our critical discussion on dance and 'scriptural principles' we have identified a series of criteria which may be useful in recognising the lawfulness or unlawfulness of an action generally, but dance specifically. Significantly none of the criteria comes from within dance itself; all have their roots in scripture.

Does it glorify God?
Is it in accordance with scripture?
Does it build up the church body?
Does it submit to judgment?
Is it spoken in love?
Is the dancer in control of herself or himself?
Does it involve a proper balance of mind, body and heart?
Do we see the good works of God in the dance?
Is the Spirit involved? Are the fruits of the Spirit in evidence?
Are we behaving decently and orderly?
Is there due reverence, fear and awe at the root of the dance?
Is it true, noble, pure, lovely, admirable, excellent and praiseworthy?
Do we preach ourselves or Christ?
Is it difficult to see the Son for the 'stars'?
Is the performance art concerned with the glory of God or man's glory?
Is the dance an entertainment in its own right or rather a means to the faith?
Am I trying to win approval for myself or God?
Is the dance and dancing God-centred or man-centred?
Am I upstaging the Word?
Is my work of a nature and condition that is foreign and unintelligible?

We must never in our eagerness to perform, minister and evangelise forget the prime importance of these criteria.

Jonah and the Whale

SECTION II
DANCE AND EDUCATION

1. EDUCATION AS INITIATION

There exists a world which we can come to know. It was here before we came into it and it will be here when we are gone. This world is both physical and metaphysical. It is a world of objects, places, things and people, which we can see, touch, smell and hear. It is a world of ideas – goodness, beauty and love. How well we come to know it or not, the extent to which we come to know it and the way in which we come to know it is dependent upon our various forms of knowing: our 'language' structures, concepts, logics and canons of truth, which we inherit from our culture and by which we construct and make meaningful our world. How we perceive the world, which is essentially external to us and impinges upon us, will depend fundamentally upon these various forms of knowing. *What* we perceive, *how* we perceive – ourselves, the world around us, dance, the Word etc. is very much dependent upon the various 'languages' or thought structures that go to make up our socio-historic traditions of knowledge and understanding.

By 'language' I do not mean the everyday, literal use of the term related to written symbols of words or verbal utterances, although this surely represents one of the most important and public 'languages' of communication and thought. I mean *any* symbolic system of thought through which man can 'make sense of', 'make meaningful', 'constructs and articulates' something of both his inner personal and outer public world and something of the mystical and transcendental world beyond everyday perception. In this sense of the term, 'languages' or 'knowledge forms' such as mathematics, physics, literature, music, dance, philosophy and theology, *all* represent various legitimate ways of coming to know the world. All in their different ways, by virtue of their peculiar media, symbolic systems, concepts, logics and canons of truth contribute in a unique way, towards the construction of reality.

When speaking of knowledge forms or 'languages', I do not have in mind what Professor Dearden[1] calls 'the rucksack theory of knowledge' – 'A theory of knowledge which sees knowledge as a jumbled mass of information such as might be exhibited to advantage on a quiz programme. A form of knowledge is a form of understanding, organised, well founded and so ingrained in the mind as to transform and not just supply more information about one's experience.'

History, within this conception of knowledge, is not so much remembering facts about particular events, although this is an important and peculiar characteristic, but rather a way of thinking about or constructing reality. Similarly with mathematics, science and art. They are all characteristically and distinctly different ways of perceiving the world. Each one represents one of many possible ways of perceiving.

2. FORMS OF KNOWING

Let us look at some of the statements made by writers on this subject in clarifying the fundamental position concerning the justification of dance. Ernst Cassirer[2] argues that 'The whole world of human meaning is expressed in several kinds of symbolic forms, each of which has its own unique legitimate function.' Cassirer nominated language, myth, religion, art and science as the main symbolic forms which determine the circle of humanity.

P. H. Phenix[3] although presenting a different list of knowing forms makes the same point: 'Meanings are of many different kinds and a full development of human beings requires education in a variety of "realms of meaning", rather than a single type of rationality.' He proposes six fundamental 'realms of meaning' each comprising a distinctive mode of human understanding and providing the foundations for all meanings that enter human experience: symbolics, empirics, aesthetics, synpoetics, ethics and synoptics. He argues that the problem of meaning for many of us is in part due to a lack of identity and development in various meaning realms. Understanding human life means understanding a complex of meanings that enter human experience. Susan Langer,[4] one of the most important contemporary philosophers of dance as an art helps to clear up some traditional misunderstandings:

> As long as sense was supposed to be the chief factor in knowledge, psychologists took a prime interest in the organs which were seen as windows of the mind in the details of their functioning. If all scientists and philosophers dutifully admitted that all true belief must be based on sense evidence the activity of the mind had to be conceived purely as a matter of recording and combining, and intelligence had to be a product of impression, memory and association. But now an epistemological insight has uncovered a more potent, howbeit more difficult, factor in scientific procedure . . . the use of symbols to attain as well as organise belief. Not higher sensitivity, not longer memory or even quicker associations sets man above animals; no, it is the power of symbols. All human behaviour is symbolic behaviour; the symbol is the universe of humanity.

The symbol is the basis of man's understanding of himself and his world; the essential act of thought *is* symbolisation, be it in art, religion, gesture or sound. The symbol-making function is one of man's primary activities and constitutes a fundamental process of mind.

It is not important for this discussion to argue specifically how many different kinds of knowing there are and what is the distinguishing criteria for each, or whether these are applicable to all cultures. What *is* important is the recognition that reality is structured from many different meanings implicit in the various forms of knowing. Education is essentially an initiation into these 'realms of meaning'.

We have established, therefore, that dance constitutes a 'language', a unique form of knowing through which man can make meaningful his world and the world in which he lives.

3. KNOWLEDGE IS BOTH OBJECTIVE AND SUBJECTIVE

Knowledge, whatever form it may take, is both objective and subjective. It should not be thought that we are mere passive recipients of public and objective knowledge. Much of the knowledge we use to construct our world is public and objective, especially if we are very young. We each inherit these public systems of thought and in this sense we might be seen as passive recipients of knowledge, but all knowledge has to be actualised and internalised within a personal, thinking/feeling system, and in this sense the objective becomes uniquely subjective. In turn, man expresses something of this subjective self – communicates and invests in the objective world again. Knowledge is the product of an ongoing process of interaction between individual man and collective society. Even for the most passive of individuals or for that sort of knowledge which by its nature leaves little room for personal interpretation, there is still a subjective dimension. That is basically how knowledge progresses and new thought forms are created.

Knowledge in the human and 'language' sense of the term is finite, but the world which we inhabit and seek to know, especially the world we seek to know as Christians, is infinite. The Word is infinite and we shall never exhaust existing human knowledge forms. Scientists and artists continually seek to go beyond what is given, seeking new thought forms with which to come to understand and express more of the nature of our world and of the truth. Psychologists estimate that man utilises less than a third of his cognitive potential. The one gigantic 'step' on the moon was one enormous step in man's extension of thinking and this development arose not out of traditional structures of thought, but new forms of symbolising, thinking and communicating. Knowledge is dynamic and constantly changing as man changes. When Vaughan Williams describes the function of music as being concerned with knowing of a kind beyond this world, and Susan Langer[4] writes that art generally and dance specifically are more concerned with '*pre*sentation' than '*re*presentation', they both have in mind a knowledge beyond what already exists.

4. 'BRIDGES AND BARRIERS OF KNOWLEDGE' (See P. H. Phenix, *Realms of Meaning*[5])

Knowledge forms are distinguishable by their unique structures or systems of thought and experiencing. No one knowledge form is sufficient to cover all man's thinking and feeling. No one knowledge form is sufficient to knowing, therefore no one knowledge form has exclusive right to truth. Each represents a unique way of structuring reality related to the Word. Some knowledge forms are 'bridges' to our coming to know and some are 'barriers'. The 'language' of mathematics may represent a most efficient 'bridge' in my coming to understand and communicate a complex series of engineering data, but it might represent a very real 'barrier' in coming to know and understand the nature of love, beauty, and art. Similarly, if during my dancing I break my big toe, or strain my back the 'language' or knowing form that I hope the nurse will bring to bear on my physical injury will not be one of music, history or philosophy, but rather physiology and anatomy. No doubt her singing to me and talking about my history and helping me to accommodate this frustration will contribute in some sense to my well being in a very general sense of the term, but they will not by themselves solve my physical problem. With coming to know the Word, as we have seen, there are many ways in which we can come to know the faith. The particular 'language' or knowing form will depend on what we are seeking to know. The concern may be essentially a theological one. It may be a historical one. It may be a geographical, scientific, sociological, philosophical, psychological question. It may be a concern that only the non-verbal knowing forms of art can articulate. When it comes to the ineffable, the mystical and knowing that arises from the heart, the 'language' of mathematics, history, theology, etc. may be 'barriers' rather than 'bridges'. Dance, within this area of perception, might very well constitute a 'bridge' to understanding.

Education, whatever its form or function, whatever fundamental philosophy may underlie its institution, is essentially an initiation into the various social/cultural, inherited forms of knowing. Fundamental to the notion of western education is this original Greek notion of a 'liberal education'. This states Hirst, 'is concerned with the comprehensive development of the mind in acquiring knowledge; it is aimed at understanding and experiencing in many different ways.'[6]

5. LIBERAL EDUCATION

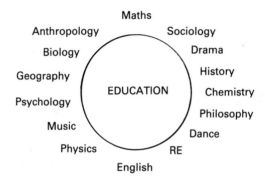

N.B. Not 'subjects' but 'forms of understanding'.[7]

Within this frame of reference it can be argued that dance represents a form of knowing, a unique way through which man can come to articulate, make meaningful in non-verbal terms something of this 'world'. As such it forms an essential part of an individual's fundamental liberal education, whatever the ultimate philosophy or specialist focus. An educated person in this sense of the term, is one who is not limited by one or two perceptual forms, however important his specialism, but possesses the range of understandings.

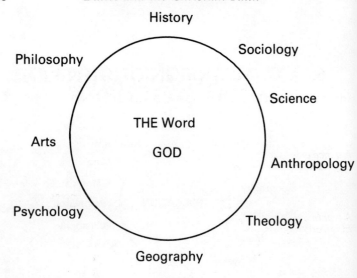

From the preceding diagram and our understanding of a liberal education we can see that all languages constitute legitimate ways of coming to know the Word. Knowledge is both objective and subjective, for while knowledge does something to us, we in turn do something to it. Reality is constructed from this interaction. Knowing God, as with knowing the Word in secular educational terms, is not exclusive to any one form of knowing, and experiencing knowing the Word involves a wide variety of understanding. It involves also an understanding of the peculiarities, the strengths and weaknesses of such systems of thought.

6. A COMPARISON OF DIFFERENT MEDIA EXPRESSIONS

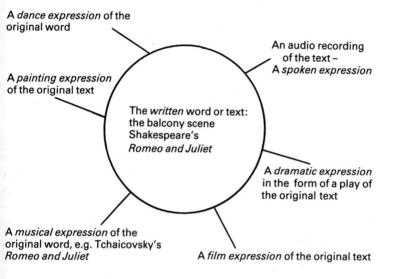

A *dance expression* of the original word

An audio recording of the text – A *spoken expression*

A *painting expression* of the original text

The *written* word or text: the balcony scene Shakespeare's *Romeo and Juliet*

A *dramatic expression* in the form of a play of the original text

A *musical expression* of the original word, e.g. Tchaicovsky's *Romeo and Juliet*

A *film expression* of the original text

In each case the original text of the balcony scene from Shakespeare's *Romeo and Juliet* remains constant. What changes is the medium or 'language' of expression. Each expressive form, by virtue of its peculiar structures, 'says' something about the original written word that the others do not. Music articulates in terms of sounds and silences; dance in movement and stillness; the painting in colour, texture, shape and form. The film, perhaps, brings together most of the art forms – music, drama, painting, dance and movement as well as its own unique expressions. It is important to note that the original word, although expressed or articulated in several different ways, nevertheless remains constant in its essential propositional

knowledge meaning. You might ask yourself just what it is
that one art form 'says' that another does not? What, for
example, can dance 'say' that the word by itself cannot?
What are the strengths and weaknesses of each with regard
to knowing God?

Let us now take a similar idea, but focus on a religious
theme.

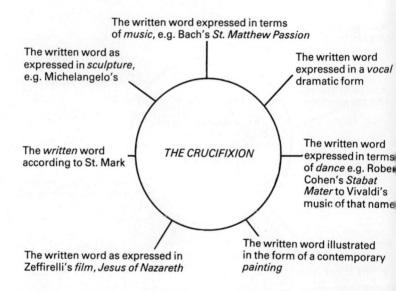

The written word expressed in terms
of *music*, e.g. Bach's *St. Matthew Passion*

The written word as
expressed in *sculpture*,
e.g. Michelangelo's

The written word
expressed in a *vocal*
dramatic form

The *written* word
according to St. Mark

THE CRUCIFIXION

The written word
expressed in terms
of *dance* e.g. Rober
Cohen's *Stabat
Mater* to Vivaldi's
music of that name

The written word as expressed in
Zeffirelli's *film, Jesus of Nazareth*

The written word illustrated
in the form of a contemporary
painting

The examples of *Romeo and Juliet* and *The Crucifixion*
illustrate this notion of different 'realms of meaning'. Each
represents a unique way of knowing and understanding.
The text, as expressed in terms of the written word, remains
constant, but the expression or interpretation of the same
differs considerably from one knowing form to another.
Furthermore, this difference of expression is different from
within each art form. Take, for example, music. Think of all
the different composers who have 'said' something about
the theme of the Crucifixion. Each artist 'speaks' differently
even within the same 'language'! No *one* knowing form and
no one human being has the exclusive way to knowing the
TRUTH. Each artistic form and each artist within the various forms helps reveal to us something of the TRUTH.

In this sense, religious education is not just R.E. in the 'theological' sense of the term. It is a religious education approached from a variety of knowing forms. If we take the crucifixion theme again, we could approach it from a wide variety of positions.

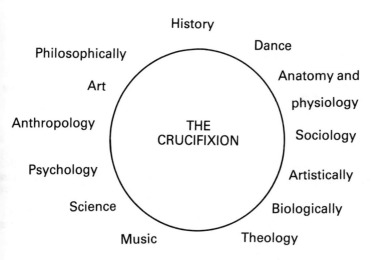

Each form tells us something about the Word. What we want to know and communicate will, of course, determine whether these knowing forms constitute 'bridges' or 'barriers'. They all represent fundamentally legitimate ways of articulating such a momentous, significant event. Ask yourselves what sort of questions, by virtue of the nature of each discipline, will each knowledge form raise, and what sort of answers can each give? Thinking about death and resurrection for example, what sort of questions would the scientist ask? What sort of questions would the historian ask, as distinct from the scientist or from the theologian? Equally, ask yourself what sort of answers would be given. And, more important, consider critically the validity of these answers to the sort of knowledge you are after.

7. EDUCATION AND THE 'WHOLE MAN'

Education, while being concerned with an initiation into various forms of knowing, is also fundamentally concerned with the education of the whole man, including the intellectual, physical, emotional, social. For a development of this within dance and physical education, see P. J. Arnold.[8]

Once again it should be recognised that these are conceptual rather than real distinctions. Each is intimately related to the other. The intellectual personality is intimately related to the physical, to our feelings and emotions and to society itself. Studies on deprivation in all these areas – cognitive retardation, emotional maladjustment, social deprivation, physical disturbance – are well documented, reinforcing the importance of wholeness. To neglect any one of these aspects of development is to neglect the whole.

Fundamental to the initiation into various forms of knowing is a recognition of the whole personality. Subjects or forms of knowing are a means to this end. My own experience of teaching dance within education was rooted in the idea that it was firstly a means to the end of individual growth and development rather than dance itself. I can remember vividly composing my dance lessons and then identifying questions concerning the nature of its intellectual, physical, emotional and social content. Dance is one of the most comprehensive of knowing forms in this sense. Very few other knowing forms have the intimate and deliberate four-fold characteristic that dance has. Although much of my work today both in teaching undergraduates in dance and leading a professional dance company is necessarily concerned with the artistic nature of dance, I am aware that one of its oldest functions is therapeutic. At one level we see this at the local disco and at barn dances; at another, we see it in therapy sessions for the subnormal.

Dance constitutes a unique means whereby the whole person becomes intimately involved in the 'language'. Above all the instrument of dance expression IS the whole person. Coming to know God, the 'WORD' as we have seen from our study of scripture involves the whole person. Body, mind and heart – all worked out within everyday living are essential to a proper knowledge and understanding of ourselves and God. If we neglect one, we undermine the whole. Dance is probably at its most efficient and effective when concerned with the emotional/feeling aspect of reality, but it must embrace the other elements of our being – mind, body and society.

8. THE EDUCATIONAL PROCESS – TEACHING AND LEARNING

Educational psychologists define learning as 'relatively permanent changes in behaviour'. Educational philosophers, on the other hand, while wanting to build into the notion of learning and teaching something of a change in behaviour, argue that changes in behaviour by themselves are not reliable criteria for teaching and learning. It is pointed out that conditioning, torture, hypnotism and blackmail are all used to bring about changes in behaviour and, in their more disguised forms, are by no means uncommon in education! (See 'Logical and Psychological Aspects of Teaching'.)[9] The *process* of learning is as important a part of education as the *product*. Above all in our developing process of coming to know, fundamental to all learning and all education, is the notion of an active, responsible participant rather than a passive, non-responsible recipient. It has always seemed incredible to me that, since learning is so fundamental to education, there is not a subject concerned with such a topic. There is

certainly plenty of research done within this field, but how
many of us in our education were ever given instruction in
learning itself?

9. THREE CO-ORDINATE SPECIES OF KNOWING

What does it mean to say that we *know* something? Let us
take the waltz. What does it mean to say that we know a
waltz, or any dance for that matter? Imagine three students
presenting their answers. The first answer is essentially
theoretical, knowing *about* the waltz. It is very much an
abstract or second-hand truth, and although valid in itself,
it is not sufficient for a reliable and valid educational notion
of knowing. This is a knowing in part. The second answer is
essentially a practical and physical re-creation or translation
of a second-hand knowledge identified in the first answer.
The student has gone to a text book on social dance and
tried to translate the instructions into physical terms. In this
sense it is true, but once again it is only a part of the truth,
not sufficient by itself. The third answer is essentially a
knowing of the heart, a genuine, intimate, emotional,
heartfelt expression of the waltz ideal. She listens to the
music and is moved from the heart to 'express herself all
over the floor'! As with the other two answers, this contains
something of the truth. But it is, by itself, insufficient. All
the answers represent significant criteria for a full sense of
the term to know, but by themselves are inadequate. Just
what, then, constitutes a reliable and valid criteria of knowing a waltz?

Knowing a waltz, like knowing any subject of the curriculum – knowing the Word and knowing the dance – involves three co-ordinate species of knowing: knowing
'that', knowing 'how' and knowing 'of'.

Knowing the waltz in the first sense means knowing

something about its social historical meaning. It evolved from the Ländler during the eighteenth century and became very popular as a ballroom couple dance in the nineteenth and twentieth centuries. It is still danced today, albeit in slightly different form, but it retains its characteristic 3/4 time involving 'turning'. One could study various books on the subject and also the music of such a dance. This sort of factual knowledge represents important preliminary information.

Knowing the waltz in the second sense, means knowing something about it in practical and physical terms. This involves working out the choreography of the dance and learning the steps, postures and gestures, floor patterns, etc. related to the dance. This aspect is in fact fundamental.

The third form of knowing is that of the heart. As Margot Fonteyn says in her biography (Pan) 'I learn the steps quickly, but it is a long time before I dance them'. Dancing the waltz means something more than mind and body. It certainly involves the mind and the body but in the end the dance comes alive as a dance because of what we invest in the steps and thoughts. This investment comes from the heart and it is there that we see the true basis of the dance. Is this so different from knowing the Word? I think not. Knowing the waltz, as with knowing the Word, involves knowing in three interrelated ways.

The following dance score, music score and dramatic score are three equivalents of the 'written word' or propositional knowledge. In each case the 'written word' *denoted* in various ways does not equal the Word in the sense of the 'dance', 'music' or 'dramatic experiences'. Rather it *represents* essential knowledge *about* the dance. The written word of the dance is knowledge about the ballet *Coppelia*. The written word of the music is written knowledge about *Tableaux d'une Exposition*. The written word of the play is knowledge about the play. In each case the ballet mistress, the conductor and the director have to give serious thought to the basic text before translating it into art. Equally the dancer, musicians and actor have to give similar attention to both their parts and the artifact or Word as a whole. This theoretical knowledge is now transferred to the practical realisation of the Word. The Word has to be made 'flesh' and be re-created in physical, everyday terms, so that it makes sense to those for whom it is intended to communicate. For the dancer this will mean working on the various physical patterns and sequences of events, trying to accommodate them all in her mind and trying to make her body realise the various ideas. When this practical knowledge has been achieved then comes the most difficult and important aspect of knowing . . . a knowing that involves a professional, personal investment of the artist into both the theoretical and practical knowledge identified so far. Here the skilled and disciplined dancer, musician and actor or the ballet mistress, conductor and director bring the whole to life, carefully negotiating with other artists and ever-conscious of the real world within which the Word has to be communicated. At this point, having mastered the denotative aspects of the composition as symbolised in the respective notation systems, the artist concerns his or her self with the ultimate and essentially, connotative aspects. The essence of the dance lies in what is connoted rather than what is denoted.

The sacred dancer, like any dancer learning a dance, has this threefold responsibility involving the mind, the body and the heart.

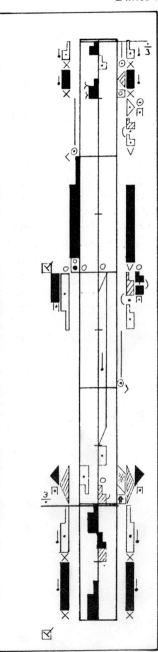

The meaning of the art symbols lies not in the symbols *per se* but rather in what each artist invests in the symbols.

This is knowledge essentially *about* the artifact rather than *how* or *of*.

TABLEAUX D'UNE EXPOSITION

PROMENADE

M. P. MUSSORGSKY
Orchestration by
Maurice Ravel

ACT ONE

A wooded hillside near AASE'S *farm. A stream is rushing down it. On the far side is an old millhouse. It is a hot summer's day.* PEER GYNT, *a strongly built youth of twenty, comes down the path.* AASE, *his mother, small and frail, follows him. She is angry and is scolding him.*

AASE: Peer, you're lying!
PEER (*without stopping*): I am not!
AASE: Well, then, swear it's true!
PEER: Why swear?
AASE: Ah, you daren't! It's all rubbish.
PEER (*stops*): It's true, every word.
AASE (*squares up in front him*): Aren't you ashamed?
  First you sneak off into the mountains
  For weeks on end in the busy season
  To stalk reindeer in the snow –
  Come home with your coat torn,
  Without the gun, without the meat.
  And then you look me straight in the face
  And try to fool me with your hunter's lies!
  Well, where did you meet the buck?
PEER: West near Gjendin.
AASE (*laughs scornfully*): Did you, now?
PEER: I suddenly smelt him on the wind.
  Hidden behind an elder-bush
  He was scratching in the snow for lichen –
AASE (*still scornfully*): Oh, yes!
PEER: I held my breath
  And stood listening. I heard his hoof
  Crunch, and saw one branching antler.
  I wormed on my belly through the stones towards
    him.
  Still hidden, I peered out.

10. AN INITIATION INTO DANCE AS A FORM OF KNOWING

We began our discussion of education and religious dance by focusing on the philosophy that education is essentially an initiation into 'forms of knowing' (Hirst)[9], 'realms of meaning' (Phenix),[10] or 'forms of knowing and experiencing' (L. A. Reid).[11] Dance and R.E. represented two of many knowing forms or 'languages' through which we can come to know and express the world. For the second part of this discussion of education and dance, we examine *what constitutes an initiation into dance as a form of knowing*.

Just as education generally involves an initiation into various forms of knowing, so, too, an education in dance involves an initiation into dance generally. The concept of dance is not rigid or fixed; it encompasses a wide and complex variety of movement expressions. 'Dance is in many and various dimensions: we are free to move in all of them' (Nureyev). The following list identifies some of these movement expressions: classical ballet, contemporary dance, ballroom dance, national dance, historical dance, modern dance, disco dance, tap dance, folk dance, creative dance, stage dance, educational dance, ethnic dance, religious dance and dance drama. A detailed description of such forms is included in *Dance – from Magic to Art* by Louis Ellfeldt.[12]

Within each of these dance forms exists a variety of differences. For example in contemporary dance there are as many different notions of dance as there are choreographers. Similarly there is great variety within ballroom dance, social-historical dance, ethnic and national dance. These titles are in themselves 'umbrella terms': the nature of dance, both in its physical form and its expressive meaning, is essentially open and this characteristic may represent one of the distinguishing features of such a 'language'. Each dance type is different from other expressions in terms of its function, its structure and form, its style, its context, its vocabulary and content. The term 'ballroom dance' denotes a particular expressive system in terms of such criteria. Its function, form, vocabulary and nature of expression are different from, say, classical ballet. (All these dance forms constitute a potential movement vocabulary for sacred dance.)

However, within dance's essentially contested and open nature there are common characteristics of the 'language' as a whole.

Firstly, all dance uses as its instrument of expression the body. Without the body, there is no dance and how we dance depends on the extent to which we can use our bodies.

Secondly, all dance uses movement as its medium of expression. There may be many other supports like music, props, costume, etc. but movement is the primary essential for all dance.

Thirdly, all dance is in some sense structured and codified. This may be manifest in a very free, intuitive, spontaneous form or in a more controlled, preconceived deliberate form. But in most, if not all, cases of dance, there is some notion of recognised form or style.

Fourthly, all dance is concerned with expression which is essentially not of words. Its meanings, even at its most literal, mimetic and narrative, are still something 'more than' and 'independent of' the narrative upon which the dance may be based. For example the *Dying Swan*, by Fokine, made famous by Pavlova and one of the most famous romantic ballets, while based on the narrative of a swan dying is not literally and naïvely a dance about a dying swan (*Art of Making Dances*[13]). Firstly it is significant that Fokine chose a swan rather than, say, a dog or a cow! The swan during the romantic period of art represented something very special and the dance lies not so much in what is *denoted*, as what is *connoted*. It is the feelings and emotions related to all that surrounds such a significant symbol that the *Dying Swan* is about. Among the most mimetic dance forms I know is that of some of the classical Indian dance, every subtle gesture, flick of an eyelash, posture, hand movement is incredibly mimetic and at one level understanding is very much dependent upon knowing the meaning of the complex range of mimetic symbolism. But in the end, as any classical Indian dancer will tell you, this is not drama *per se*, but a unique language which expresses dramatic feeling and emotion. It is expression of feeling through movement that distinguishes the dance from the drama of words. This is so also in social dance, be it ballroom, folk or national dance. All dance is in some sense concerned with expression and communication in non-verbal/bodily terms, even at the most literal level. The primary purpose of dance is not so much in what it *denotes* as in what it *connotes* (*Movement and Meaning*[14]).

Fifthly, all dance is characterised by its multiplicity of meaning. We have already spoken of the variable specificity of 'language' in previous sections, asking the question in relation to coming to know the Word – 'Just how specific must the meaning of the Word be?' The answer really depends upon the nature of the particular form of knowing. Clearly in such 'languages' as mathematics and normal public language of words, the meanings are fairly fixed and not open to too wide an interpretation. Two plus two is always four: there is no room for negotiation. The meanings of mathematical concepts are relatively fixed and this is their strength. Similarly with certain use of words, for example, words used in law and the social sciences. It would make nonsense for me to say that 'all unmarried men are spinsters', since an unmarried man is a bachelor and an unmarried women is a spinster. This sort of logic is not that of dance, in fact quite the opposite. While a logic of this kind is expressed in the *denotative* aspect of the dance, the essential *connotative* nature of the dance is much more open. The steps, rhythms, context, structure, form, etc. of such a dance as the waltz are fixed and unnegotiable in the denotative sense, but the actual dance expression, i.e. what the steps connote, is not. In the denotative sense of the term *Swan Lake*, I can say that a dancer 'is' or 'is not' dancing *Swan Lake*; that is right or wrong. And right or wrong is defined by fairly fixed public criteria. If the dancer puts in some of her own steps or borrows steps from say, *Giselle*, then, as with mathematics, we can say that it is wrong since these meanings are fixed. So too, with music and drama. If we return to our three examples of art: *Coppelia, Tableaux d'une Exposition*, and *Peer Gynt*, we see in the symbols the artifact in denotative terms. This is fixed and not negotiable. What is negotiable and, indeed, expected of the artist is an expressive interpretation of the symbols. This is open to a wide variety of meanings from the audience – almost as many meanings as there are audience. This connotative element is open to meaning. There is layer upon layer of meaning. We sometimes in fact use this multi-dimensional nature as a criteria for good dance and certainly in dance as art.

We must recognise both the denotative and the connotative element of religious dance. Like Fokine's *Dying Swan* and Cohen's Mary the Mother of Jesus at the foot of the cross, in *Stabat Mater*, these expressions are much 'more than' and 'independent of' the narrative!

Stabat Mater is rooted in scripture and this is an important denotative element, but the essential dance meaning lies in what the dance ultimately connotes – for the choreographer firstly, then the dancer, and finally the audience. In these three different perceptive focuses we see three very different notions of meaning, expressions and communication – and in all probability each perceiver will see different meanings. The audience will all be *looking* at the same artifact which is non-negotiable in both the physical movement and the scriptural sense of the term upon which the dance is based, but they will all be *seeing* very different things. A dance colleague of mine, speaking at a recent seminar on dance and Christian faith, was emphasising that dance must communicate clearly. She was right in the sense that the dance must be presented in such a way that it is intelligible to the perceiver, and that its Christian expression upon which it is based is clear, but quite wrong in the sense that there is but *one* meaning – the meaning that she, as the choreographer, had in mind for the dance. The empirical, psychological fact as well as the logical fact of art suggests quite the opposite. Those who dismiss religious dance because of its 'layer upon layer' of meaning misunderstand the nature of the language. They are applying the logic of another form of knowing to dance. They are making a 'categorical mistake' (Ryle, *Concept and Mind*[15]) and as such denying the essential and unique truth of meaning in dance. The fact that art generally and dance specifically is open to many interpretations is its strength, and not a weakness. Just how specific does the meaning of the Word have to be? When I listen to Bach's *St. Matthew Passion*, or watch Robert Cohen's *Stabat Mater*, not only is the nature of the art such that it is open to a variety of meanings, each time I come to it I 'see' different things! One of the reasons for our returning to a work of art is partly to recognise what we already know, but partly also to know something more by comparing different interpretations and by bringing more and more of our knowledge and understanding to the experience. When the artist is a great exponent we invariably see something never seen before.

The cartoon opposite represents a common and amusing criticism of what is sometimes referred to as 'creative dance'. The implication is that there is no real communication because all are perceiving differently. For true communication, it is argued all should be thinking about the dancer's 'daisy'! It displays to my mind an extraordinary ignorance and naïvety as to the nature of dance meaning and artistic meaning generally. The essential nature of art is that, as with an icon, we are encouraged to look and contemplate and begin to see from within our own unique perception. (See *Icons* by Ouspensky – and the transformation of matter, i.e. we 'go into' the icon.)[16] This is not a seeing separate from looking.

Sceptical view of non-verbal communication by C.E.M. From
The New Yorker.

The act of looking is a conscious and deliberate, disciplined
act to attend and to concentrate, to contemplate, and in
doing so we necessarily bring to the artifact a vast specialist
range of categories by which we then begin to see.

11. WHAT ARTISTS AND PHILOSOPHERS SAY ABOUT DANCE

'No art suffers more misunderstanding, sentimental
judgment and mystical interpretation than the art of
dance' (Susan Langer, dance philosopher).

'The artist aims not at beauty but objective self expression' (Ducasse, philosopher).

'Art may be defined as the practice of creating perceptible
forms, expressive of human feeling. The work of art expresses a conception of life, emotion, inward reality. But it
is neither a confessional nor a frozen tantrum; it is a
developed metaphor, a non-discursive symbol that articulates what is verbally ineffable – the logic of consciousness
itself' (Susan Langer, dance philosopher).

'Art is the evocation of one's inner nature. Through art – which finds its roots in man's unconscious race-memory – is the history and psyche of race brought into focus. Great art never ignores human values. Therein lies its roots. This is why forms change' (Martha Graham, dancer/choreographer).

'Art is like a hall of mirrors or a whispering gallery. Each form conjures up a thousand memories and after-images' (Lancelot Law Whyte, philosopher).

'A great work of art is like a dream; for all its apparent obviousness, it does not explain itself and is never unequivocal' (Carl Jung, psychologist).

'My dancing is just dancing. It is not an attempt to interpret life in a literary sense. It is the affirmation of life through movement. Its only aim is to impart the sensation of living, to energise the spectator into keener awareness of the vigour, of the mystery, the humour, the variety and wonder of life; to send the spectator away with a fuller sense of his own potentialities and the power of realising them whatever the medium of his activity' (Martha Graham, choreographer).

'Art cannot be known but only experienced, and art belongs to man. When great art is so deeply felt and understood, it ceases to be a collection of beautiful objects and becomes instead a succession of gateways. And whenever this happens art reveals the path of beauty' (Alexander Elliot, critic).

'Art forms do not give directly: we get their meanings indirectly from the imagery of the creator who embodies the experience. The real value of a work of art lies not so much in what we actually see as how we react to all that we perceive' (Margaret H. Doubler, dance teacher). (See *Dance – from Magic to Art*).[17]

12. WHAT SHOULD WE UNDERSTAND BY 'RELIGIOUS DANCE'?

We have been discussing dance in a very general sense and while we have identified some common elements, dance nevertheless remains an essentially multi-faceted phenomenon with a wide variety of forms, functions and contents. So we must examine what constitutes religious dance.

Firstly, in the sense that 'God created the earth and all that is in it and saw that it was good', then all dance is religious. This general sense of the term 'religious' has two significances:

(i) Even though some dance is abused and misused and, in the religious sense, unlawful and unrighteous, nevertheless it is in essence good, since it comes from God.

(ii) A Christian involved in such non-specific religious dance as classical ballet, stage dance, ballroom dance, national dance, etc., may still be seen as involved in religious dance. The Christian dancer in the classical ballet, *Swan Lake*, or the stage musical *Cats*, may not be dancing a specific scriptural theme, but as a Christian she is a Christian professional artist expressing something of her faith in the work that she is committed to and within an activity that is good and God given. There is no theological reason why a Christian dancer cannot legitimately commit herself wholeheartedly to such dance forms and not see her dancing as an expression of her faith in the same way as all Christians are involved in life.

There was a time not so long ago when some Christian professional dancers thought that for a true Christian dance witness the dance had to be specifically biblical and the dancer should commit herself to outreach and renewal. Although an admirable and much needed focus in our society, it is not the only way that one can express oneself as a Christian dancer. For the religious person, all activities are religious in nature in that they come from God, glorify him, and are given back to him. (See *Art Needs No Justification*.[18])

In the more specific sense of the term, there is such a religious dance form which, in the context of this study, has the distinguishing characteristic of communicating and propagating the Christian faith either within the Church or outside it. Its repertoire although not exclusively scriptural in the Word sense is, in the main, deliberately focused on communicating the Word. It may be entertaining, aesthetically pleasing, physically satisfying, emotionally expressive, formally significant, socially conducive, etc. – all the functions that other dance forms fulfil, but with the vital and fundamental difference that all this is a means to the end of the Word. The distinguishing feature of religious dance is not steps, forms or even content *per se*, but rather motivation and intention. While there are many movements, postures and gestures that we normally associate with religion they do not by themselves constitute the sufficient distinguishing feature of 'religious dance'. It is the context and the intention, the function of the dance that is the primary distinguishing feature of religious dance. In this sense of our definition all dance vocabularies represent potentially acceptable movement ideas and a dance vocabulary for the sacred dance. Disco, ballet, contemporary, stage, national and folk dance all constitute legitimate movement vocabularies and ideas for the sacred dance. In the end what makes a dance religious or not is not the dance itself but what each one of us, choreographer, dancer or spectator, invests in the dance. Those who write to ask for 'religious' steps believing that (a) there is such a thing and (b) that this step makes the dance religious, misunderstand the nature of both dance and religious dance. In the general sense all dance is religious. In the more specific sense, dance is religious by virtue of its motivation and function. In the repertoire of Springs there are dances incorporating most dance styles – classical ballet, modern, stage, jazz, spectacular in the style of *Fame*, body popping, historic, national and ethnic dance. None is used as an *end* in itself; all represent *means* of communicating the Word of God.

13. CREATIVITY

In discussing creativity and dance I do not have in mind a conception of dance and creativity as a natural and innate ability that, if left alone and not imposed upon, will come to 'blossom like a blooming flower'! A view marvellously epitomised by Joyce Grenville as the school teacher, saying, 'Now then children, I want you to listen to this music and – express yourselves all over the floor!' While I do not deny we may have an innate ability to move and to express ourselves through movement and that within this expression there is positive growth and development in terms of cognitive, emotional, physical and social development, I do want to deny that this is necessarily dance. In a burst of joy children jump. In response to their inner physical drives and needs they leap and turn, skip, roll and hop. In a rage they stamp their feet. When they are bored and restless they fidget. These are all legitimate and common movement expressions, but they are not dance expressions. They are *symptoms* of an inner state rather than *symbols* of a disciplined, conscious state. 'In order to elevate these manifestations to the heights of an art we must give it definite form' (Vaganova).[19] 'There is such a lot of sentimental babble of the beauty of children (and adults) dancing spontaneously in a natural self expression delightfully unconscious of the effects of their creations' (Beryl Grey).[20] The art of dance is a conscious, considered and intended activity, not something unconsidered and haphazard, mere sporadic outbursts of impulsive movement, unplanned, unintended and uninformed.

I am not implying a return to the rigid and highly formalised rote-learning situation of creativity and learning that characterised much of the traditional subject-centred educational philosophy. In dance terms, I dread the thought of everyone struggling at the ballet barre, being bullied and moulded passively into a 'swan'! I want to retain the emphasis on freedom and individual creativity, on spontaneity and intuitive thinking, which grew out of the child-centred educationists' reaction to the traditional subject-centred repressive views of education. But I want to support such a freedom with a disciplined framework from within which the individual 'artist' can grow properly. Some of the manifestations of the more extreme child-centred freedom is expressed in the many 'nymphs' and 'fairies' that have come increasingly to represent Liturgical Dance. I want to retain this marvellous and refreshing, uninhibited expression, *but* I want to give it some basic disciplined structure, form and content. The art of dance, whatever its form, is a learned phenomenon.

> It is a skill which resides in and derives from an expansion of perception, and a skill like other skills must be cultivated and trained. We learn to do things not by 'first nature', but 'second nature'. (Professor L. A. Reid)[21]

> We learn to become 'natural' to acquire a new kind of spontaneity through passing the stages of hard discipline. The ability to perceive is a learned ability. We are not born with sight; we acquire it with experience through trial and error. To see something is to have constructed intelligibly a perceptual realisation. (E. W. Eisner)[22]

> Discipline is a prerequisite of the artist although this is not the popular view held today. But without discipline, there can be no freedom to attain anything worthwhile, and it is the joy of attaining that freedom that makes it so worthwhile. Movement is common to us all, but the artist makes it more telling and uses it as a means of expression. (Beryl Grey)[23]

These statements insist on a disciplined initiation into both creativity and a particular subject or 'form of knowing'.

Creativity and dance both presuppose mastering some mode of experience and being trained in techniques appropriate to that particular form of articulation.

14. CRAFTSMANSHIP AND DANCE

Applying this concern for a disciplined initiation into dance we now focus upon four functional prerequisites of dance.

The instrument of expression – body

Every artifact, whatever its form, be it a musical composition, a painting, a play or a dance, is realised firstly in physical terms, through the expressive instrument peculiar to that form. The instrument is fundamental to any form of expression. It is the means by which the expression is realised. Throughout the creative process it represents a highly significant variable on which the nature of expression, its structure and content all depend. The effectiveness and efficiency of the instrument itself and of how we use it is an intimate part of expression. To ignore the instrument of expression is in effect to ignore the expression itself. In dance terms, the extent to which we can move will in a very real sense equal the extent to which we will dance.

In dance, the body is the beginning and the end. We teach dance, but we teach about the body first – how it works, what its anatomy is. Dancing is a science that transforms into an art. (Rosella Hightower – dancer/teacher)[24]

Each art has an instrument – the instrument of dance is the human body . . . my aim is to dance significantly, i.e. through the medium of discipline and means of a sensitive, strong and agile instrument, to bring into focus unhackneyed movement in a human being. It is here in the studio that the dancer learns his craft, the mastery of his instrument which is his body. (Martha Graham – dancer/teacher)[25]

The dancer's medium is his body which is an extremely tangible piece of goods, much more than words, notes or paint – it already has a definite complex system of levers, limbs, nerves and muscles . . . plus a lived-in personality with entrenched ways of its own. Knowledge about, awareness of, and a curiosity about the body are essential. (Doris Humphrey – dancer/teacher)[26]

Dance as an art form reveals the beauty of the body and more important the beauty of motion . . . a very beautiful instrument, much more like an orchestra than like a single instrument. The task of controlling a complex orchestra, forming it into a unified voice achieving complex contrapuntal effects and meeting the variety of demands is both difficult and time consuming. The control of so many and so varied factors as are represented by the human body requires a similar discipline. (M. H. Nadel)[27]

The physical skill necessary for dance does not come about naturally. It is rather based upon a disciplined understanding of the body and an initiation into dance is necessarily an initiation into physical skill. 'It is emphatically not enough merely to provide the educand with opportunities for physical self discovery' (A. D. Monrow).[28]

In arguing for physical skill I do not have in mind necessarily a full-time, professional training in classical ballet or contemporary dance technique. Although such training is essential for the full-time dancer, it is not so for the ordinary dancer in the church. What I have in mind when arguing for skill is a disciplined concern for such things as: body shape, strength, stamina, clarity, precision, control, flexibility, balance, suppleness, co-ordination. These are the means whereby the body looks good, moves comfortably, goes above the normal everyday moving, can jump, leap, turn, twist and 'speak' in a wide variety of ways. Such qualities are best obtained within such disciplines as classical ballet technique or modern dance classes, but they may be attained through a good knowledge and understanding of 'keep fit'. There are very few places in this country where it is not now possible to take classes in dance, led by qualified and experienced teachers. The dance magazines *Dancing Times* and *Dance and Dancers* provide addresses to write to for help in finding a good teacher. The local educational authorities usually have evening classes in such activities. If you are an established religious dance group or intend to form such a group then careful attention should be given to this first prerequisite. If you are a performing and travelling group, it requires serious concern since you deliberately put yourselves forward as performers, implying that you have something extraordinary to offer.

The medium of expression – movement

Although a skilful instrument of expression is a first and fundamental prerequisite of dance, it does not by itself automatically produce dance. One of the traditional educational criticisms of ballet training was that all too often the concern for technique became a concern for itself, instead of being a means to dance. Being able to move skilfully is one thing, but being able to 'say' something is quite another. I have met many professionally trained dancers who, because of their training, find it very difficult to say anything themselves either by making up their own dances, i.e. choreographing, or when dancing other persons' dances. Skill by itself cannot bring about dance. Similarly with regard to the worst sort of child-centred, educational dance. All too often it was assumed that a child had an innate vocabulary. The teacher would put on a record of, say, Handel's *Water Music* or Tchaikovsky's *1812 Overture* and then invite the children to 'express themselves all over the floor'. Apart from the fact that these musical works are inappropriate to dance – the first is not evocative of water at all, and the second is so complex and dramatically overwhelming that the children are not stimulated and end up wallowing on the floor, moving in order not to upset teacher – it wrongly assumes that the children have something to say. Education is as much to do with impressions as expressions: the latter frequently depend on the former. Education, by definition, is an initiation and in this case it is an initiation into movement possibilities. The student has to be introduced to movement ideas, encouraged to explore such ideas in his own terms and in the terms of specialists, gradually building up and developing his or her own vocabulary. In religious dance we see so much of the same very limited movement vocabulary usually dominated by 'arms' and 'grapevine' steps. I do not want to undermine the use of the arms or the use of that very common folk motif called the 'grapevine step', but dance has so much more to say. As I have already pointed out, the 'language' of dance is not a homogeneous phenomenon. It embraces a wide variety of styles. Dance is not just classical ballet or contemporary dance. The vocabulary of national, folk, historical and jazz dance is as legitimate for religious dance as is your own dance vocabulary. The 'language' of dance is not plié, arabesque, pirouette, or contractions, 'falls' and 'triplets' – although they may be incorporated in dance either implicitly through technical skill or explicitly in terms of vocabulary. The language of dance is 'movement' and all movement constitutes a legitimate vocabulary of dance.

Let us consider how we might build up a dance vocabulary appropriate for religious dance.

One of the best ways is to use already existing vocabularies. From your practical and theoretical knowledge of folk, national, ethnic, jazz, social and historical dance, for example, it is possible to develop a very rich language of expression, which by its very nature and function is applicable to the non-professional dancer.

Another way is carefully to watch and analyse professional dance companies. Whenever I go to the theatre I take a pencil and paper with me so that I can jot down in words, matchstick men or even dance notation anything that attracts me. It may be a particular step, an interesting shape, an unusual sequence or development of material. It may be something to do with floor patterns of the dance, with groupings of the dancers. It may be costume, music, drama, etc. I take the ideas home with me and then make them my own. *← Don't say how • this is the crucial info we need*

A dance vocabulary can be built up from drama, from various musical stimuli, paintings, poetry, and architecture which can be translated into movement. Traditionally this has been one of the main ways of encouraging dance ideas in education. The infamous example of, 'Now then children I want you to be a tree, or a flower, or a bunch of bananas,' sounds very silly to the uninitiated but with the right thinking and understanding on the part of the teacher and the learner, within a limited range, some interesting ideas *disagree* can arise. The problem with the method is that dance tends to become associated exclusively with the literal and mi- *+ with* metic rather than movement expression, i.e. dance itself. *careful use*

The problem for the previous vocabulary stimuli is that it *encourage* requires a vocabulary to do justice to the stimuli. However *ment of* *not set* moved we may be by the story, the music, the painting, or *symbolic* the poem, there still remains the problem of translating this *thinking* into dance. *← Aha! take my comment back*

One of the most positive things to come out of twentieth-century 'educational dance' is that of Laban's classification of movement.[29] Laban was one of the great educational *3* dance innovators in the early part of the twentieth century. *CHEERS* His analyses of movement in relation to education, dance *Mr Blogg* and life generally have proved an extraordinary source of inspiration. Within dance generally, and that includes pro-fessional dance, this classification is proving to be most fruitful. For classical ballet, there already exists a codified vocabulary of movement and movement descriptions, *that are* Classical ballet dancers and choreographers still tend to *generally* choreograph in terms of ballet dance steps and postures, *lacking in* but even within this conservative field, there is a trend *meaning* towards ballet which includes all movement rather than the traditional codified steps. It is this classification of move-ment, this notion of a dance vocabulary, that I propose to concentrate on both in this section and also in Section III where I introduce a variety of potential religious dance projects.

Laban's classification of movement

Laban identified four major categories of movement: space, body, effort or dynamics, relationship. Any movement embraces an element from each of these.

(i) *Space* – refers to *where* I move. Do I move in my own space, or the more general space about me? Do I move forwards, backwards, sideways, diagonally? Do I move upwards, or downwards, around, through, over, under, etc.?

(ii) *Body* – refers to *what* moves. Do I move my whole body or a part? Do I move my arm, head, leg, hip, etc.? Do I run, walk, hop, skip?

(iii) *Effort* – refers to *how* I move. Do I move suddenly, or do I move in a more sustained manner? Do I move heavily or lightly, freely or bound?

(iv) *Relationship* – refers to *what or who* I move with or respond to. Do I move with a partner, or a group? Do I move in relation to the drama, the music, the poetry, etc.?

Under each of these classifications there exist various movement/dance themes which the dancer is encouraged to consider from a theoretical, practical and emotional point of view. For example, in exploring body shape the dancer should consider from a theoretical point of view all the possible shapes the body could produce, and shape should be related to the body, space, effort and relationship. The dancer might also study shape in existing dances – ballet, folk or ballroom dance, for example.

Having studied theoretical conception of 'body shape', this should now be experienced in practical dance/movement terms.

Finally, dancing should be considered in artistic and feeling terms. 'Body shape' is studied in terms of the mind,

the body and the heart – knowledge 'that', knowledge
'how' and knowledge 'of'.

SPACE – where?	BODY – what?

personal space
general space
floor patterns and air
    patterns
levels –
    deep/medium/high
directions:
  backwards
  forwards
  sideways
  diagonal – forward or
    back
  circle
over, under, through,
    round, near far,
on to, into, etc.
	stillness and motion
	body parts:
	  arm
	  leg
	  head
	  hip
	  shoulder
	  knee
	  hand
	locomotion: run, walk,
	    hop, skip, crawl, slide,
	    jump, leap, turn, etc.
	body gestures
	body shape
	balance
	leading with body parts

RELATIONSHIP – in relation to what?	EFFORT – how?
solo duo in relation to others in relation to body parts unison counterpoint music drama poetry costume staging	Time: sudden/sustained Weight: firm/light Space: flexible/direct Flow: bound/free wringing thrusting gliding flicking dabbing floating pressing slashing

[handwritten annotation:] SHOULD EXPLAIN WHERE these words come from!

In seeking a vocabulary for a dance idea, any and all of these themes can be used. For example, in approaching the altar 'where' do I move/dance, 'what' moves/dances, 'how' does it move/dance, and 'in relation to what' does it move?

This may be rather abstract for those who know nothing of this classification. However, I hope that it will become more meaningful within Section III, where I will be drawing heavily on this classification with the intention of building up a good theoretical and practical working knowledge of a potential dance vocabulary.

The structure of expression – form

We have a skilful instrument of expression – the body. We have a rich vocabulary of expression – movement. But a rich vocabulary of movement, like a skilful body, does not, by itself, equal the dance. A third prerequisite is necessary. This rich vocabulary of movement skilfully performed needs to be carefully structured and shaped so that it becomes communicable. Structure and form are about punctuation and it is the grammar and punctuation that allow the dance to be perceived and understood. A dance is always much more than a series of movements put together. The choreographer carefully shapes his ideas, moves towards pauses and climaxes, accents, highlights and moments of repose. He carefully considers such perceptual tools as motifs, repetition and development of material. Just as the musical conductor has to study the score, identifying the main ideas or themes and their development, the various sections that make up the work, the relationship between ideas and various subtle nuances, like crescendos, accelerandos, repetitions, grades of volume, and many other such focuses, so too does the ballet mistress and the dancer have to consider such focuses in the dance.

Whenever I am teaching a dance to a dancer, I give fundamental consideration to such focuses, usually illustrating some of the more visual ideas on a blackboard. I have seen dances with an exciting and original vocabulary, but unrealised simply because of this lack of structural concern. Some are little more than a series of unconnected movements, some meander over a period of time (sometimes a very long time) and never get anywhere. Some seem bland and flat. The writer punctuates in order to communicate his ideas. In terms of dance, which is essentially a time/space form of expression, recognising basic ideas and seeing connections and developments is usually very important and if these ideas are not presented in such a way that the perceiver can grasp the material and make it intelligible then no matter how rich the vocabulary or skilful the dancer, the dance will not come across.

As with developing your knowledge and understanding a dance vocabulary, I strongly recommend that you look analytically at dances and dancing, carefully identifying structures, motifs and development of material. Notice how the dancer shapes the material in physical and emotional terms. Notice in particular the relationship between the dance and the music which invariably accompanies dance. For the beginner in choreography, the dance can represent a valuable and legitimate structure, but there has to be a good theoretical and emotional knowledge and understanding. Similarly with drama, it is important if you use a narrative as the basis of your dance that you and the dancer recognise the dramatic and emotional 'shape' and relationships of the narrative and of the characters. The dances in national, ethnic and folk dance are usually very simple, their forms being mainly two- or three-part structures based upon simple contrasting ideas. A recurring motif is not uncommon. Study these dances and identify the form as well as the vocabulary of expression.

> To compose is not an inspirational experience. Composition is based on two things; a conception of a theme and the manipulation of that theme. Whatever the chosen theme may be it cannot be manipulated, developed, shaped without knowledge of rules of composition. (Horst and Russell)[30]

In dance as in poetry, music and all other arts material must be arranged in a pattern of some order if it is to become a composition. This orderly arrangement which provides a recognisable structure or contour is its form. Because the form of a composition develops according to a logical plan, it contributes to the total impression of unity and completeness of meaning whilst at the same time imposing a disciplined method of working upon the choreographer! (Lockhart and Pease)[31]

The art (craft) of expression – dance

Physical skill, a vocabulary of movement ideas and a sense of structure and form are fundamental prerequisites of all dance, but by themselves they do not make the dance. Just as an ability to read a script, translate it into sounds and movements, and recognise the structure and form of the drama does not make an artistic performance, so too with dance. What transforms these artistic elements into art has something to do with the artist himself. Until the knowledge, imagination and performance skills are applied to and invested in the artifact, these elements remain elements, and as such they are dead in terms of art. Although this expressive prerequisite is essentially subjective, there are objective elements which can contribute to our knowledge and understanding of this aspect of art.

The objective element is related firstly to such theatrical skills as projection and 'stage' communication – all that is implied by the term 'performance'. It also implies an awareness and sensitivity to the performance space, i.e. the nature and condition of where one is performing, the occasion, the atmosphere and audience response. A performance is always a dynamic affair and involves a continual negotiation of the artistic material. It is never the same even though the elements may remain, and hopefully remain the same. The nature of an artistic performance is that it is different every time one performs it.

A second objective focus is that related to the pluralistic notion of art expression. As already indicated, there is no

one, all-embracing theory of art. Although we have identified a major focus within this writing, that of 'emotionalism' as defined by Susan Langer, this by no means exhausts
the possibilities of dance as art. 'Art may be defined as the
practice of creating perceptible forms expressive of human
feeling. The work of art expresses a conception of life,
emotion, inward reality, but is neither a confessional
nor a frozen tantrum; it is a developed metaphor, a non-
discursive symbol that articulates what is verbally
ineffable.'[32] There are many other philosophies of dance
and we are free to move in them all, and yet still retain this
basic focus. A recognition, if not a knowledge and understanding of such alternatives, will not only extend our
present understanding, but will sharpen and refine it. Art is
an 'essentially contested concept'. Its nature is dynamic,
open and constantly changing and there are, in a sense as
many theories of 'dance as art' as there are choreographers.
I do not mean to imply necessarily an identification with
this or that theory. Rather I hope that you will recognise in
these theories, insights and possibilities into the artistic
process, the nature of choreography and expression as a
means to identifying our own expression, and expression
possibilities for religious dance. In making a study of such
contemporary choreographers as Balanchine, Ashton,
Graham, Humphrey, MacMillan, Robert Cohen and
Twyla Tharp, for example, we can greatly enhance our
objective understanding of dance expression. Ten years
ago, of course, this would have not been possible, unless
one lived in London and could afford to go to the theatre.
But with the recent explosion of dance we now have many
opportunities to see dance on television, there are more and
more touring companies in the provinces and, above all,
there is the innovation of the video. Already some libraries
have a video section. So it is not impossible to study
choreographers.

15. SOME THEORIES OF DANCE AS ART

First, let us recognise the problematic nature of theory with regard to art.

'To understand the role of theory in aesthetics is not to conceive it as definition – logically doomed to failure – but to read it as summaries of seriously made recommendations to attend in certain ways to certain features of art' (M. Weitz).[33]

'Enough has been said in this essay to suggest that our initial hope of eliciting a definition of art, or work of art, was excessive' (R. Woolheim).[34]

With the above in mind, I will identify four major basic dance/art theories, to consider both in terms of choreographers and their choreographies. (See Stolnitz, *Aesthetics and Philosophy of Art Criticism*.[35])

Imitation theory

'The art object is the imitation of nature' (Plato).

 eg BALLET, TAP *etc.*

'I deplore the artist who makes his art withdraw from the travail of his time; who sterilises and dehumanises it into empty formalism and who forgets that the artist's function is perpetually to be the voice and conscience of his time' (Limon, dance/choreographer).

This is perhaps the oldest of theories of dance. Here the emphasis is on narrative and drama. The dance tells in movement/dance terms something that we can relate to in everyday human terms. Sometimes this reality is a romantic one as, for example in *Giselle*, and *Swan Lake*, or sometimes it is expressed in the social realism of Kurt Jooes' *Greentable* which tells the story of war and man's inhumanity to man, the hypocrisy of politicians. Most of the religious dance that I have seen tends to be within this theory. The dance tells a story or mimes a scriptural passage.

Formalism

'Art is defined as the elements of the media organised into formal pattern which is essentially valuable' (Bell).

'The visual aspect not the story is the essential element' (Balanchine).

Here the focus is less on the narrative and more on the line, form, pattern and colour of the dance. Much of the work of the American choreographer, Balanchine, provides the best example of this dance theory. His *Serenade* and Ashton's *Symphonic Variations* and *Monotones* are good examples. One of the strengths of this theory is that it focuses on the dance itself. With the imitation theory, dance is so often parasitic on drama or music, with the result that we sometimes lose much of the dance interest. One of the most famous 'formalist' dances is Fokine's *Les Sylphides*. There is very little notion of a story; the 'meaning', the expression and what is communicated lie more in the actual dance and dancing itself, in the patterns, shapes and working of material, in the costume and the lighting effects, in the changing moods of the dance and music. Dance does not have to be rooted in a narrative. Indeed, my experience is that dance says so much more in terms of dance than trying to be drama. Drama is a language in its own right, as is music. Dance is at its best when it expresses that which cannot be put into words. Which brings us to the third theory – that of emotionalism.

Emotionalism

'Art is the manifestation of emotion obtaining external interpretation' (Veron). Yes.

'Art is the evocation of one's inner life' (Martha Graham, choreographer). ⟶ vague

Emotionalism represents the main focus of this study and much has already been said about it. In identifying with this particular philosophy I am not rejecting the other theories but hope that a study of them will extend this primary focus. A strong narrative, form in the sense of pattern, shape and design etc., as well as the fourth theory 'Aesthetic Fineness', all constitute valid potential elements of religious dance provided that they work towards the end of the faith rather than concentrating on themselves. Dance examples under this heading include: Martha Graham's *Lamentations*, music by Cohen; MacMillan's *Gloria*, music by Poulanc; Pina Bausch's *Rite of Spring*, music by Stravinsky; Robert Cohen's *Stabat Mater*, music by Vivaldi.

'Aesthetic fineness'

'A disinterested and sympathetic attention to an art object for its own sake' (Stolnitz).

'Let the movement speak for itself' (Nikolais, choreographer). Ho Hum.

On the face of it, this theory seems out of place within religious dance since it is quite explicit in concentrating on itself. In the sense that it does this and ignores or undermines the faith then in religious dance terms, of course, it is not legitimate. But in the sense that it reminds us that dance movement is in itself a legitimate focus of art, and that stories, form and emotion, while being traditional focuses are nevertheless three among many focuses for dance as art, we can lawfully accommodate it within religious dance.

This theory, more than the others, has greatly extended the dance vocabulary of movement possibilities. Much of contemporary dance falls into this category and such choreographers/dancers as Merce Cunningham, Twyla Tharp, David Bintley and Douglas Dunn et al. would fit comfortably into this model of dance.

I strongly recommend that you try to obtain videos or attend performances in order not just to identify the different artistic focuses but also to see something of how dancers work within such focuses, i.e. how they project, express or communicate such varied dance ideas. All represent a legitimate concern for the religious dancer. There are also innumerable dance history and appreciation books available. For examples of such books and where to obtain the same, see 'Further Reading' towards the end of this book.

What ultimately makes a dance – dance as art – is what each artist invests in the various elements we have been discussing. These objective elements can quite easily be learnt from the mind and taught to us from the outside but the subjective element, which ultimately makes the dance art, can only come from within. It is uniquely you.

The art of dance, whatever form it may take, is a conscious and deliberate one moving within a variety of prerequisite skills. The notion of an innate ability, both in creativity and dance, separate from a disciplined initiation into the same is rejected. This does not mean to say that we should reject the positive elements of individual expression, intuitive thinking and feeling, spontaneity and all that goes to make up so-called creative dance and above all that great sense of freedom and fun which so often characterises much of this sort of dance, but it does mean that we underpin such positive expressions with a disciplined concern for the various elements that go to make up dance and that in doing so, greatly extend and refine individual dance experiences.

Before we leave this second section of dance and education and move into the practical third section, I would like to draw attention to some very interesting revealing parallels between the pursuit of dance and the pursuit of the Christian faith. The two major focuses of this book both represent extraordinary and, to a certain extent, unnatural pursuits. Both are long-term activities. Both involve a fundamental faith in the pursuit, considerable sacrifice and a pilgrimage which is characterised by a sustained struggle, pain, uncertainty, failure and disappointment – all in the pursuit of an ideal. Both involve a strange paradox – in that while growth and development are characterised by much failure and hurt, it is from this failure and hurt that one succeeds, attains satisfaction, joy and fulfilment.

16. SIGNIFICANT PARALLELS BETWEEN PURSUIT OF DANCE AND PURSUIT OF THE CHRISTIAN FAITH

   (i) Both activities are extraordinary and unnatural in worldly terms at least.

   (ii) Both involve pain and struggle, failure and constant disappointment.

   (iii) Both are fundamentally verbs rather than nouns – i.e. the essential nature of both is they are 'doing' activities.

   (iv) Both include a commitment to rules, to a discipline – one has to submit to the activity and to a formal social body.

   (v) Both require a selfless commitment.

   (vi) Both involve a regular, daily renewal and struggle.

   (vii) Both involve a long-term commitment and single-mindedness.

   (viii) Both involve all or nothing.

   (ix) Both involve necessarily a combination of mind, body and heart.

   (x) Both belong to a universal, ongoing tradition of struggle and fulfilment.

   (xi) Both involve faith.

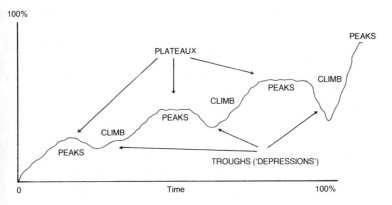

The above graph is based upon a fairly free interpretation of a motor learning graph, e.g. physical skill – dance.

   (i) We notice first of all that progress takes time.

  (ii) More difficult skill development takes more time than simpler skill.

 (iii) Troughs or 'depressions' together with 'plateaux' and 'climbs' are characteristic of progress.

 (iv) Troughs and plateaux become:
     (A) progressively more frequent
     (B) plateaux become progressively longer
     (C) troughs or 'depressions' become deeper.

  (v) 'Climbs' become steeper, higher and more difficult to attain.

For both the dance and the Christian faith, this is a 'great race', there is much in common. However, there is an important difference between dance and the faith, and this is made clear in 1 Cor. 9:24–5: 'Do you not know that in a race all the runners run, but only one gets the prize? Run in such a way as to get the prize. Everyone who competes in the games goes into strict training. They do it to get a crown that will not last; but we do it to get a crown that will last forever.'

'I am worn out, O Lord; have pity on me' (Ps. 6:2). 'Do not let
your heart be troubled' (John 14:1). 'Everyone who competes
in the games goes into strict training' (1 Cor. 9:25). 'After you
have born these sufferings a very little while, the God of all
grace who has caused you to share his eternal splendour
through Christ will himself make you whole and secure and
strong.' (1 Pet. 5:10). 'Weeping may remain for a night but
rejoicing comes in the morning' (Ps. 30:5).

SECTION III
RELIGIOUS DANCE – PRACTICAL

The OXFAM poster on the wall of my study reads:

> Give a man a fish and you feed him for a day;
> Teach a man to fish and you feed him for life.

The principle underlying this caption is significant in relation to our previous discussion on the nature and conditions of teaching and learning. It sees teaching and learning as investment rather than consumption. It is a 'putting in' rather than a 'taking out' and the student is seen not in terms of the first part of the caption, i.e. a passive recipient of information, non-responsible and dependent upon the 'teacher', but an active participant ultimately responsible and independent of the teacher. The function of education, the caption implies, is to teach a man to fish, i.e. to learn for himself, be responsible for himself and his learning.

The focus of this third section identifies with this positive conception. It is my concern not simply to 'give' you, or 'feed' you with a dozen or so dances, but rather to 'teach' you and encourage you to 'feed' yourselves, i.e. become actively responsible for making up your own dances. The following dances are means to that end.

In the first part the focus is on set dances. The creative act lies more in re-creating the set steps and patterns than in making up your own. It is hoped that from these varied 'impressions' you will begin to see possibilities for your own 'expressions'. Each dance focuses on a particular expressive/scriptural idea and has its own structure or form, vocabulary of movement ideas and movement development.

From a practical and theoretical working of these dances you will begin to build up a rich vocabulary of dance possibilities from which you will eventually choreograph your own ideas.

The second part is concerned more with open ideas than set steps, with plenty of scope for your own creativity. In each case I have identified a scriptural/dance idea and have suggested a number of clearly defined possibilities within which to work. I have concerned myself more with questions than answers. Your answers will hopefully help you to begin to identify and articulate both in dance and scriptural terms something of your own dance expression.

1. ANGELUS AD VIRGINEM

'The Angel Unto Mary Came' Fourteenth-century advent hymn

A simple line dance taking the form of a farandole.

With this first dance – a Christmas 'carol' i.e. a song-dance – I introduce one of the oldest and simplest of traditional dances. The farandole is a sort of 'follow the leader' dance for as many as will, each person joining when her or she likes and taking up the step motifs of the leader.

The 'carol', *'Angelus Ad Virginem'*, might be used most effectively as a means of Christmas communal celebration. The leader may be the minister himself! In any case he or she moves among the assembled company inviting all to join the dance. The destination of the 'farandole' might be symbolically Bethlehem, a special destination symbolising peace and goodwill to all men as well as tidings of great joy. The destination might be the blessing of the crib, the lighting of the candles for the Christmas tree, the bringing of gifts for the poor and needy. It might be a coming to receive the Christmas communion. Above all it is a coming together to celebrate his name.

The farandole in this form represents a communal, heart-felt expression of joy and properly belongs to the Christmas family service where young and old alike may join in as a church body expressing something of the unity, peace and goodwill to all men that characterises this great and glorious event. 'God became man and dwelt among us.'

As with all dance, religious meaning does not lie in the steps and floor patterns themselves but rather in what each dancer brings to and invests in them, and this in turn is dependent upon the nature and condition of the religious occasion. The dance, in this instance the farandole, represents a means whereby the church fellowship expresses something of the communal and heartfelt meaning of this celebration.

I suggest that you keep the steps of the pathways fairly simple – perhaps a walking or a skipping motif. This allows everyone to take part. If, on the other hand, you have an experienced and skilful group of young people, then by all means invent a complex series of developed motifs related to jubilation – skips, hops, jumps, turns, elaborate body gestures, etc. In any case, give care and attention to the role of leader. All too often the leader(s) in their enthusiasm forget those at the back of the line; if the leader moves away too fast the whole becomes a shambles and the scriptural focus is forgotten or at best seriously undermined.

The music has some irregular phrasing which is characteristic of early music. This need not bother you since the essential beat remains the same. The irregularity of the phrasing, in fact, helps keep the tune alive.

N.B. The 'carol' is not exclusive to Christmas. It is a song-dance and as such belongs to any religious celebration, as does the farandole. This dance form and expression is appropriate for Harvest, Good Friday, Easter Sunday, Whitsun etc. The occasion will dictate the sort of expression of the dance, but the basic movement idea remains the same. In our discussion of Miriam's dance I suggested that her dance may have taken the form of the farandole.

A possible development of this idea is to have several farandoles going on at the same time, joining and leaving as each leader feels best.

Remember the two features of a farandole, floor patterns and step patterns are both underlined by an expression arising out of scripture.

2. BROKEN FOR ME

A quiet, meditative dance based upon four simple dance motifs and presented in the form of a four-part movement canon.

Broken for me, broken for you;
The body of Jesus broken for you.

Music	Bar	Beat	Movement
Audience			*Starting Position* All kneel, sitting back on the heels with arms crossed at the wrists and held in front of the chest. The head is tilted slightly forward. The whole is an attitude of prayer.
A	1/4		*'Broken for me'* Slowly the head comes up. The eyes focus up to the cross and the face comes to express something of the mystery, wonder, love and praise related to the text. At the same time as the head comes up there should be an overall feeling of awakening in the body. Be careful to sustain the movement throughout the full four bars of the text. Do not come up in one or two beats and then hold 'dead'. Take as much of the time as possible.
B	5/6		*'The body of Jesus'* Slowly rise up on to the knees letting the arms stretch out before you. Wrists are still crossed. *'broken for you'*
	7/8		Open the arms wide to the side with palms upwards. At the same time discreetly bring the L leg forward and put your weight on it, ready to get up. Lift the torso 'high' in this kneeling position.

C	9/12		*'He offered his body, he poured out his soul'* As if lifted up by one hair of your head, slowly come to stand quietly tall and erect, assured in his saving grace. Let the arms hang loosely at the side. An expression of joy and wonder lights up the face. Leading with your right shoulder, as if slowly drawn, turn a full circle on the spot. Keep your eyes focused on the cross for as long as possible and as you come out of your circle pick up the cross again.
D	13/16		*'Jesus was broken that we might be whole'* With the face gazing up in wonder at the cross, slowly and confidently sink to original starting position ready to start the sequence all over again.

Although the music is not in canonic form the dance may be presented as such. Each group of dancers identified as A, B, C, and D, are placed specifically, entering one after the other in order and performing the dance sequence outlined above in four part canon.

I suggest the following placings for this dance – eight people in all.

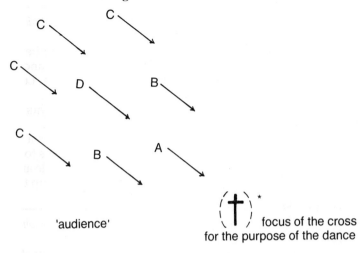

'audience'

focus of the cross
for the purpose of the dance

N.B. For other place settings see *There's a quiet understanding*, No. 4.

Suggested plan for this dance

(i) *Quiet instrumental introduction* during which the dancers enter group by group in order of the movement canon, eventually coming to their positions and kneeling ready to perform the dance at the end of the introduction.

(ii) *Four-part canon* performed four times corresponding to the four verses. Each group enters at the appropriate point in the dance.

N.B. Because of the canon the instrumental accompaniment needs sensitively to accommodate the extra three phrases as each group of dancers finishes one after the other, ending with a solo dancer D quietly standing in the middle of the group. After a moment she kneels and joins her colleagues. The music comes to an end.

* The broken line brackets indicate an imaginary cross as opposed to a real cross which in most churches will be behind the dancers.

Possibilities for development

(i) Explore other placings.

(ii) Consider different fronts and even maybe changing the front for each verse, thus affording the audience various visual focuses.

(iii) You might consider doing the whole first verse in unison either all at once or more and more dancers joining and gradually building up the dance in both visual and emotional expressive terms.

(iv) The unison could then go into the canon, thus greatly extending the dance.

(v) In the unison setting the congregation can perhaps be encouraged to join in. If this is so you might use one of the more traditional settings illustrated in *There's a quiet understanding*.

3. JESUS CAME

Jesus came and died on the tree,
rose again for you and me;
now he lives so we can be free.
Praise the name of Jesus.

A simple, uninhibited, communal dance of praise and thanksgiving within the English folk dance tradition and specifically *Sellinger's Round*.

Music	Bar	Beat	Movement
			Starting Position The dancers, identified as A and B, alternately *and* as partners, form a circle facing the centre with hands joined low, feet together ready to side skip to the left.
CHORUS	1	1	Step L/f side L ⎫
		&	Close R/f to L/f
		2	Step L/f side L
		&	Close R/f to L/f
	2	1	Step L/f side L ⎬ = side skip to L
		&	Close R/f to L/f
		2	Step L/f side L
		&	Hop on L/f ⎭
	3	1	Step R/f side R ⎫
		&	Close L/f to R/f
		2	Step R/f side R
		&	Close L/f to R/f
	4	1	Step R/f side R ⎬ = side skip to R
		&	Close L/f to R/f
		2	Step R/f side R
		&	Hop on R/f ⎭

	5	1	Step L/f forward	Move into the centre. Release partner and bring up arms high and wide above the head in praise.
		2	Step R/f forward	
	6	1	Step L/f forward	
		2	Step R/f forward	
	7	1	Step L/f back	
		&	Hop L/f	
		2	Step R/f back	
		&	Hop R/f	
	8	1	Step L/f back	
		&	Hop L/f	
		2	Step R/f	
		&	Turn R/f to face partner – A turn right B turn left	

VARIATION ONE – 'SET AND TURN' – partners turn to face each other.

	1	1	Step L/f to L
			Place R/f next to L/f
	2	1	Step R/f to R
		2	Place L/f next to R/f
	3/4		Both change places with partner passing R shoulder to R shoulder coming to face each other as in bar 1.

	5	1	Step L/f to L
		2	Place R/f next to L/f
	6	1	Step R/f to R
		2	Place L/f next to R/f
	7/8		Both change places with partner passing R shoulder to R shoulder coming to face the centre of the circle, joining hands once again ready to side skip to the L returning to the dance chorus.

CHORUS   See beginning.

VARIATION TWO – 'SIDINGS' – partners turn to face each other.

	1	1	Step L/f side L	The whole takes the form of a greeting, moving to face each other with arms outstretched to side with palms open, moving first to the left and then to the right within a shallow semicircle.
		2	Step R/f front L	
	2			
		1	Step L/f side L	
		2	Bring R/f next to L	
	3	1	Step R/f side R	
		2	Step L/f front R	

	4	1 2	Step R/f side R Bring L/f next to R
	1/4		Bars 1–4 repeated. N.B. On the fourth bar come to face the centre once more for the return of the chorus.

CHORUS   See beginning.

VARIATION THREE – 'ARMING' – partners turn to face each other.

	1/4		Facing each other, link arms R arm to R arm, walking around each other for four bars. Moving clockwise, at the end of the fourth bar turn round and link L arm to L arm, ready to move the opposite way.
	5/8		Walk around anticlockwise linking L arm to L arm releasing at the end of the phrase, facing the centre and ready to take up the chorus for the last time.

CHORUS   On the completion of the final chorus I suggest that all stand perfectly still with arms high and wide above the head. It is such an anticlimax if all suddenly collapse! Hold the energy, the dramatic expression and the geometric form and line.

I suggest that the congregation be encouraged to sing the verse for each of the choruses leaving the variations to the musicians.

The dance may be extended if so desired by taking the whole into a farandole. As with No. 1 simply break at the point of the leader and move off into the congregation encouraging the fellowship to join in. You might even like to come back to the original setting and perform the folk dance once more.

A word of warning to the accompanying musicians. As with most of these dances it is very important to keep the repetition fresh and 'alive'. Consider the following:

instrumental colour changes
instrumental *obligato* variations
modulation for each variation
an established instrumentation for the return of the
    chorus
changes in harmonic structure
all join in the chorus with singing while the variations
    are reserved for the instrumentalists

Chorus
Variation one 'set and turn'
Chorus
Variation two 'sidings'
Chorus
Variation three 'arming'
Chorus

N.B. Once again, I remind you that what makes a dance religious is not so much its steps and form as what each one of us invests in them, which comes from our knowledge and understanding of the religious occasion.

4. THERE'S A QUIET UNDERSTANDING

A quiet, meditative dance incorporating 'the peace' based upon four simple motifs and presented in the form of a four-part movement canon.

There's a quiet understanding when we're gathered in the spirit.
It's a promise that he gives us when we gather in his name.

Music	Bar	Beat	Movement
			Starting Position Dancers identified as A, B, C and D stand quietly tall and confident in the 'placings' suggested, with eyes focused forward high, feet together and arms held loosely at the side.
A	1/2		*Motif one* 'There's a quiet understanding' Take the R leg back and slowly come to kneel on the R knee. Lower the eyes and tilt the head forward slightly. Arms continue to hang loosely at the side. The attitude of the body is one of peace and humility, quietly enjoying the Lord's presence.
B	3/4		*Motif two* 'when we're gathered in the spirit' In the kneeling position slowly lift the head to focus forward high on the cross. At the same time let the arms breathe, away from the side, with palms upwards
C	5/6		*Motif three* 'It's a promise that he gives us' Slowly rise again standing tall and assured. Try to rise with a strong straight back, keeping the torso vertical. Keep your eyes focused on the cross.
D	7/8		*Motif four* Carefully walk a small circle on the spot to the R, all the time keeping your eyes focused on the cross.

> N.B. These movements are not intended as mimetic but rather as ineffable and heartfelt expressions of the text. Accordingly some considerable investment is required on the part of the dancer for this meditation to become meaningful.

Placing

There are a number of possibilities with regard to the placing of this dance – or any dance. Placing tends to be a neglected and underestimated element within choreography. Where the individual is standing and how the group is arranged within the performance space are important elements of the dance.

Consider the following placing possibilities.

PLACING

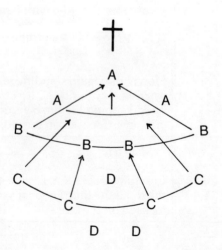

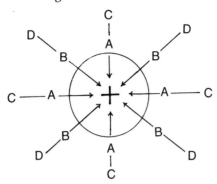

As well as considering the actual placing of your dance and dancers, consider also the possibility of using *different levels*. If, for example, you have steps in your church try to incorporate them into your dance rather than pretend that they are not there! Consider also the heights of your dancers and use them for aesthetic effect.

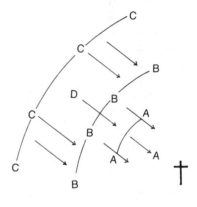

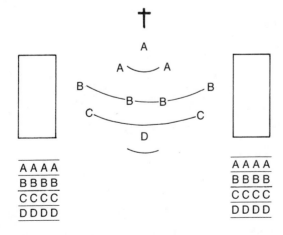

Suggested plan for this dance

(i) *Instrumental introduction* allows the dancers to move carefully into their places but at the same time sets the appropriate spiritual atmosphere for the dance. The musicians should recognise the nature of this introduction and perform accordingly.

(ii) *With the congregation singing* the dancers perform the whole, i.e. thirty-two bars, either in unison, four-part canon or a combination of both.

(iii) This section takes the form of 'the peace' and I suggest that this is also an *instrumental interlude* allowing the congregation the freedom to greet each other. This instrumental interlude may continue for as long as is necessary but at the appropriate point someone should indicate its completion and also indicate that the whole is going to be repeated. The dancers will need to get into their original positions.

(iv) Following 'the peace' everyone returns to the *original singing* and dancing of section (ii). The congregation might be encouraged to perform these simple movements also where they are sitting.

N.B. The musicians must remember that the dancers are performing in canon and therefore will not be finishing together. A codetta will be needed to round off the whole.

5. TURN YOUR EYES UPON JESUS

A quiet, meditative, movement expression based upon simple mimetic postures and gestures related to the text of the song.

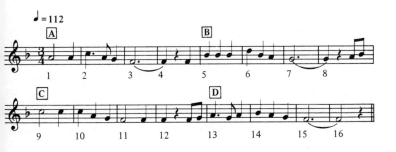

Turn your eyes upon Jesus,
Look full in his wonderful face
And the things of earth will grow strangely dim
In the light of his glory and grace.

Music	Bar	Beat	Movement
†			*Starting Position*
			Dancers identified as A, B, C and D place themselves in the suggested positions. All kneel, sitting back on the heels. Arms are held loosely at the sides. The head is tilted slightly forward.
			N.B. The rear cross behind the dancers is the important focus of the dance.

A	1/2 3 4		*Motif one* 'Turn your eyes upon Jesus' Slowly bring head up to face forward high ahead. Rise up on to knees and turn head to R, looking over your shoulder as best you can to the cross behind you. Bring L leg forward and the weight of the body forward ready to get up.
B	5/8		*Motif two* 'Look full in his wonderful face' Let the head continue to turn, taking the rest of the body with you. Keep your weight forward on the L leg and slowly rise. At the same time turn 180 degrees coming to stand opposite to where you started. Let the face continue to turn looking over your shoulder at the cross on the altar.
C	9/12		*Motif three* 'And the things of earth will grow strangely dim' Let the arms slowly come up from the side to high and wide above the head, psalm in an attitude of growing realisation and adoration. *At the same time turn* another 180 degrees, taking you back to your original facing. When the face comes round, the congregation should see a dramatic transformation from the opening expression reflecting the meaning of the text.
D	13/16		*Motif four* 'In the light of his glory and grace' Slowly bring the arms down to the sides and sink confidently to the original kneeling position timing the arrival for the end of the phrase, ready to start motif A once again.

How you might use this dance material

(i) Firstly, this can be done in unison, either all together at once or a build-up of dancers on each repeat, perhaps starting with one dancer then adding three more, five more and one more, the four groups corresponding to the four motifs.

(ii) Secondly, this may be done as a four-part movement canon with each dance group entering the dance at an appropriate time so that eventually all four motives are being performed at the same time rather than in unison.

(iii) Thirdly, consider alternative placings and numbers of dancers.

Suggested plan for this dance

(i) *Instrumental introduction* allows the dancers to walk quietly into their placings. Remember *how* you walk is already a part of the dance expression. Consider also your entrance. It might be an interesting idea if you came in from different entrances. Consider also the lines that these walks will bring about. This needs to be carefully choreographed.

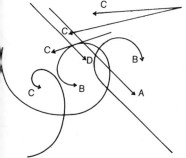

Just as placing tends to be neglected as an important choreographic element so, too, does concern for floor patterns – and in this case entrances. Floor patterns, entrance and exits should be given careful consideration.

(ii) *Performance of the dance.* Four performances of this song would be effective if you were using the canon idea. When the whole is completed, leaving one D to perform the last phrase on her/his own, I suggest that D remains standing for a moment before slowly kneeling, in silence.

N.B. See dance No. 5 for alternative placings.

6. HOLY, HOLY, HOLY LORD

Holy, Holy, Holy Lord
God of power and might
Heaven and earth are filled with your glory

Hosanna, Hosanna in the highest
Hosanna, Hosanna in the highest.

A circle dance for as many as will, using motifs from within
the folk dance tradition.

Music	Bar	Beat	Movement	
			Starting Position Dancers identified as A and B alternately stand in a circle facing the centre. Arms are held loosely at the sides. Eyes are lowered and feet are together. The body attitude initially is one of quiet submission.	
			A	B
A	1	1	Step R/f forward	Take R leg back and slowly come to kneel. Arms come diagonally forward 'deep' and the head and eyes remain lowered.
		3	Step L/f forward	
	2	1	Step R/f forward	Slowly rise. Let the arms return to the original position and slowly let the eyes focus upon the cross.
		3	Step L/f forward	
	3	1	Step R/f back	Step R/F forward ⎫
		3	Step L/f back	Step L/f forward ⎬
	4	1	Step R/f back	Step R/f forward ⎭
		3	Bring L/f to R/f	Step L/f forward
			In bars 1–2 let the arms come up high and wide above the head. They gradually come down in bars 3–4.	In bars 3–4 move out of the circle to the R and make a small tight individual circle on the spot. Keep your focus on the centre cross.

Starting Position diagram: A circle of dancers facing the centre, with dancers labelled A and B alternately around it: O (top), then B A B, then OA ... AO, then B A B, O (bottom), with the centre marked.

Music	Bar	Beat	A	B
	5	1 2 3 4	Take the R leg back and slowly come to *kneel*. Arms come diagonally forward and the head and eyes are lowered.	Step R/f forward Step L/f forward
	6	1 2 3 4	*Slowly* rise. Let the arms return to the sides and let the eyes come to focus up on the cross.	Step R/f forward Step L/f forward
	7	1 2 3 4	Step R/f forwards Step L/f forwards	Step R/f back Step L/f back
	8	1 2 3 4	Step R/f forwards Step L/f forwards Small indiv. circle to the R.	Step R/f back Bring L/f to R/f
			In bars 7–8 move out of the circle to the R and make a small, tight, individual circle on the spot.	In bars 5–6 let the arms come up high and wide above the head. They come down gradually in bars 7–8.
A²	9–16		REPEAT BARS 1–8 for 9–16	

Music	Bar	Beat	Movement
B^1	17		Join hands at shoulder level.
		1	Step R/f over L/f
		2	Bend R knee
		3	Step L/f side L
		4	Bend L knee
	18	1	Step R/f under L/f
		2	Bend R knee
		3	Step L/f side L
		4	Bend L knee
	19	1	Step R/f over L/f
		2	Bend R knee
		3	Step L/f side L
		4	Bend L knee
	20	1	Step R/f under L/f
		2	Bend R knee
		3	Step L/f side L
		4	Bend L knee
	21	1	Step R/f over L/f
		2	Bend R knee
		3	Step L/f side L
		4	Bend L knee
	22	1	Step R/f under L/f
		2	Bend R knee
		3	Step L/f side L
		4	Bend L knee
	23	1	Step R/f over L/f
		2	Bend R knee
		3	Step L/f back under R/f
		4	Bend L knee
	24	1	Step R/f over L/f
		2	Step L/f back under R/f
		3	Step R/f over L/f
		4	Step L/f back under R/f

Bars 1–24 can be repeated as they are or a slightly more difficult step could be used for as in bars 25–32, i.e.   B²

B²	25	1	Step R/f over L/f
		2	Step L/f side L
		3	Step R/f under L/f
		4	Step L/f side L
	26	1	Step R/f over L/f
		2	Step L/f side L
		3	Step R/f under L/f
		4	Step L/f side L
	27	1	Step R/f over L/f
		2	Step L/f side L
		3	Step R/f under L
		4	Step L/f side L
	28	1	Step R/f over L/f
		2	Step L/f back under L
		3	Step R/f over L/f
		4	Hop R/f
	29	1	Step L/f back under R/f
		2	Step R/f side R
		3	Step L/f over R/f
		4	Step R/f side R
	30	1	Step L/f back under R/f
		2	Step R/f side R
		3	Step L/f over R/f
		4	Hop L/f

	31	1	Step R/f forward	Make a small
		2	Bend R knee	individual circle
		3	Step L/f forward	on your spot to
		4	Bend L knee	the L with hands
				raised in praise.
				Finish facing the
				centre of the
				circle ready to
				return to the
				beginning, i.e.
				A's walking into
				the centre and B's
				kneeling.
	32	1	Step R/f forward	
		2	Bend R knee	
		3	Step L/f forward	
		4	Bend L knee	

N.B. An alternative to bars 31 and 32 is that in bar 31 take four running steps in a small circle and in bar 32 take a pivot turn on R foot to the R. As with all these set dances, feel perfectly free to add or subtract within the frameworks, making them more difficult or simplifying as the case may be.
Back to the beginning and repeat as many times as required.

7. THE LORD IS PRESENT

This is a strong, almost aggressive community dance rooted in the Jewish folk-dance tradition.

The Lord is present in his sanctuary,

  (1) Let us praise the Lord!
  (2) Let us sing to the Lord!
  (3) Let us delight in the Lord!
  (4) Let us love the Lord!

The Lord is present in his people gathered here,

  (1) Let us praise the Lord! Praise him, Praise him! Let
  (2) Let us sing unto the Lord! Sing to him, sing to him!
  (3) Let us delight in the Lord! Delight in him, delight in
  (4) Let us love the Lord! Love him, love him! Let us love

(1) Let us praise the Lord! Praise him, praise him! Let us praise Jesus.
(2) Let us sing unto the Lord! Sing to him, sing to him! Let us delight in Jesus.
(3) him! Delight in him, delight in him! Let us delight in Jesus!
(4) the Lord! Love him, love him! Let us love Jesus!

Music	Bar	Beat	Movement
			Starting Position Dancers form a circle, face the centre, join hands standing strong and erect with feet together and head held high. Release hands on the advance forward.
A	1	1 2 3 4	Step L/f forward Bend L knee Step R/f forward Bend R knee
	2	1 2 3 4	Step L/f forward Bend L knee Step R/f forward Bend R knee As you advance forwards slowly and confidently bring the arms up high and wide above the head. Make the steps quietly emphatic!
	3	1 2 3 4	Step L/f back – Accent! Hop L/f Step R/f back – Accent! Hop R/f

	4	1	Step L/f back – Accent!
		2	Hop L/f
		3	Stamp R/f back
		4	Stamp L/f alongside R/f but keep weight on R/f
			Slowly bring arms down bars 3–4
	5	1	Step L/f forward
		2	Bend L knee
		3	Step R/f forward
		4	Bend R knee
	6	1	Step L/f forward
		2	Bend L knee
		3	Step R/f forward
		4	Bend R knee
	7	1	Step L/f back – Accent!
		2	Bend L knee
		3	Step R/f back – Accent!
		4	Bend R knee
	8	1	Stamp! L/f
		2	Stamp! R/f
		3	Stamp! L/f
		4	Join hands
			(Arms as for bars 1–4)
			The steps quicken now as they take the circle to the left with a smooth and careful speed.
B	9	1	Step R/f over L/f
		2	Step L/f side L
		3	Step R/f under L/f
		4	Step L/f side L
	10	1	Step R/f over L/f
		2	Step L/f side L
		3	Step R/f under L/f
		4	Step L/f side L

	11	1	Step R/f over L/f
		2	Step L/f side L
		3	Step R/f under L/f
		4	Step L/f side L
	12	1	Step R/f over L/f
		2	Step L/f back under R/f
		3	Step R/f over L/f
		4	Hop on R/f
	13	1	Step L/f back under R/f
		2	Step R/f side R
		3	Step L/f over R/f
		4	Hop L/f
	14	1	Step R/f
		2	Step L/f = Perform a tight individual circle on the spot to the L
		3	
		4	Step R/f
			Step L/f
	15	1	Step R/f
		2	Close L/f
		3	Step R/f
		4	Close L/f = Pivot turn on the R/f to the R
	16	1	Step R/f
		2	Close L/f
		3	Step R/f
		4	Close L/f
	17	1	Stamp R/f
		2	Stamp L/f
		3	Stamp R/f
		4	
			Wait – prepare to go back to the beginning stepping forward on the L/f. For the repeats bring down arms on the fourth beat. For the final repeat leave the arms held high and still.
			N.B. Clapping may accompany the stamps with good effect!

8. GOD HAS SPOKEN

God has spoken to his people, hallelujah!
And his words are words of wisdom, hallelujah! (Repeat)

A strong dramatic community dance based upon simple Jewish steps expressing with uninhibited urgency the fundamental importance of listening to God's word.

Music	Bar	Beat	Movement
			Starting Position
			Dancers identified as A and B alternately form a circle facing the centre with arms held at shoulder level and palms of hands in contact with the person on either side. The whole is ready to move off clockwise facing the centre.
A	1	1 2 3 4	Step R/f across L/f Step L/f side L Step R/f behind L/f Step L/f side L
	2	1 2 3 4	Step R/f across L/f Step L/f side L Step R/f behind L/f Step L/f side L
	3	1 2 3 4	Step R/f across L/f Step L/f *back* behind R/f Step R/f across L/f Step L/f *back* behind R/f The effect of bar 3 is to mark time on the spot.
	4	1 2 3 4	Step R/f across L/f Step L/f side L Step R/f behind L/f Step L/f side L
	5	1 2 3 4	Step R/f across L/f Step L/f side L Step R/f behind L/f Step L/f side L
	6	1 2 3 4	Step R/f across L/f Step L/f *back* behind R/f Step R/f across L/f Hop R/f

	7	1	Step L/f back behind R/f
		2	Step R/f side R
		3	Step L/f across R/f
		4	Step R/f side R
	8	1	Step L/f back behind R/f
		2	Step R/f side R
		3	Step L/f across R/f
		4	Hop L/f
	9	1	Step R/f Release hands and complete a
		2	Step L/f small individual circle to the
		3	Step R/f left on the spot with the arms
		4	Hop R/f raised in praise.
	10	1	Step L/f back behind R/f
		2	Step R/f side R
		3	Step L/f across R/f Take up
		4	Step R/f side R original hand positions.
	11	1	Step L/f back behind R/f
		2	Step R/f side R
		3	Step L/f across R/f
		4	Hop L/f
	12	1	Step R/f
		2	Step L/f Release hands as for bar 9.
		3	Step R/f
		4	Hop R/f
B	13	1	Step L/f back
		2	Hop L/f
		3	Step R/f back Arms high and wide
		4	Hop R/f above the head.
	14	1	Stamp! L/f forward Arms down to the
		2	Stamp! R/f forward side, fists
		3	Stamp! L/f forward clenched.
		4	Stamp! R/f forward
	15	1	Step L/f back Arms high and wide
		2	Hop L/f above the head.
		3	Step R/f back
		4	Hop R/f

	16	1	Step L/f forward
		2	Hop L/f and swish R/f across L
		3	Step R/f forward
		4	Hop R/f and swish L/f across R
	17	1	Step L/f backward · Join hands and
		2	Hop L/f · hold at shoulder
		3	Step R/f backward · level.
		4	Hop R/f
	18	1	Stamp! L/f forward · Arms down to the
		2	Stamp! R/f forward · side, fists
		3	Stamp! L/f forward · clenched.
		4	Stamp! R/f forward
C		19/20	*Arming R/arm*
			A's turn to L and B's turn to R so that both face each other. Both link R arm to R arm and run in a clockwise direction. The free arm is held high above the head. Lean away from partner. On the last beat of bar 20 both turn to link L arm to L arm and ready to travel the opposite direction.
		21/22	*Arming L/arm*
			As above but travel in the opposite direction. On the last beat of bar 22 make sure that you are in a position ready to start to dance from the beginning.
			Back to the beginning.

9. OSTENDE NOBIS

Lord, show us your mercy. Amen! Come soon!
Principal Canon

An extended dance composition incorporating the sixteenth-century basse dance, the seventeenth-century courante and eighteenth-century minuet, for solo dancer and dance choir, giving expression to a prayer of confession.

Introduction
Solo 'cello – 8 bars in 3/4 time. For these first 8 bars there is no dance. The space remains empty, the atmosphere is still and an appropriate spiritual mood is evoked by the music. The 'cello's melody is based upon the bass line.

Recitation of the prayer of confession.
Following the solo 'cello's introduction the flute joins the bass line with the melody of *Ostende Nobis* and continues for 16 bars during which time the congregation recite the following prayer carefully responding to the atmosphere and shape of the music:

Almighty God, our heavenly Father,
We have sinned against you and against our fellow men
In thought, word and deed,
In the evil we have done and in the good we have not
   done
Through ignorance, through weakness,
Through our own deliberate fault.
We are truly sorry and repent of all our sins.
For the sake of your son, Jesus Christ, who died for us,
Forgive us all that is past;
And grant that we may serve you in newness of life to
   the glory of your holy name.

Amen

SOLO DANCE (S)

4 bars interlude – 'cello

Towards the end of the prayer of confession the solo dancer quietly gets up and moves into the performance space. The interlude allows her time to place herself, standing for a moment looking up at the cross, then kneeling sitting back on the heels, arms across the chest with wrists crossed and head tilted slightly forward.

Music	Bar	Beat	Movement
1			*Petition Motif*
	1/2	1–6	Head slowly comes up to forward, high, gazing at the cross. 6 counts.
	3	1–3	The arms with wrists crossed reach forward with palms upwards.
	4	1–3	Arms open wide to diagonally forward, palms facing upwards.

	5	1–3	Rise up on knees with the body slightly held back. Head is held high.
	6	1	Place the L leg forward ready to get up. Keep the torso lifted high.
	7	1–3	Lean the body forward in an attitude of submission and humility. Stretch the arms out wide behind you with palms facing forward. Head is tilted forward.
	8/10		Put the weight of the body forward on to the L leg and come to stand tall with the head held high and the eyes focused on the cross.
2			*Courante Motif* – slowly, quietly and formally you approach the cross with the courante figure.
	1		Slow courante step with R leg (see details of this step at the end of the dance).
	2		Slow courante step with L leg
	3		Slow courante step with R leg
	4	1 2 3	Quick courante step with L leg Quick courante step with R leg Quick courante step with L leg – on the second half of the beat bend the L leg and turn to face diagonal R. Extend the R leg back and point the foot. Keep the face focused on the cross.
	5		Slow *ronde de jambe* with R leg – supported on a bent L leg. Gradually rise on half toe in the next bar (i.e. trace a half circle on the floor with an extended leg and pointed toe).

	6	1–2	Bring R leg in front of the L tightly and stand tall in classical ballet fifth position. Keep the eyes on the cross.
		3	Lower the R leg and bend the same on the second half of the third beat in preparation for . . .
	7		Slow *ronde de jamb* with L leg – supported on a bent R leg. Gradually rise on half toe in the next bar.
	8	1–3	Bring L leg in front of the R tightly and stand tall in classical ballet fifth position. Keep the eyes on the cross. Slowly swivel to turn and face the congregation (this movement is in fact a *soutenu* in classical ballet terms) and the waiting dance choir and then walk back to join the latter, taking up a leading position in front of them.

Transition – 4 bars of music

As the solo dancer turns it is as if she is inviting her fellow dancers to join her in the dance. The dance choir move into their placings and kneel ready to perform the whole of the solo sequence with the soloist who kneels also.

Dance Choir Plus Soloist

N.B. These placings are only suggestions: you might prefer the dancers to face the congregation.

1			*Petition Motif* Bars 1–8
2			*Courante Motif* Bars 1–8
			Transition – 4 bars of music. All turn to face the congregation and quietly and carefully return to your original placings.

Music	Bar	Beat	Movement
3			*Horizontal figure 8 basse danse motif*
	1	1 2 3	Step R/f across L/f 'high' Bring L/f to R/f 'high' Lower both heels gently to the ground
	2	1 2 3	Step L/f forward 'high' Bring R/f to L/f 'high' Lower both heels gently to the ground
	3	1 2 3	Step R/f forward 'high' Step L/f forward 'high' Step R/f forward 'high'
	4	1 2 3	Step L/f forward 'high' Step R/f forward 'high' Sink on R knee and extend L leg across R
	5	1 2 3	Step L/f across R/f 'high' Bring R/f to L/f 'high' Lower both heels gently to the ground
	6	1 2 3	Step R/f forward 'high' Bring L/f to R/f 'high' Lower both heels gently to the ground

	7	1	⎧ Step L/f forward 'high'
		2	⎨ Step R/f forward 'high'
		3	⎩ Step L/f forward 'high'
	8	1	⎰ Step R/f forward 'high'
		2	⎱ Step L/f forward 'high'
		3	⎩ Sink on L leg and extend R leg across L

N.B. Make sure that the geometry is performed carefully in unison, each dancer keeping her original distance.
N.B. Throughout this figure keep your head focused whenever possible up to the cross.

4			*Minuet Motif*
	1	1	Step R/f back 'high' ⎫
		2	Sink on R knee
		3	Step L/f back 'high' ⎬ = One minuet step
	2	1	Step R/f back 'high' ⎫ backwards
		2	Step L/f back 'high'
		3	Sink on L leg ⎭
	3	1	Step R/f forward 'high' ⎫
		2	Sink on R knee
		3	Step L/f forward 'high' ⎬ = One minuet
	4	1	Step R/f forward 'high' step forward
		2	Step L/f forward 'high'
		3	Sink on L knee ⎭
	5	1	Step R/f side R 'high' ⎫ One
		2	Sink on R knee minuet
		3	Step L/f behind R/f 'high' ⎬ = step
	6	1	Step R/f side R 'high' sideways
		2	Step L/f across R 'high' R
		3	Sink on L knee ⎭

	7	1	Step R/f behind L 'high'	
		2	Sink on R knee	One
		3	Step L/f to L 'high'	minuet
				= step
	8	1	Step R/f behind L/f 'high'	sideways
		2	Step L/f to L 'high'	L
		3	Sink on L knee	

N.B. During bars 1–2 as you retreat gradually lift the head high so that when you advance in bars 3–4 a quiet confidence and assurance is expressed on your face.

Do be very careful in this minuet step that you melt on the sink and rise, otherwise you tend to produce a bobbing up and down which can be rather comical. The melting of the knee is in effect a reverence and should be performed as such.

5

Coming and going motif

At this point the dancers perform their own variation of the minuet sequence involving going towards the cross and turning away or going away from the cross and turning towards it. The effect that I am after is a sort of business among the dancers all coming and going at different times. The following sequences will help you to understand what I mean:

Variation One

2 minuet steps forward and turn away from the cross into
2 minuet steps away from the cross and turn towards the cross

5				*Variation Two*

Variation Two

1 minuet step towards the cross and turn into
3 minuet steps away from the cross and turn into
2 minuet steps forward

Variation Three

Turn immediately and take 1 minuet step away from the cross and turn into
3 minuet steps towards the cross and turn into
1 minuet step away

Variation Four

1 minuet step towards the cross. Do not turn
3 minuet steps backward
1 minuet step forward

Variation Five

2 minuet steps retreat from the cross but remain facing the cross then turn into
2 minuet steps towards the cross but with the back towards the cross.

This 'coming and going' needs very careful direction. Above all be conscious of the problem of spacing and not bumping into one another. Use the turn as an intimate part of the dance; it creates a special dynamic and punctuates the minuet step with something slightly different. Each dancer will need to identify her own variation.

This motif can continue for 16 bars or so but from that point on I suggest that each dancer one at a time 'breaks' the sequence and quietly comes to kneel before the cross. Some should begin this before the end of the 16 bars. Finally let one dancer remain on her own just for a moment until the music ends and then sink to the ground. The whole is finished with everyone kneeling in formation.

This dance can be done by any number of persons but the more dancers involved the more problems there are related to spacing and form.

There is a record from Taize TZ 040 3004 and this dance almost fits the music up to the point we have come to in the dance. There is just one point – 'Petition motif' No. 1 at the end of bar 8 – where in the Taize music there is an extra few bars. Treat these as transition bars before going into the courante.

Music	Bar	Beat		Movement
				Slow courante motif – R leg
		1		Keep the body weight on the L leg and extend the R leg *back* with a straight leg and a pointed foot.
		&		Draw a quarter circle on the floor with the extended R leg bringing to the *side* R.
		2		Draw another quarter circle with the extended leg and pointed foot bringing it in *front* of the L. Still keep the weight of the body on the L leg.
		3		On the third beat *place* the weight of the
		&		body evenly between the extended front leg and the leg behind. There should be a gap of six to twelve inches between the feet.
				As you trace the half circle, i.e. a *ronde de jambe*, on the floor let the shoulder of the working leg, i.e. R leg, come slightly forward with the leg. Let the head look over the shoulder. Do not tilt the head forward but lower the eyes. The arms should be held loosely at the side, moving just slightly with the shift of the shoulders.

			For the *slow courante on the L leg* do exactly the same as the above except on the opposite legs.
			Quick courante Exactly the same as the above except that the step is performed within one beat rather than three. Try to keep the clear geometric floor pattern and above all do not let the leg lose its clarity and strength of line and become sloppy. Equally do not make this movement appear busy or fussy.
			Minuet arms The arms for the minuet hang loosely slightly away from the sides of the body with hands fully extended and wrists slightly upturned. There is just the hint of 'breathing' as you travel, rising and falling.
			Ronde de jambe Circular pathway of the leg as in the courante step.

DANCE PROJECT NO. 1

Gloria
Music: Bach, *Brandenburg Concerto* No. 2, First Movement

It has been said throughout this book that an essential characteristic of Christian worship is rejoicing and being glad, giving thanks and praise to the Lord. Such heartfelt psycho-physical expressions, as we have seen, dominate both the Old and New Testament. In the New Testament we are told to rejoice in the Lord *always*. I raised the question in Section I with regard to such exhortations and suggested that dance might very well constitute a legitimate and appropriate means whereby such expressions may be articulated.

In *Gloria*, danced to the first movement of J. S. Bach's *Brandenburg Concerto* No. 2, we have a marvellous vehicle whereby such expressions may be realised. For me all of Bach's music, both religious and secular, has an extraordinary spiritual quality which I have found lends itself to religious dance. The first movement is jubilant, characterised by a clear and consistent energy and vigour, powerful rhythmic drive and perfect for giving expression to such emotions as rejoicing and being glad. It sparkles with enthusiasm. Within the context of Christian worship and performed by Christian dancers who have an intimate knowledge and understanding of why we should at all times rejoice and be glad and who are able both intellectually and physically to invest something of this heartfelt, ineffable knowledge into the steps, we have here, potentially at least, a very exciting dance.

Unlike the dances of the first part of Section III where I gave precise and detailed instructions as to the nature and condition of the dance expression, I propose in this section only to give general introductory ideas, allowing you to explore these themes and make them your own. I shall be using Laban's classification of movement as a means of analysis. With *Gloria* let us consider the following questions in the hope of building up a potential dance vocabulary.

Body – What moves?

The basic body focus of this dance is locomotion, i.e. with transporting the body. This dance is essentially concerned with running, jumping, skipping and walking. The arms, the head, facial expressions should all contribute to the overall expression of rejoicing and being glad, but it is in the motion of the body that the primary focus lies. Do not, of course, neglect stillness. Apart from the very real need in this dance to have a rest, stillness also acts as a dramatic contrast to movement and can be very effective if used carefully. When discussing structure and form I emphasised the importance of punctuation in dance. Various grades of stillness may prove to be very important in structuring the dance and enabling the 'audience' to perceive your composition.

Space – Where do you move?

With such a dance as this which is based upon travelling, attention must be given to *where* the dancers are to go – both in functional and expressive terms. Consider the floor patterns of the dance. Consider the geometry of the dancers both individually and collectively. The dance might move forward, backward, sideways, diagonally and in circles, etc. Introduce variation in your travelling by using levels – deep, medium and high, i.e. bent knees, normal, and on the balls of the feet.

Effort – How do you move in terms of dynamics?

There is little choice with regard to the basic dynamic for this dance since the music is so dominantly strong, sudden, free and direct. But having said that, do not hesitate to use slow, sustained movements where desirable over and against the music. This frequently produces an interesting effect. Consider also various groups moving with different dynamics at the same time.

Relationship – In relation to what do I move?

SCRIPTURE: 'Rejoice and be glad, come before him with praise and thanksgiving.'

MUSIC: listen very carefully to the music with both heart and mind, identifying the emotional/dramatic character, the phrasing and general shape of the music structure, the instrumentation, the climaxes, pauses and transitions.

DANCE: consider various possible formations of your

dancers both geometrically and physically/emotionally. Consider the possibility of having solo interludes, small groups and unison groups. Give care to the setting that you propose to dance within. Make the structure of your church an intimate part of the dance, whatever the problems!

If you are going to use a recording of the *Brandenburg Concerto* remember that there are many versions and nearly all are different! If possible listen to some recordings and select the one that you feel comfortable with. In particular the tempo of the music is very important: a tempo which is too slow or too quick will undermine your dance.

One final point, I strongly recommend that those who can read music get hold of a score of this concerto. It will help you to make sense of a very long composition. Incidentally, you do not need to dance the complete work; there are many points at which you may conveniently stop or gradually fade out.

Here, then, are some simple ideas to get you off the ground:

Music	Bar	Beat	Movement
	1–8		*Introduction* 8 bars Consider how you might use these introductory bars in getting the dancers into the performing space. You might like the idea of each running across the space from different entrances, perhaps some going off and bringing a friend with them. The idea of generally disturbing the space can help create an excitement and an atmosphere appropriate to the dance.
			Placing ◯ ◯ ◯ ◯ ◯ ◯ ◯ ◯

♩ = 96			The following directions refer to little running steps unless otherwise stated.
	9	1	Step L/f forward
		2	Step R/f forward
		3	Step L/f forward
		4	Step R/f forward
	10	1	Step L/f forward
		2	Step R/f forward
		3	Step L/f forward
		4	Step R/f forward
	11	1	Step L/f back
		2	Step R/f back
		3	Step L/f back
		4	Step R/f back
	12	1	Step L/f forward
		2	Step R/f forward
		3	Step L/f forward
		4	Step R/f forward
	13	1	Step L/f forward
		2	Step R/f forward
		3	Step L/f forward
		4	Step R/f forward
	14	1	Step L/f forward
		2	Step R/f forward
		3	Step L/f forward
		4	Hop on L/f

N.B. ♩ = 96

Bars 13–14 } = small individual circle on the spot to the left

	15	1	Step R/f forward ⎫
		2	Hop on R/f
		3	Step L/f forward
		4	Step R/f forward
	16	1	Step L/f forward
		2	Step R/f forward
		3	Step L/f forward
		4	Step R/f forward ⎭

⎫ = small individual circle on the spot to the right

	17	1	Step L/f across R/f 'deep'
		2	Step R/f side R 'high'
		3	Step L/f across R/f 'deep'
		4	Step R/f side R 'high'
	18	1	Step L/f across R/f 'deep'
		2	Step R/f side R 'high'
		3	Step L/f across R/f 'deep'
		4	Hop on L/f
	19	1	Step R/f across L/f
		2	Step L/f side L 'high'
		3	Step R/f behind L/f
		4	Step L/f side L
	20	1	Step R/f across L/f
		2	Step L/f forward
		3	Step R/f forward
		4	Hop R/f

⎫ = small individual circle on the spot to the left (covers counts 1–4 of measure 20)

	21	1	Step L/f forward
		2	Step R/f forward
		3	Step L/f forward
		4	Hop on L/f

	22	1	Step R/f forward
		2	Step L/f forward
		3	Step R/f forward
		4	Hop on R/f
	23	1	Step L/f back 'deep' and accent
		2	Hop L/f
		3	Step R/f back 'deep' and accent
		4	Hop R/f
	24	1	Step L/f back 'deep' and accent
		2	Hop L/f
		3	Step R/f back
		4	Step L/f back
	25	1	Step R/f across L/f 'deep'
		2	Step L/f side 'high' L
		3	Step R/f across L/f 'deep'
		4	Step L/f side 'high' L
	26	1	Step R/f across L/f
		2	Step L/f side L
		3	Step R/f across L/f
		4	Hop R/f
	27	1	Step L/f across R/f
		2	Step R/f side R
		3	Step L/f behind R/f
		4	Step R/f side R
	28	1	Step L/f across R/f
		2	Step R/f forward
			= small individual circle on the spot to the R
		3	Step L/f forward
		4	Hop L/f

Music	Bar	Beat	Movement
	29	1	Step R/f forward
		2	Step L/f forward
		3	Step R/f forward
		4	Step L/f forward
	30	1	Step R/f forward
		2	Step L/f forward
		3	Step R/f forward
		4	Hop R/f
	31	1	Step L/f back 'deep'-accent
		2	Hop L/f
		3	Step R/f back 'deep'-accent
		4	Hop R/f
	32	1	Step L/f back 'deep'-accent
		2	Hop L/f
		3	Step R/f back 'deep' – accent
		4	Hop R/f
	33	1	Step L/f across R/f 'deep'
		2	Step R/f side R
		3	Step L/f across R/f
		4	Hop L/f and throw L leg to side
	34	1	Step R/f across L/f 'deep'
		2	Step L/f side L
		3	Step R/f across L/f
		4	Hop R/f and throw L leg to side
	35	1	Step L/f behind R/f
		2	Hop L/f and throw R leg to side
		3	Step R/f behind L/f
		4	Hop R/f and throw L leg to side
	36	1	Step L/f behind R/f
		2	Hop L/f and throw R leg to side
		3	Step R/f behind L/f
		4	Hop R/f and throw L leg to side

	37	1	Step L/f forward
		2	Step R/f forward
		3	Step L/f forward
		4	Step R/f forward
	38	1	Step L/f forward
		2	Step R/f forward
		3	Step L/f forward
		4	Hop L/f
	39	1	Step R/f back 'deep' – accent
		2	Hop R/f
		3	Step L/f back 'deep' – accent
		4	Hop L/f
	40	1	Step R/f back
		2	Step L/f back
		3	Step R/f back
		4	Hop R/f

Continue . . . consider ways of travelling, turning and changing your front, move in to a circle formation rather than linear formation. Consider short solo or group interludes corresponding to the solo instrumental interludes in the music. Try moving at half the time rather than on every beat, as has been the case so far. You will recognise from my sequence that I return frequently to a main, simple theme. This is good both for the dancers and the audience. It is a psychological relief, a recognition of something familiar in a constantly changing dance. You might find it effective to continue this idea.

Do not feel that you have to complete the whole. There are suitable moments in the music where it is possible to finish. You can always simply fade the music out sensitively at an appropriate point.

DANCE PROJECT NO. 2
PRAYER OF HUMBLE ACCESS

Music: Vivaldi, *La Notte*

The music I propose to use for this dance is Vivaldi's concerto *La Notte*, fifth movement. If you listen to the music carefully a number of times hopefully you will come to identify at least two emotional/spiritual moods. On the one hand there is a great sense of mystery and wonder, an awesome sense of fear, something beyond ourselves and much greater than ourselves. There is a longing to know this 'other', in some sense to be united with it. At the same time there is a growing sense of peace, of becoming, of being warmly and lovingly accepted, an ineffable sense of well-being. You can begin to see how this might fit the Prayer of Humble Access, and it is against such an emotional/spiritual background I propose to explore a dance interpretation of this prayer. With the *Brandenburg Concerto*, the music we used for the previous dance project, we were moving closely and deliberately with the detailed rhythmic and formal structure of the music. I propose to use *La Notte* more as a general impressionistic background against which you can perform your movements. Rather than work within the structure of the music I want to suggest that we move across it, finding our own 'punctuation' in the main In the previous dance we explored the exuberant and joyful expression of the faith. In this dance we explore the more ineffable and mystical expression.

Study the text carefully and begin to identify the dramatic and the emotional/spiritual content of this prayer, especially the two focuses identified in the music.

We do not presume to come to this thy table, O merciful Lord, trusting in our own righteousness, but in thy manifold and great mercies. We are not worthy so much as to gather up the crumbs under thy table. But thou art the same Lord whose nature is always to have mercy. Grant us therefore, gracious Lord, so to eat the flesh of thy dear Son Jesus Christ and drink his blood, that our sinful bodies may be made clean by his body, and our souls washed through his most precious blood, and that we may evermore dwell in him, and he in us. Amen.

Once again I am thinking in general Laban terms of movement.

Body – What moves?

The basic body focus of this dance is, I suggest, travel, pause, gesture and posture.

Within the context of this dramatic/spiritual text, how will you come into the Lord's presence – run, skip, walk? If you walk into the presence, will the emphasis be on the whole body or body parts? Will you lead with a body part? For example, will you come with your back to the cross and eventually lead with your head, or your shoulder, or a hand reaching up to the cross etc?

Consider the shape of your body, i.e. its posture. Will you come bowed down, shuffling your feet? Will you be huddled on the floor, fearful to show your face? Will you stand tall and confident in his mercy and love? Will you kneel?

In terms of gestures, which parts of your body will you use to express the humility, the unworthiness, the longing and joy of forgiveness, having our bodies washed by his precious blood? Consider body parts other than the hands or the face.

In this dance expression give particular attention to stillness as well as movement.

Space – Where do you move?

Consider first the floor patterns you might use in your travelling and coming into the Lord's presence. Where will you enter from? Will you move in a direct pathway or an indirect pathway? What do you think is the emotional/ dramatic significance of the different pathways? You might use a combination of 'lines' – zig zag, meandering pathway, circular pathway, linear and curve. Experiment with various ideas both individually and collectively, carefully identifying what you think is the most appropriate series of pathways for this expression.

In your travelling and the pathways you create give attention to levels. For example, you might begin to enter the presence of the Lord at the 'deep' level, probably on your knees, but gradually as you come closer and closer to him, being forgiven and accepted by him, rise until you are walking 'high'. Remember that levels are not exclusive to walking. The arms, the head, the other parts of the body all involve different levels. In your 'pauses' or 'stillnesses' you might consider a sculptural posture with a particular level, e.g. a sculptural expression of humility and longing held at 'medium' level or 'deep' level, and this might be placed upon a diagonal pathway coming in from front stage R going across to back stage L.

Effort – How do you move?

With the impressionistic background of *La Notte* it seems to me that the effort, quality and dynamic of this dance is essentially slow and sustained, light or fine touch, a combination of 'free' and 'bound' flow, 'flexible and direct'. But a careful and sensitive use of sudden and strong movement might help with the punctuation of the dance as well as give a certain 'salt and pepper' to the expression.

Relationship – In relation to what do you move?

Obviously the text and the context of the prayer are fundamental to this expression and you should have the meaning clear in your mind before you embark upon creating a dance expression of it. Consider the whole area of 'the holy', the mystery and ineffability, sin and forgiveness etc.

Become intimately familiar with the music. Although I have suggested an impressionist background there is a basic pulse of four beats that you might find useful and clear sections and phrasing which again you might like to relate to. The extended ending of the music needs careful thought. Try not to finish too early and be left 'standing'. If anything, finish after the music in silence.

Consider the physical and emotional/dramatic relationships between the dancers. The entrances and the floor patterns or pathways will need to be given some thought. Why not explore the dance in individual terms first of all? This will allow a rich and varied vocabulary; then with one of the members standing outside the dance, begin to put the various ideas together making a coherent whole.

There is always the fundamental physical space in which the dance has to be performed. Try to use what you have, however difficult that space may be, and usually is! If you have steps, levels, pillars, try to incorporate them into your dance rather than pretend that they are not there.

DANCE PROJECT NO. 3

The Wondrous Cross
Music: Byrd, *Ave Verum*
The final dance project takes the form of a dance drama and focuses upon the cross today through the minds and hearts of various biblical characters who go to make up the Easter

story and provide the core of the New Testament faith. We will be exploring in dramatic/emotional scriptural terms such persons as Peter, Mary the mother of Jesus, Barabbus Judas, Mary Magdalen, Thomas, Pontius Pilate, the Centurian, and asking such questions as, 'If we came face to face with Jesus today in terms of these persons, what would we say, how would we react?' and, 'If we came face to face with each other, what would we say and how would we react – (a) in normal immediate human terms and (b) in light of the cross?'

The music I propose to use for this dance drama is William Byrd's *Ave Verum*.

For this project I suggest that you consider the use of illustrative material in the form of religious and secular paintings as a source for dance ideas. Dance is a visual art form. All too often the concern of dancers and choreographers is with movement, with steps, with the result that the visual, although always necessarily there, is not altogether recognised as an important part of the choreographer's repertoire.

Among the many paintings I have found useful for religious dance are: Bosch's *Bearing of the Cross*, Raphael's *Crucifixion*, El Greco's *Christ Driving the Traders from the Temple*, Botticelli's *Mystic Nativity*, Munch's *The Scream*, Picasso's *The Cry*, Seurat's *Sunday Afternoon on the Island of La Grande Jatte*.

Within the context of *The Wondrous Cross* specifically consider the use of distortion in Munch's *The Scream* and Picasso's *The Cry* – distortion in the body or groups of bodies, distortion in the costume. With regard to Raphael's *Crucifixion*, consider the postures and gestures of those characters at the foot of the cross. Consider also the structure and form of this visual expression, the way the various elements that go to make up the painting are composed. There are many ideas here for your dance composition made up from the various characters suggested for this project.

Finally, consider the painting by Seurat of *Sunday Afternoon on the Island of La Grande Jatte* in relation to this dance project.

Notice first of all the overall linear structure and balance of various visual ideas in terms of line – the horizontal lines, the diagonals, the verticals and the curve. See such focuses in terms of the whole and individual ideas. All these are implicit in the standing, kneeling, sitting and lying persons, the trees, the costumes, the umbrellas. Think exactly how you might place your dance characters in terms of the performance space generally and their individual postures and gestures.

Notice the curve motif, a common theme which occurs within different contexts, e.g. umbrellas, hats, the women's dresses, the chest and back of bodies and the trees, but all the time the curve remains the important structural element. Think how you might have such a theme as a unifying element within *The Wondrous Cross*.

Notice the bold general lines that help to hold the whole together – the diagonal lines across the picture from top right-hand corner to bottom left-hand corner implicit in the lake line. Notice the horizontal lines of the top left lake, the shadows, the man in the forefront reclining. Think how you might use such an idea in your composition.

Notice the various groups' formations and their placings. There are groups of two, three, four or just individuals.

Notice the general focus of the groups – forward and down towards the lake.

Notice the different heights of the characters in their placing.

Notice the various characters, their costume, their postures and gestures. Consider *how* they might move, *where* they might move to and *whom* they might go with.

All these paintings can easily be found in any general book on art and certainly the local library will help you locate the appropriate books. I strongly recommend this illustrative source for your choreography, not just for *The Wondrous Cross* but for all dance, including the previously discussed projects in this book.

For examples of dance in relation to this visual focus I would recommend Fokine's *Les Sylphides*, Balanchine's *Serenade*, Ashton's *Monotones*, Kirian's *Symphony of Psalms*. All are excellent for body shape and floor patterns, interest-

'The Lord is my light and my salvation – whom shall I fear?
The Lord is the stronghold of my life – of whom shall I be
afraid?' (Ps. 27:1). 'Let us be strong and of good courage,
neither frightened nor dismayed; for the Lord our God is with
us wherever we go' (Josh. 1:9). 'His love endures for ever'
(Ps. 107:1).

ing placings and geometric composition. They are all concerned essentially with dance material rather than a story.

Martha Graham's *Lamentation* is an excellent example of Munch's *The Scream* or Picasso's *The Cry*.

Robert Cohen's *Stabat Mater* is a marvellous example of all the points I have been discussing and an excellent model to study with regard to this project, *The Wondrous Cross*.

SOURCES OF DANCE MUSIC

1. *Angelus ad Virgenem* Fourteenth-century Advent hymn arranged by Elizabeth Poston in *The Penguin Book of Christmas Carols*, 1965. Copyright Elizabeth Poston

2. *Broken for Me* Colin and Janet Lunt arranged by Mia Farra in *Cry Hosanna*, Hodder and Stoughton. Copyright 1978 Mustard Seed Music, Berkhamsted, Herts

3. *Jesu Came* Jan Harrington, Celebration services in *Cry Hosanna*, Hodder and Stoughton

4. *There's a Quiet Understanding* Ted Smith in *Cry Hosanna*, Hodder and Stoughton. Copyright 1973, Hope Publishing, Carol Stream, Il 60188

5. *Turn your Eyes upon Jesus* H. H. Lemmel in *Fresh Sounds*, Hodder and Stoughton. Copyright 1922. Assigned to Singspiration Inc., Grand Rapids Mich 49506

6. *Holy, Holy, Holy Lord* Composer unknown in *Sing Praise Unto God*, Dales Bible Week

7. *The Lord is Present* Gail Coe in *Cry Hosanna*, Hodder and Stoughton. Record: *Rejoice with the Fisherfolk*. Copyright 1975, Church of the Messiah, Detroit, Mich 48207

8. *God Has Spoken*   Rev. W. F. Jabusch in *Cry Hosanna*, Hodder and Stoughton

9. *Ostende Nobis*   *Music from Taize*, Collins. Record: *Taize*

BIBLIOGRAPHY

Section I – Dance and Scripture

Part I – Dance as explicitly recorded in scripture

1. B. H. Edwards, *Nothing But the Truth*, Evangelical Press, 1972
2. R. Frances, *Concise Biblical Handbook*, Lion, 1984
3. R. Nicole, 'Revelation and the Bible' in K. Hawkins, *Concise Lion Handbook*, 1980
4. L. Boattner, 'Roman Catholicism' in K. Hawkins, *Concise Lion Handbook*, 1980
5. K. Hawkins, *The Concise Lion Handbook*, Lion, 1980
6. B. H. Edwards, *Nothing But the Truth*, Evangelical Press, 1972
7. W. O. E. Oesterley, *The Sacred Dance*, Dance Horizons, 1923
8. *Encyclopaedia Biblica*
9. *Encyclopaedia Judaica*, Macmillan, 1972
10. D. Adams, *Congregational Dancing and Christian Worship*, Sharing Company, 1971
11. W. O. E. Oesterley, *The Sacred Dance*, Dance Horizons, 1923
12. A. G. Clarke, *Analytical Studies of the Psalms*, Kreger Press, 1979
13. John Stott, *The Canticles and Selected Psalms*, Hodder and Stoughton, 1966
14. A. Cole, *Exodus*, Tyndale Commentary, 1973
15. J. H. Dobson, *Exodus*, SPCK, 1977
16. J. Blanchard, *Pop Goes the Gospel*, Evangelical Press, 1983
17. J. White, *Flirting with the World*, Hodder and Stoughton, 1982
18. D. H. Gross, *The Parson on Dancing*, Dance Horizons, 1879
19. *Encyclopaedia Biblica*
20. *Interpreters' Dictionary of the Bible*, Abingdon Press, 1962
21. J. Blanchard, *Pop Goes the Gospel*, Evangelical Press, 1983
22. T. M. Morton, *Christian Graduate*, March 1981
23. J. Blanchard, *Pop Goes the Gospel*, Evangelical Press, 1983
24. P. Bassett, *God's Way*, Evangelical Press, 1981
25. A. Cole, *Exodus*, Tyndale Commentary, 1973
26. J. D. Martin, *The Book of Judges*, Cambridge, 1975
27. J. Klatzkin et al., *Encyclopaedia Judaica*, Macmillan, 1972

28. T. K. Cheyne and J. S. Black, *Encyclopaedia Biblica*, 1899–1903
29. *The Interpreters' Dictionary of the Bible*, Abingdon Press, 1962
30. *The Illustrated Dictionary of the Bible*, IVP, 1980
31. *The Interpreters' Dictionary of the Bible*, Abingdon Press, 1962
32. D. Adams, *Congregational Dancing and Christian Worship*, Sharing Company, 1971
33. W. O. E. Oesterley, *The Sacred Dance*, Dance Horizons, 1923
34. J. Hastings (Ed.), *Encyclopaedia of Religion and Ethics*, T. and T. Clarke, 1908
35. W. G. Blackie, *II Samuel*, Hodder and Stoughton, 1950
36. S. Langer, *Problems of Art*, Charles Scribner and Sons, 1957
37. *The Book of Common Prayer*, Cambridge University Press
38. W. G. Blackie, *II Samuel*, Hodder and Stoughton, 1950
39. *Encyclopaedia Judaica*, Macmillan, 1972
40. W. G. Blackie, *II Samuel*, Hodder and Stoughton, 1950
41. Spurgeon, *Exodus*, Commentaries, 1876
42. John Stott, *The Canticles and Selected Psalms*, Hodder and Stoughton, 1966
43. R. Glover, *Matthew*, Zondervan, 1956
44. J. Blanchard, *Pop Goes the Gospel*, Evangelical Press, 1983
45. J. White, *Flirting With the World*, Hodder and Stoughton, 1982
46. *The Catholic Encyclopaedia*, Encyclopaedia Press, 1907–1914
47. J. J. Smith, in *Commentary of the Psalms*, G. Horner, 1813
48. St. Gregory of Nazianzus, *Oration V: Contra Julianum*, Migne, Cambridge, 1899

Section I – Dance and Scripture

Part II – Dance implicit in biblical principles

1. R. Abba, *The Nature and Authority of the Bible*, Clark and Clark, 1958
2. E. Brunner, *The Divine Human Encounter*
3. J. J. von Allmen, *The Vocabulary of the Bible*, Lutterworth, 1958
4. C. H. Dodd, *The Authority of the Bible*, Nisbet, 1928
5. J. J. von Allmen, *Vocabulary of the Bible*, Lutterworth, 1958
6. J. G. Ryle, *Knots Untied*, J. Clarke, 1954
7. M. Marshall, *Renewal in Worship*, Marshalls, 1982
8. J. F. White, *New Forms of Worship*
9. A. W. Tozer, *When He Comes*, Christian Pub. Inc., 1968
10. J. F. White, *The Fight*, IVP, 1977
11. A. W. Tozer, *Born After Midnight*, Christian Pub. Inc., 1959
12. L. Morris, *I Believe in Revelation*, Hodder and Stoughton
13. Warren W. Wiersbe, *Romans*, Victor Books, 1977
14. J. Blanchard, *Right With God*, Banner of Youth Trust, 1971
15. J. A. Robinson, *The Difference in Being a Christian Today*, Penguin
16. J. Darnell, *Life in the Overlap*, Lakeland and Scott, 1977

17. A. Redpath, *The Royal Route to Heaven*, Pickering and Inglis, 1971
18. F. Wendal
19. A. W. Tozer, *Born After Midnight*, Christian Pub. Inc., 1959
20. A. W. Tozer, *When He Comes*, Christian Pub. Inc., 1968
21. A. Redpath, *The Royal Route to Heaven*, Pickering and Inglis, 1971
22. J. Anderson, *Worship the Lord*, IVP, 1980
23. D. Watson, *I Believe in Evangelism*, Hodder and Stoughton, 1976
24. M. Marshall, *Renewal in Worship*, Marshalls, 1982
25. Michael Green, *To Corinth With Love*, Hodder and Stoughton, 1982
26. J. Young, *Worship the Lord*, IVP, 1980
27. P. Tournier, *The Gift of Emotion*, 1979
28. D. and R. Bennett, *The Holy Spirit and You*, Kingsway, 1971
29. William Temple
30. J. Young, *Worship the Lord*, IVP, 1980
31. G. Harkness, *Mysticism*, Olivants 1973
32. R. Gordon, *How Much More*, Marshall and Scott, 1983
33. A. W. Tozer, *Born After Midnight*, Christian Pub. Inc., 1959
34. L. Morris, *I Believe in Revelation*, Hodder and Stoughton
35. W. Jonstone, *The Inner Eye of Love*, Collins, 1978
36. M. Marshall, *Renewal in Worship*, Marshalls, 1982
37. G. Harkness, *Mysticism*, Olivants, 1973
38. W. James, *Kinds of Religious Experience*, Fontana
39. J. A. Robinson, *The Difference in Being a Christian Today*, Penguin
40. S. Langer, *Problems in Art*, Charles Scribner's Sons, 1957
41. C. S. Lewis, *Letters to Malcom*, Fontana
42. D. Watson, *My Path of Prayer*, Ed. D. Hares, Henry E. Walter Ltd., 1981
43. Vaughan Williams
44. S. Langer, *Problems in Art*, Charles Scribner's Sons NY, 1957
45. A. W. Tozer, *Born After Midnight*, Christian Pub. Inc., 1959
46. J. Hastings (Ed.), *Dictionary of Christ and the Gospels*, T. T. Clark, 1906
47. J. G. Davies, *New Forms of Worship Today*, SCM, 1978
48. J. Hastings, *Dictionary of the Apostolic Church*
49. J. G. Davies, *New Forms of Worship Today*, SCM, 1978
50. J. G. Davies, *New Forms of Worship Today*, SCM, 1978
51. Liz Attwood, and Joy Potter – unpublished article.
52. M. Marshall, *Renewal in Worship*, Marshalls, 1982
53. J. G. Davies, *New Forms of Worship Today*, SCM, 1978
54. J. White, *Eros Undefiled*, IVP, 1978
55. J. Young, *Worship the Lord*, IVP, 1980
56. C. S. Lewis, *Letters to Malcom*, Fontana
57. J. White, *Eros Undefiled*, IVP, 1978
58. J. G. Davies, *New Forms of Worship Today*, SCM, 1978
59. J. White, *Eros Undefiled*, IVP, 1978
60. J. Packer, *Evangelism and the Sovereignty of God*, IVP, 1961
61. D. Watson, *I Believe in Evangelism*, Hodder and Stoughton, 1976
62. Margot Fonteyn, *Margot Fonteyn*, Star Books, 1976
63. J. Perry, *Christian Leadership*, Hodder and Stoughton, 1983

64. *The Book of Common Prayer*, Cambridge University Press.
65. M. Marshall, *Renewal and Worship*, Marshalls, 1982

Section II – Dance and education

1. R. F. Dearden, *The Philosophy of Primary Education*, RKP, 1968
2. Ernst Cassirer, *The Philosophy of Symbolic Forms*, Yale
3. P. H. Phenix, *Realms of Meaning*, McGraw-Hill, 1964
4. S. Langer, *Philosophy in a New Key*, Harvard Un. Press, 1963
5. P. H. Phenix, *Realms of Meaning*, McGraw-Hill, 1964
6. P. H. Hirst, *Knowledge and the Curriculum*, RKP, 1974
7. R. F. Dearden, *The Philosophy of Primary Education*, RKP, 1968
8. P. J. Arnold, *Education, Physical Education and Personality Development*, Heinemann, 1968
9. P. H. Hirst, *Knowledge and the Curriculum*, RKP, 1974.
10. P. H. Phenix, *Realms of Meaning*, Mc Graw-Hill, 1964
11. L. A. Reid, *Ways of Knowing and Experiencing*
12. Louis Ellfeldt, *Dance – from Magic to Art*, Wm. C. Brown, 1976
13. Doris Humphrey, *Art of Making Dances*, Dance Books, 1978
14. Eleanor Mettheny, *Movement and Meaning*, McGraw-Hill, 1968
15. Ryle, *Concept of Mind*, Penguin, 1970
16. Ouspensky, *Icons*, SVS Press, New York, 1978
17. Lois Ellfeldt, *Dance – from Magic to Art*, Wm. C. Brown, 1976
18. H. R. Rookmaaker, *Art Needs No Justification*, IVP, 1978
19. A. Vaganova, *Basic Principles of Classical Ballet*, Dover Press, 1946
20. Beryl Grey, speaking at a conference of dance educationalists
21. L. A. Reid, *Meaning in the Arts*, Allen and Unwin, 1969
22. E. W. Eisner, *The Mythology of Art Education*
23. Beryl Grey, speaking at a conference of dance educationalists
24. Rosella Hightower, *Dance – from Magic to Art*, Wm. C. Brown, 1976
25. Martha Graham, *A Dancer's World* (Film)
26. Doris Humphrey, *Art of Making Dances*, Dance Books, 1978
27. M. H. Nadel, 'The Spirit of Dance' in *The Dance Experience*, Universe Books, 1978
28. A. D. Monrow, *Physical Education*, G. Bell and Sons, 1972
29. V. P. Dunlop, *A Handbook for Modern Educational Dance*, Macdonald and Evans, 1963
30. Horst and Russell, *Modern Dance Forms*, Dance Horizons, 1961
31. Lockhart and Pease, *Modern Dance*, Dance Horizons
32. S. Langer, *Problems in Art*, Charles Scribner and Sons, 1957
33. M. Weitz, 'Role of Theory in Aesthetics' in *Philosophy Looks at the Arts*, Margolis
34. R. Woolheim, *Art and its Objects*, Penguin, 1968
35. J. Stolnitz, *Aesthetics and Philosophy of Art Criticism*, Houghton Mifflin, 1960

FURTHER READING

Practical dance books
Martin H. Blogg: *Time to dance*. Collins, London, 1984.
Priscilla & Robert Lobley: *Your book of English country dancing*. Faber & Faber, London, 1980.
Cecil Sharp: *Country dance books*. (Many editions, all out of print, but obtainable from libraries.)
Joan Lawson: *European folk dance*. Imperial Society of Teachers of Dancing, London.
Melusine Wood: *Historical dances*. Dance Books, London, 1982.
Mabel Dolmetsch: *Dances of England & France, 1450–1600*. Da Capo, New York, 1976.
Mabel Dolmetsch: *Dances of Spain & Italy, 1400–1600*. Da Capo, New York, 1975.
Ann Hutchinson: *Your move*. Gordon & Breach, London, 1983.

Notation books
Ann Hutchinson: *Labanotation*. Dance Books, London, 1977.
Ann Kipling Brown and Monica Parker: *Dance notation for beginners – Benesh movement notation and Labanotation*. Dance Books, London, 1983.

Theoretical books on dance composition
Lois Ellfeldt: *A primer for choreographers*. Dance Books, London, 1974.
Doris Humphrey: *The art of making dances*. Dance Books, London, 1976.
Valerie Preston-Dunlop: *A handbook for dance in education*. Macdonald & Evans, Plymouth, 1985.
Betty Redfern: *Concepts in modern educational dance*. Dance Books, London, 1982.

Theological discussion of dance in worship
J. G. Davies: *Liturgical dance*. SCM Press, London, 1984.
J. B. Gross: *The parson on dancing*. Dance Horizons, Brooklyn, 1975.
W.O.E. Osterley: *The sacred dance*. (Several editions, all out of print, but obtainable from libraries.)
B. Edwards: *Shall we dance?* Evangelical Press, Welwyn, 1984.
Geoffrey & Judith Stevenson: *Steps of faith*. Kingsway Publications, Eastbourne, 1984.

Dance aesthetics and criticism

Jean Morrison Brown: *The vision of modern dance*. Dance Books, London, 1980.

A. V. Coton: *Writings on dance, 1938–68*. Dance Books, London, 1975.

Deborah Jowitt: *The dance in mind*. David R. Godine, Boston, 1985.

Susanne K. Langer: Feeling and form. Routledge & Kegan Paul, London, 1979.

Betty Redfern: *Dance, art and aesthetics*. Dance Books, London, 1983.

The books on this list, and many others on dance, may be obtained from Dance Books Ltd., 9 Cecil Court, St. Martin's Lane, London WC2N 4EZ. (Tel. 01-836 2314).

APPENDIX

Processions

(I am grateful to Canon David Ford from Ripon Cathedral for this information on contemporary religious processions and celebrations.)

The main difference between a secular and a religious procession is that a secular procession is either to share fun and enjoyment, e.g. a carnival, or to honour a high official, e.g. a monarch. In some countries it can also be political, e.g. in Russia with the May Day procession, or for sport, e.g. the Olympics, but in all these it is to pay honour to mankind. In all religious processions the aim is to honour Almighty God and the participants themselves have no importance except in relation to God who is being worshipped. Usually in a secular procession the most important people go last. A religious procession is normally preceded by the cross of Christ and the more 'important' the person is the further back he is in the procession as a sign of humility and of being a servant. The bishop, etc. therefore comes last, not because he is important but because he is 'the servant of the servants of God'.

The Church sometimes becomes involved in processions which are also concerned with the State and confusion can arise as to who is receiving honour and praise, e.g. mayor-making, Armistice Day processions. This confusion can sometimes be regarded as a compromise and it is to be noted the upset which was caused in the minds of some over the Falklands service when the Church emphasised the family of all nations and the State appeared to want to give glory to the power of Britain!

There are processions in Mediterranean countries to honour saints, very often Virgin Mary, by carrying a statue of the Virgin through the streets, by having fireworks and singing hymns to the glory of the saint. These occasions often have a carnival atmosphere, and religious and secular are clearly seen, yet also very mixed up.

However, in Western Christianity and within the Church there is a greater and tighter rein on processions so that they can clearly be seen to be acts of worship to God and to give him glory (a kind of dance). In Ripon we have a special procession at Candlemas (2 February). This procession has gone on almost continuously since before the Reformation and at the gradual (the hymn before the gospel) everyone receives a candle, the celebrant lighting his first and the servers taking their light from his candle and passing it on so that everyone in the congregation lights his candle from his neighbour's. We all then process out of the choir into the nave singing praises to God. The whole cathedral is in total darkness and lit only by the people's candles and this is a symbol that we each receive a light from the Light of the World and each bear witness to him. The cathedral appears to become a place of light when the whole of the nave is filled with people in procession with their candles. We all then return to the choir and the gospel is read. The service then continues with the minimum of electric light. This is to celebrate the Presentation of Jesus in the Temple and to rejoice with Simeon for 'our eyes have seen the salvation of the Lord'. There are other churches, of course, which have this ceremony but few can claim that it has normally taken place with an almost unbroken line as we can claim at Ripon.

Another ceremony is on Easter Eve and is taken from the early Church, where, on the night before Easter, the Church waits with expectancy for the Resurrection of Christ and the whole congregation goes in procession to the font where there is normally a baptism and all present renew their baptismal vows. Also the Paschal candle is brought into the body of the church and is lit from the new fire and the deacon says, 'The Light of Christ', three times. The candle is then placed in the candle-stand and all receive a light from that flame, again as an indication of receiving light from Christ and their willingness to be a disciple.

In Ripon we also have a street procession around the beginning of August when a person dressed like a bishop and representing St. Wilfrid mounts a horse and follows the carnival procession with floats, singing and dancing through the streets of the city. The procession finally ends up in the cathedral with the person representing St. Wilfrid sitting in a bishop's chair in front of the nave altar and there is a short service honouring St. Wilfrid and looking to Jesus. Other civic and city occasions include processions of banners and flags.

Quite recently a new tradition of bringing the bread and wine to the altar at the offertory has been adopted by many Anglican and Roman Catholic churches and this symbolises the ordinary people bringing their own work and industry, e.g. bread and wine, to the altar to Christ for him to feed his people. In all religious processions the pilgrims are looking and walking towards God and usually the 'arrival point' is the altar of God.

Many other processions with great significance take place within the Eastern Orthodox Church and emphasise the numinous and the mystical nature of God. These are often far more ritualistic than those within the Anglican and Roman Catholic churches and almost every move or action symbolises a spiritual truth.

AUDIO CASSETTE

An audio cassette designed specifically to accompany the enclosed dances is available from the following address:

Christian Sound Services,
43 Linden Road,
Enfield,
Middlesex.
Tel. 01-363 2337

The price, including postage and packing, is £4-50 p.

Further information about Christian Dance Ministries, about workshops, lecture/demonstration and performances may also be obtained from the above address.

'Let us praise his name with dancing' (Ps. 149).